KEY CONCEPTS IN ACCOUNTING AND FINANCE

Palgrave Key Concepts

Palgrave Key Concepts provide an accessible and comprehensive range of subject glossaries at undergraduate level. They are the ideal companion to a standard textbook, making them invaluable reading for students throughout their course of study and especially useful as a revision aid.

The key concepts are arranged alphabetically so you can quickly find terms or entries of immediate interest. All major theories, concepts, terms and theorists are incorporated and cross-referenced. Additional reading or website research opportunities are included. With hundreds of key terms defined, **Palgrave Key Concepts** represent a comprehensive must-have reference for undergraduates.

Published

Key Concepts in Accounting and Finance
Key Concepts in Business Practice
Key Concepts in Human Resource Management
Key Concepts in International Business
Key Concepts in Management
Key Concepts in Marketing
Key Concepts in Operations Management
Key Concepts in Politics
Key Concepts in Strategic Management
Linguistic Terms and Concepts
Literary Terms and Criticism (*third edition*)

Further titles are in preparation

www.palgravekeyconcepts.com

Palgrave Key Concepts
Series Standing Order ISBN 1–4039–3210–7
(*outside North America only*)

You can receive future titles in this series as they are published by placing a standing order. Please contact your bookseller or, in case of difficulty, write to us at the address below with your name and address, the title of the series, and the ISBN quoted above.

Customer Services Department, Macmillan Distribution Ltd, Houndmills, Basingstoke, Hampshire RG21 6XS, England

Key Concepts in Accounting and Finance

Jonathan Sutherland and Diane Canwell

First published 2004 by
PALGRAVE MACMILLAN
Houndmills, Basingstoke, Hampshire RG21 6XS and
175 Fifth Avenue, New York, N.Y. 10010
Companies and representatives throughout the world

PALGRAVE MACMILLAN is the global academic imprint of the Palgrave Macmillan division of St. Martin's Press, LLC and of Palgrave Macmillan Ltd. Macmillan® is a registered trademark in the United States, United Kingdom and other countries. Palgrave is a registered trademark in the European Union and other countries.

ISBN 1–4039–1532–6

This book is printed on paper suitable for recycling and made from fully managed and sustained forest sources.

A catalogue record for this book is available from the British Library.

A catalogue record for this book is available from the Library of Congress

10   9   8   7   6   5   4   3   2   1
13 12 11 10 09 08 07 06 05 04

Printed and bound in Great Britain by
Creative Print & Design (Wales), Ebbw Vale

Contents

Introduction

You could be mistaken for believing that accounting and finance represent the only true sciences of business; in fact, in the right hands, the disciplines are more like arts. Solid, staid, restrictive, impersonal number-crunchers, grey-suited and humourless – all descriptions levelled at practitioners, yet in truth the disciplines are as forward looking and vibrant as any other field of business operations.

Accounting provides the primary means of examining, recording, analysing and assessing performance and quantifying the financial data of a business. Finance is a broader church, which addresses issues such as investment, the securities markets and currency exchange, which require practitioners to be conversant in financial data and the truths that are hidden within these figures.

Both accounting and finance present additional complications, particularly for those involved in the practice or the study of international techniques, definitions, processes and interpretations. Gradually, international conventions on the formatting, presentation and interpretation of accounting and finance data are being established, but there is still a gulf in style, notably between the two sides of the Atlantic Ocean. Once we look beyond the different terminologies, the techniques become remarkably familiar, and meaningful comparisons may be made.

The plethora of accounting and finance ratios and calculations may at first appear daunting, but once the purpose of these mathematical computations has been established, the simplicity of many belie the more complete science of interpreting what the resulting figures actually mean. It is increasingly difficult for business studies generalists or, for that matter, specialists in the field of marketing or human resources to ignore the implications of either accounting or finance. In addressing these two disciplines even those with a fundamental fear of figures can begin to see the broader and more complete picture.

The structure of the glossary

Every attempt has been made to include all of the key concepts in this discipline, taking into account currently used terminology, ratios and jargon common throughout accounting and finance in organizations around the world. There are notable differences in legislation and procedure when we compare the basic performance measurements and formatting of financial data in the United Kingdom, Europe, the United

States and Japan. Increasingly there are attempts to harmonize the way in which financial statements appear, the way in which they are interpreted, and a process is in train which is gradually seeking to standardize regulations and procedures.

The key concepts have been arranged alphabetically in order to ensure that the reader can quickly find the term or entry of immediate interest. It is normally the case that a brief description of the term is presented, followed by a more expansive explanation.

The majority of the key concepts have the following in common:

- They may have a reference within the text to another key concept identified by a word or phrase that is in **bold** type – this should enable readers to investigate a directly implicated key concept should they require clarification of the definition at that point.
- They may have a series of related key concepts which are featured at the end of the definition – this may allow the reader to continue to research and investigate subsidiary or allied key concepts.
- They may feature book or journal references – a vital feature for the reader to undertake follow-up research for more expansive explanations, often written by the originator or by a leading writer in that particular field of study.
- They may include website references – it is notoriously difficult to ensure that websites are still running at the time of going to print, let alone several months beyond that time, but in the majority of cases long-established websites have been selected, or governmental websites that are unlikely to be closed or have a major address change.

Glossary terms – a guide

Whilst the majority of the key concepts have an international flavour, readers are cautioned to ensure that they access the legislation, in particular, which refers to their native country.

It is also often the case that there are terms which have no currency in a particular country as they may be allied to specific legislation of another country. Readers are cautioned to check whether the description does include a specific reference to such law, and not to assume in every case that the key concept is a generic one and that it can be applied universally to accounting or finance.

In all cases, references to other books, journals and websites are based on the latest available information. It was not always possible to ensure that the key text or printed reference is in print, but the majority of well-stocked college or university libraries should have access to the original materials. In the majority of cases, when generic accounting, finance or investment books have been referenced, these are, in the view of the writers, the best and most available additional reading texts.

Above the line

Whilst 'above the line' may be most closely associated with a marketing expenditure related to advertising, it has two distinctly different definitions in relation to finance and accounts.

'Above the line' may refer to the horizontal line which can be found on a business's **profit and loss account**, which effectively separates the entries related to the profit itself (above the line) and entries dealing with the distribution of that profit, or sources of finance to fund that loss (below the line).

The term can also be used to describe business transactions which are concerned with revenue rather than capital, in national accounts.

Absolute priority rule

This term relates to the notion that creditors' claims always take precedence over shareholders' claims in the event of **liquidation** or a reorganization of the business. **Shareholders** are compensated only after the creditors have been fully paid.

For many years, in US bankruptcy law, it has been the case that only after major creditors have been paid during a reorganization plan, or have given their consent for the company to reorganize, have smaller creditors received their payments. In practice, smaller creditors and shareholders often receive some kind of payment as compensation for allowing the settlement process to take place.

Absorbed

This term actually has three different definitions:

- In accountancy, 'absorbed' refers to costs which are actually treated as an expense, rather than that cost being passed on to customers. Examples of absorbed costs are insurance and property taxes.
- In the equities markets, 'absorbed' is a description of the process of trading securities without necessarily affecting the market price.

- More generally, however, the term 'absorbed' refers to a business that is acquired and merged into another business, with all of its **assets** and operations becoming part of the purchasing business.

Accelerated depreciation

Accelerated depreciation is a **depreciation** method which allows a business to write off **assets** faster than by the straight-line method. Businesses with large tax burdens may choose to use accelerated depreciation methods. It does reduce the income shown on financial statements. The method is often used to write off equipment which will be replaced before the end of its useful life. Typically, items of equipment such as computers will become obsolete before they have actually worn out. An example of the accelerated depreciation method is the modified accelerated cost recovery system (**MACRS**).

During the 1990s US businesses alone invested $2 trillion on computers, software and technological products. This dramatically accelerated US **productivity**. The US Government is moving to recognize the value of changing tax rules on accelerated depreciation in order to re-stimulate the US economy. Currently, for example, the US recognizes a 5-year life span for most technological equipment.

Accounting rate of return (ARR)

The accounting rate of return is a means by which a business can calculate the expected **net profit** from a particular investment. It is usually calculated as a percentage of the **book value** of the **assets** invested.

See also **average accounting return (AAR)**.

Friedlob, George T., Schleifer, Lydia F. and Plewa, Franklin J., *Essentials of Corporate Performance Measurement*. New York: John Wiley, 2002.

A

Accounting standards

See **Accounting Standards Board (ASB)** *and* **Financial Accounting Standards Board (FASB)**.

Accounting Standards Board (ASB)

The Accounting Standards Board (ASB) is a UK-based organization which issues accounting standards, and which took over the responsibility of setting accounting standards from the Accounting Standards Committee (ASC) in 1990. The accounting standards developed by the

ASB are detailed in the Financial Reporting Standards (FRSs). Initially the ASB adopted the standards issued by the ASC, many of which were known as Statements of Standard Accounting Practice (SSAPs). Some have been superseded by the FRSs.

The ASB routinely collaborates with other accounting standard setting agencies and organizations around the world, including the **International Accounting Standards Committee (IASC)**.

www.asb.org.uk

International Accounting Standards Committee, *International Finance Reporting Standards 2003*. London: International Accounting Standards Board, 2003.

Accounts payable

Accounts payable are monies owed by a business to suppliers for products and services essentially purchased on credit. These debts are shown on a business's **balance sheet** as a **current liability**. Once the accounts have been paid, the debts represent a negative **cash flow** for the business.

Effectively, accounts payable encompasses all payments or reimbursements for non-payroll **expenditures**. Accounts payable tend to use purchase orders to track payments made. Analysts will compare accounts payable with the figures for purchases in order to make an assessment of daily financial management.

Accounts receivable

Accounts receivable are monies owed to a business by a customer in exchange for products and services provided on credit. These monies are treated as **current assets** on a **balance sheet**. Each sale is only treated as an account receivable once the customer has been sent an invoice.

'Accounts receivable ageing' is a periodic report which shows all outstanding receivable balances, usually broken down by customer and month due.

'Accounts receivable turnover' is the average duration of an account receivable, which is equal to the total credit sales divided by accounts receivable.

'Accounts receivable financing' is the selling of a business's accounts receivable at a discount to a **factoring** company. The factoring company then assumes the risk of the debt and receives the payment from the debtors when they settle their accounts. Businesses will often sell their accounts receivable, particularly if they do not feel confident in being able to collect the debt. In other cases it may cost more to collect the debt than the cost of the discount to the factoring company. The amount sold on is then deducted from the business's **balance sheet**.

Accrual basis accounting

Accrual basis accounting is one of the most commonly used accounting methodologies. The system reports **income** when earned and **expenses** when incurred. It is seen as an alternative to **cash basis** accounting, which reports income when received and expenses when paid. Using the accrual method, businesses have greater discretion as to when to count income and expenditure.

Businesses using this system need to make estimates against revenues that may be recorded, on the assumption that some may not be paid.

Accrued expense

An accrued **expense** is an expense which has been incurred during a given accounting period, but that has not yet been paid.

Accumulated depreciation

Accumulated **depreciation** is the sum total of the depreciation that has taken place on a particular asset.

Accumulated earnings/accumulated earnings tax

Accumulated earnings are earnings which were not paid out as **dividends** by a business, but were reinvested in core activities or used to pay off a debt.

An accumulated earnings tax may be payable on earnings which a business retains, in an attempt to avoid higher income taxes. The owners would have been subject to higher taxation had the earnings been paid out to them as a dividend.

A

Acid-test ratio

This is a fundamental business-health test or formula. The acid-test ratio measures **current assets** less **stock** against total **current liabilities**. This ratio shows how well a business is able to cover its short-term obligations, in other words, its liquidity. It is considered to be one of the most stringent tests as it simply considers current assets which can be turned into cash immediately, hence it does not consider stock as being immediately convertible into cash. The ratio shows creditors or potential investors what proportion of the business's short-term debts can be met by selling liquid assets.

Current assets – stock = current liabilities

An alternative way of working out a business's ability to turn assets into cash in order that sufficient money will be available when the creditors require payment is

Debtors + cash balances = current liabilities

Acquisition

The most common use of 'acquisition' is in describing the process of one business purchasing another business, or indeed individuals purchasing an existing business.

'Acquisition' can also refer to the process of obtaining a loan or another form of finance.

Acquisition can equally be applied to the purchase of a property by a business.

See also **acquisition cost** *and* **acquisition evaluation.**

Weston, J. Fred and Weaver, Samuel C., *Mergers and Acquisitions.* New York: McGraw-Hill, 2001.

Acquisition cost

Acquisition, also known as a take-over or merger, is when one business acquires control over another business, usually by the purchase of shares. This can be either a hostile (unwanted) take-over or a friendly (expected and desired) take-over.

'Acquisition cost' refers to **expenses** incurred in the purchasing of equipment or property of either an **asset** or another business.

Acquisition evaluation

An **acquisition** can normally be typified by six distinct phases. Four of these deal with the actual acquisition itself and the last two consider the post-acquisition phase. The first stage is to create a pre-acquisition team, which carries out a review of the industry and examines the business's existing strategic goals, identifying benefits and costs related to any proposed acquisition. The next phase is to evaluate whether the target business fits with the strategic criteria of the purchasing organization. Risk analyses are carried out, as well as a search for synergy. It may also be appropriate for the business to examine the organizational, financial and legal structure of the target. The third stage is to examine any restructuring or changes in the assets which may be required in order to integrate the target business. Once these stages have been undertaken the acquisition itself, specifically the transaction which needs to be carried out to obtain the business, can go ahead, subject to the full approval of the board or owners of the business and provided there are no legal issues which arise in respect of acquiring the business. In some cases government involvement may be necessary, particularly if the acquisition will affect the balance of the market (the acquisition may result in a monopoly situation).

Once the acquisition has been undertaken there is a period of integration, when issues raised in the pre-acquisition period are dealt with, including the modification and implementation of any required integration. The final period of evaluation considers what lessons could be learned for future acquisitions in respect of integration, structuring and management.

Thompson, Samuel C., *Business Planning for Mergers and Acquisitions*. Durham, NC: Carolina Academic Press, 1997.

ACRS

See **MACRS (Modified ACRS)**.

Activity-based costing

Essentially, activity-based costing is an accounting method, or information system, which seeks to link costs with activities that generate those costs. The key aspect is the identification and measurement of cost drivers. Each complex activity is broken down into specific activities, which could include how long it might take to set machinery up to begin producing a product, any associated delays while production is under way, movement of materials to and from the machine during production, and all other activities associated with the production period.

Activity-based costing can be applied to all types of activities, including, for example, the delivery of products to customers, which may include time taken to load the vehicle, the number of miles between each delivery point, the number of stops made and any known or predicted hold-ups during the delivery process. Each of these individual activities represents a part of the accumulated costs for the whole process. Each activity can thus be assessed in terms of its cost in order to identify ways in which the costs can be driven down.

Activity-based management (ABM) is the process of controlling and improving factors identified during activity-based costing. Typically, an organization may consider solutions to specific activities which defy attempts to drive down costs. Outsource work, for example, may be a solution. ABM also considers the impact on costs if operations are expanded or reduced, and attempts to discover whether the costs will be constant regardless of the level of operation, or whether they are related directly to the levels of operation.

Cockins, Gary, *Activity-based Cost Management: An Executive's Guide*. New York: John Wiley, 2001.

See also **activity-based management**.

Activity-based management (ABM)

Activity-based management (ABM) is the application of the results from **activity-based costing (ABC)** for process and profit improvement. ABM aims to generate a number of improvement initiatives and provide the business with a clearer view of the profitability of its products or services. The associations can be best shown as in Figure 1.

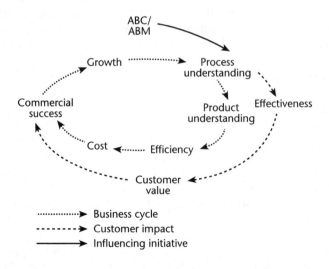

Figure 1   Activity-based management

Whilst ABC is calculated by the finance department, ABM needs to be a more widespread concern as it can identify the main resource-consumption drivers. In most cases, teams are deployed to undertake ABM activities.

See also **activity-based costing**.

Pryor, Tom, *Using Activity Based Management for Continuous Improvement*. Arlington, TX: ICMS, 2000.

Adjustable-rate mortgage (ARM) and adjustable-rate preferred stock (ARP)

An adjustable-rate mortgage is a mortgage in which the interest rate is periodically adjusted, normally in line with the prevailing rates of interest. Businesses or individuals who take out an adjustable-rate mortgage are protected, in effect, by a cap or a ceiling. The interest rate cannot rise above this level. Either the cap is reviewed on an annual basis, or it is applicable for the whole term of the mortgage. Under normal circumstances ARMs begin at a lower rate than fixed-rate mortgages as a primary means of attracting borrowers.

'Adjustable-rate preferred stock' refers to stock or cumulative **preference shares** in the US. These ARPs are linked to Treasury Bill interest rates and the maximum and minimum interest rates are specified by what is known as a 'collar'. Collars determine the cap (the highest rate of interest applicable) and the floor (which is the lowest rate of interest). A variant of ARPs is convertible adjusted-rate preferred stock, which has the facility to be converted into common stock at fixed prices on specific dates.

Adjusted basis

The term 'adjusted basis' refers to the base price of a specific **asset** or security, which reflects deductions that have been taken, or improvements to the asset or security. The adjusted basis is used to calculate any gains or losses when the asset or security is subsequently sold. The adjusted basis, or the basis, can be used to calculate not only gains or losses, but also **depreciation**, depletion and **amortization** of a business. In the US, for example, the Internal Revenue Service attributes to an owner of an investment the annual depreciation, or the gain on the sale of an asset. In this case if an investment was acquired by purchase, the owner's basis is the cost of the property plus any expenditures for improvement, minus allowable depreciation.

Adjusted book value (modified book value)

The adjusted book value is the **book value** of a business's **balance sheet** once **assets** and **liabilities** have been adjusted to their market value. This technique is also known as 'modified book value'. The adjusted book value technique takes into account that, with the exception of the time of purchase of an asset, the book value is unlikely to be the same as the current market value of that asset.

Adjusted-balance method

The adjusted-balance method is a technique which is used to calculate financial charges. Typically it is used for bank accounts, charge accounts or credit card accounts. The finance charges are calculated on the basis of the account balance which remains after adjustments have been made for payments and credits during a given billing period. It is normally the case that interest rates are lower under this method than using any other methods, such as the average-daily-balance or the previous-balance method.

The average-daily-balance method is an alternative technique for calculating financial charges and is based on the average balance which existed each day. The previous-balance method is usually used for credit card accounts. It takes the outstanding balance at the end of the previous billing period and then applies the interest rate to that total. Charges during the current billing period are not included.

Adjusting entry

An adjusting entry is a **bookkeeping** entry which is made at the end of an accounting period in order to assign specific incomes or expenses to a different period. The adjusting entries are made using accrual counting systems which aim to correctly identify the time when income and expenditure actually occurred. In other words, they should reflect the timings of those events. Adjusting entries may include **accounts receivable**, **accounts payable**, **depreciation** and **amortization**.

Advising bank

An advising bank handles **letters of credit** for a foreign bank and notifies the exporter that credit has been opened. The bank operates in the exporter's own country and informs the exporter of the conditions of the letter of credit, but without taking responsibility for payment.

A

Allowance for depreciation and for doubtful accounts

The term 'allowance' usually refers to a particular sum of money which was set aside for a particular occurrence which may or may not eventually happen. Funds may well be earmarked for expenses and in time it may be clear that the additional funds are not necessary. Allowance for depreciation, therefore, refers to the accumulated expenses which write off the cost of fixed assets over their useful time-span.

Similarly, 'allowance for doubtful accounts' is an estimate of the degree of bad debt which must be subtracted from the business's **balance sheet** (as noted in **accounts receivable**).

Amortization

The term 'amortization' has a number of implications in accounting and finance. 'Amortization' can refer to the annual expenses related to a fixed asset, such as a **lease**. Given the fact that a business may continue to pay lease charges over a fixed period, at the end of that time the lease will have no value. The business therefore divides the cost of the lease by the number of years the lease will run and then treats the result as an annual charge against profits. This technique does not necessarily give a true value of the lease at any time over the lease period, but it is a means by which the business can apportion the original cost over the period.

Similarly, an intangible asset may be amortized. **Goodwill** is a prime example and it is common practice to write off in the year of purchase all purchased goodwill. The charge is assigned to the reserves and not to the profit and loss account.

Amortization can also be applied to the gradual elimination of a **liability**, such as a **mortgage**. Regular payments are made over the period of the mortgage which are sufficient to cover the original loan and the interest due. Clearly as the mortgage period proceeds the actual liability in real terms is reduced by the payments.

The phrase 'amortization term' is used to describe the period of time over which the loan will be amortized. This is usually expressed in months or years.

A

Angel investor

Angel investors are most closely associated with new start-up businesses. Angel investors can be differentiated from **venture capital** funds as they directly inject the cash into the start-up business, rather than operating under a specific fund. For the most part, angel investors tend not to invest huge amounts in any one business, but provide what is known as seed money to a wide variety of different businesses in order to spread their risks. The seed money, as the name implies, is sufficient funding to allow the new business to begin to grow, and to develop systems, technologies, products and services which might not otherwise be able to reach the market. Angel investors are seen as a viable and more immediate alternative to conventional bank loans, as the cash is usually available straight away and there may not be the degree of conditions attached to the investment. Angel investors in the US, for example, provide $20 billion each year in seed money. Angel investors are never assured of a significant return on their investment and may well invest in a business for the longer haul rather than providing a short-term loan.

Van Osnabrugge, Mark and Robinson, Robert J., *Angel Investing: Matching Startup Funds with Startup Companies – A Guide for Entrepreneurs, Individual Investors and Venture Capitalists.* New York: Jossey-Bass, 2000.

Annual report

An annual report, or more precisely an annual account and director's report, is a document which is prepared by a business and issued to its **shareholders**. In the UK, for example, the business must file its annual report at Company's House in line with the prevailing requirements of the Companies Act. Alongside the annual report, the business also makes an annual return, which is usually prepared shortly after the business's Annual General Meeting (AGM). Again it is a requirement of the Registrar of Companies and the relevant Companies Acts. The annual return, which is usually a part of the annual report, details the share capital and any assets of directors, the company secretary and the shareholders of the business.

Pasewark, William R., *Understanding Corporate Annual Reports: A Practice Set for Financial Accounting.* Scarborough, Ontario: Irwin, 2003.

A

Annualize

As the term implies, this is a technique which seeks to reflect a value which may be expected over a full year. It may also refer to calculations which are made for periods of less than a year, but which treat the period as if it was a whole year.

Annuity

An annuity is a contract in which a business, or an individual, pays a premium to an insurance company in order to provide that business owner, or an individual, guaranteed payments for an agreed period of time, or for the rest of their natural life after retirement.

An annuity is, in effect, the complete opposite of life assurance in as much as the policy holder tends to pay the premium as a lump sum, whilst the insurer makes regular payments. Annuities tend to be purchased by individuals in order to convert capital which may otherwise be subject to taxation into an income that they can receive in old age.

There are several different forms of annuity:

- Deferred annuity – which delays payments until the holder wishes to receive them.
- Equity-indexed annuity – an annuity whose returns are based on the performance of the equity market.
- Fixed annuity – which guarantees fixed payments over the life of the annuity.
- Hybrid annuity – which combines the features of both fixed and variable annuities.
- Immediate-payment annuities – which are purchased with a single payment and begin to pay straight away.
- Joint life annuity – which is issued on two individuals and continues to be paid in whole or part until both die. These are also known as 'joint' and 'survivor' annuities.
- Life annuity – any annuity which continues to pay as long as the policy holder is still alive.
- Pre-retirement survivor annuity – which allows the dependants of the policy holder to collect the benefits should the policy holder die before reaching retirement age.
- Qualified joint and survivor annuity – which pays out at a particular level during the policy holder's life and then at a lower level for the duration of the policy holder's spouse's life.
- Qualifying annuity – which is normally purchased in order to receive favourable tax treatment.
- Single life annuity – which provides income benefits only for a single individual.
- Variable annuity – this is an annuity which makes payments on the basis of the performance of the portfolio of securities purchased by the insurance company on behalf of the policy holder.

Desoutter, Nicholas L., *Annuity Systems and Administration*. Atlanta, GA: Life Office Management, 2001.

A

Anti-trust law

Anti-trust laws seek to encourage competition by attempting to curb a business which has a monopoly and to limit unfair business practices. Anti-trust laws aim to prevent abuses of market power by large businesses, and in some cases the government will step in to prevent a merger or an **acquisition** which would create a monopoly.

Different countries have different views on what constitutes a monopoly and, indeed, what kind of business behaviour is considered to be an abuse of power. In the United States, for example, their monopoly policy is firmly built on the Sherman Anti-Trust Act (1890). It prohibits contracts or conspiracies which restrain trade. During the 1970s the Act was used against IBM but it failed. In 1982 the Act was successfully used to break up the monopoly which AT&T had established in the telecoms industry.

One of the highest-profile cases was launched against Microsoft in 1998; it was found guilty of anti-competitive behaviour. It was proposed that Microsoft be broken up; negotiations continue as to how this case will be resolved.

In the UK, successive governments seem to have followed the US trend in basing their anti-trust policies on situations which could ultimately harm consumers. Throughout the rest of Europe, however, particularly within the European Union, national governments have allowed selected businesses to become virtual monopolies in an attempt to create national companies capable of competing throughout the world. However, from the 1990s the European Commission, keen to promote competition within the European Union, has become increasingly active in anti-trust policy. It is possible that as the markets become more globalized, it will be necessary to establish an anti-trust watchdog operating throughout the world. Currently it seems that the World Trade Organization may ultimately take up this challenge.

Hylton, Keith N., *Antitrust Law: Economic Theory and Common Law Evolution*. Cambridge: Cambridge University Press, 2003.

A

Appreciation

Appreciation is an increase in the value of a particular asset and is the direct opposite of **depreciation**. The value of assets may increase as a result of a rise in market prices, interest earnings, or perhaps by inflation. Typically, appreciation is applied to the value of buildings or land. A business must adjust the nominal value of these assets and indeed any other relevant assets on its **balance sheet** in order to take into account appreciation.

The term appreciation can also be applied to the value of a currency which has a **floating exchange rate**. 'Appreciation' in this sense refers to an increase in the value of a particular currency relative to another currency.

Appropriation

Appropriation is the allocation of **net profits** of a business in its accounts. In certain cases some payments can be treated as expenses and can be deducted before the business states its net profit. Other payments must be treated as appropriations of profit after the profit has been calculated. An example of **expense** includes the wages and salaries of employees, whereas appropriations from net profits include **dividends** paid to **shareholders**, transfers of cash to reserves, or payments of income tax or corporation tax.

The term 'appropriation' can also be applied to the allocation of payments to a particular debt amongst several debts owed by a debtor to a single creditor. The debtor chooses which debts to appropriate payments to, but in some cases the creditor can choose to make the appropriation.

Arbitrage

Arbitrage is the process of purchasing foreign currency, securities or commodities in one market and simultaneously selling them in another market. Profits are made on the basis of the different rates of exchange or the different prices of securities or commodities in different markets. In other words, an **asset** will be purchased in one market and then the identical asset will be sold in another market at a higher price. An example would include the purchasing of Euros in London at a cheaper $ rate than is available elsewhere and then selling the identical amount of Euros in New York at a higher price.

Increasingly, however, arbitrage is becoming more difficult as a result of the globalization of the financial markets.

Graham, Mike (ed.), *The Arbitrage Handbook*. London: Fleet Street Publications, 2001.

A

Asset

An asset is any item of economic value which may be owned by an individual or a business. The term especially applies to items which can be converted into cash if necessary. Assets can be either **tangible assets** or **intangible assets**. Equally, they can be **current assets** or **fixed assets**.

Examples of tangible assets include plant, machinery, land, buildings, stock, fixtures, fittings, money owed by debtors, and cash. Intangible assets can include copyrights, patents, trademarks and **goodwill**.

Oberuc, Richard E., *Dynamic Portfolio Theory and Management: Using Active Asset Allocation to Improve Profits and Reduce Risk.* New York: McGraw-Hill Education, 2003.

Asset coverage

Asset coverage is the extent to which a business's net assets are able to cover its debt obligations, and/or its **preferred stock**. The asset coverage is expressed in cash terms or as a percentage.

Asset management

Asset management is an investment service which is offered by a number of financial institutions. In effect the service combines elements of banking and brokerage. More generally the term can be applied to a business's actions in respect of managing and maintaining its assets through periodic review, assessment and reassessment, **acquisition** and divestment.

Asset stripping

Asset stripping involves the **acquisition** or take-over of a business whose shares do not reflect the business's actual asset value. Having acquired the business at a comparatively low cost in relation to its true value in terms of assets, the asset stripper then sells the business's most valuable assets, achieving a higher value from the sales than was originally invested in the purchase of the shares in the first place. Entrepreneurs acquire controlling interests in businesses by buying shares openly on the Stock Market. They then revalue the assets of the business and sell them for cash. The difference between the value of the shares and the actual value of the assets of the business is lost to the former **shareholders**. Typically, asset strippers have no interest in the welfare of other shareholders, the employees, the creditors of the business, or indeed the suppliers. The primary aim is to sell off the assets of the business at the earliest possible point and, probably, close the business down.

A

Asset to equity ratio

The asset to equity ratio is equal to the total assets of a business, divided by the **shareholder** equity.

Klein, Robert, A. and Lederman, Jess, *Equity Style Management: Evaluating and Selecting Investment Styles.* London: Irwin Professional, 1995.

Asset valuation

Asset valuation is a means by which a business can determine the value of its own assets. Several of the techniques are somewhat subjective as they rely on the business making a credible case as to the true value of its own assets. Accurate assessments of current values of assets and their residual life expectancy aids corporate decision making. Asset valuation has a number of benefits:

- It can provide a means of capitalizing on resources.
- It can be used to protect shareholders' interests.
- It can provide security in consideration of capital funding.
- It can provide the firm basis for a market floatation.
- It allows the business to negotiate from a strong position in questions of **acquisitions**, mergers or take-overs.
- It can provide independent information when considering joint venture projects.
- It can help a business maximize on capital allowances and taxation issues.
- It can help to provide accurate product costing.

Copeland, Tom, Koller, Tim and Murrin, Jack, *Valuation: Measuring and Managing the Value of Companies.* New York: John Wiley, 2000.
Damodaran, Aswath, *Investment Valuation: Tools and Techniques for Determining the Value of any Asset.* New York: John Wiley, 2002.

Audit

An audit is an inspection of a business's annual accounts. Many businesses have internal **auditors** who carry out internal audits, and these are devised to report to management on the efficiency and security of internal systems. An audit carried out by an external auditor aims to provide an opinion as to the accuracy of the accounts which have been prepared by the business. In the UK, for example, businesses are required to appoint an auditor to pass opinion on whether their annual accounts actually give a true and fair view of the business's affairs and, indeed, whether they comply with any provisions under relevant Companies Acts. The auditors examine the business's internal accounting systems. They also inspect the business's **assets** and make spot checks on their accounting transactions.

Spencer Pickett, and Spencer, K. H., *The Internal Auditing Handbook.* New York: John Wiley, 2003.

Audit trail

An audit trail is, in effect, either the paper or the computer records which allow an internal or external **auditor** to trace the details of past transactions.

Auditing standards

Auditing standards define to the **auditor**s what the business, government and public expect of them and provide a guide for practising auditors. They also assure the public that the auditor is competent. Auditing standards provide the controls and content of a typical **audit**, and they also ensure that auditors are trained and proficient and, above all, independent. They also imply that auditors must show 'due professional care'.

Auditing standards require auditors to prepare financial statements so that they conform to the **Generally Accepted Accounting Principles (GAAP).** They also ensure that the auditor discloses inconsistencies with any report of the preceding period. The auditor must also disclose the business's financial position and the results of operations.

In reality, however, auditing standards are difficult to control and perfect compliance is virtually impossible. This is as a result of compliance monitoring being prohibitively expensive and the fact that audit standards are not the only measure of an acceptable audit. Audit standards seek to provide precedent for action against auditors if they have breached standard and minimum levels of professionalism.

O'Regan, David, *International Auditing: Practical Resource Guide.* New York: John Wiley, 2003.

Auditor

An auditor is an individual who carries out an independent **audit** of a business's annual accounts. The external auditor is usually a qualified accountant who is authorized under the Companies Act in the UK, or a similar form of legislation in an overseas country. The external auditor is an independent and professionally qualified individual and engaged to assess whether the business's annual accounts and its internal accounting systems comply with the legislation of the country in which it operates.

In the majority of cases businesses must have properly qualified, appointed auditors. Failure to do so in some countries, such as the UK, can result in the business's officers being fined. In the UK, for example, auditors are appointed at a business's Annual General Meeting (AGM). In the majority of circumstances, the removal of an existing auditor or

A

the appointment of a new auditor requires a special notice to be circulated to all **shareholders** of the business. In the event of the resignation of an auditor, any statement made by that auditor which pertains to the business itself must be brought to the attention of the business's shareholders and creditors. Auditors are liable to charges of negligence by the business, its shareholders, or any third party which relies on the information provided in the audited accounts. At a business's AGM the auditor's scale of charges must be approved and distinguished from any other accounting costs incurred by the business itself.

Sobel, Paul J., *Auditor's Risk Management Guide*. New York: Aspen Publishing, 2003.

Auditor's report

The nature of an auditor's report may very much depend upon who has appointed the **auditor**, and on the primary purpose of the **audit** itself. At the very least, an external auditor who has been engaged as an independent individual to assess the true and fair nature of a business's profit or loss over a given period, must simply state whether, in their opinion, the accounts meet this imperative.

An auditor's report should technically be addressed to the **shareholders** of the business and, in the UK for example, under the terms of the Companies Acts, the report must be filed, with the accounts, with the Registrar of Companies. The auditor's report may also include an audit of the directors' report.

Automated Broker Interface (ABI)

The ABI is part of the US government's automated commercial system. It permits the transmission of data related to products being imported into the United States. Information is passed between brokers, carriers, importers, port authorities and data processing businesses which operate as service centres.

www.customs.ustreas.gov

Average Accounting Return (AAR)

The average accounting return is used as a measure in order to judge the return on an investment over a given period of time. The average accounting return is equal to the average projected earnings, less taxes, divided by the average **book value** of the asset over the duration of the investment.

AAR is also used to calculate average projected earnings without excluding taxes, and indeed for average projected earnings less taxes and **depreciation**. In whatever form, AAR seeks to show how well **assets** are being used to generate income by the business.

See also **accounting rate of return.**

Average collection period

The average collection period is also known as the collection ratio. It is the average time for which receivables are outstanding. It is equal to the **accounts receivable** divided by the average daily sales.

Average cost

Average costs are simply calculated by dividing the relevant cost by the quantity of output. In Figure 2, the line marked MC refers to the marginal cost, which is the extra cost of increasing output by one unit. The AFC line refers to the average fixed cost, which declines as a proportion of the cost of each unit produced as output increases. The average variable cost (AVC) clearly increases as output increases, but in direct proportion to the increase in the level of output. Therefore the AC line, which is the average cost line, a sum of the AFC and AVC, also increases in proportion to increases in output.

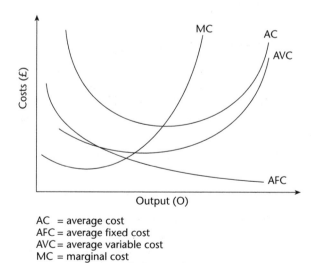

AC = average cost
AFC = average fixed cost
AVC = average variable cost
MC = marginal cost

Figure 2   Marginal, variable and fixed costs

Average rate of return (ARR)

The average rate of return is an **investment appraisal** methodology which seeks to identify the annual profits to be made from a particular investment, expressing it as a percentage of the original amount paid. Average rate of return can be expressed in two different formulae, these are:

$$APR\ (\%) = \frac{Total\ profit}{Project\ life/number\ of\ years \times 100/capital\ outlay\ on\ project}$$

Alternatively,

$$APR\ (\%) = \frac{Net\ return\ (profit)\ per\ annum}{Capital\ outlay\ (cost)} \times 100$$

A

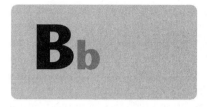

Bad debt

Bad debts are debts which are unlikely to be repaid to a business, possibly because the customer has become insolvent. In many cases businesses will set aside a sum of money to cover bad debts. This fund is referred to as the **bad debt reserve**.

Jasper, Margaret C., *The Law of Debt Collection*. Dobbs Ferry, NY: Oceana Publications, 1997.

Bad debt reserve

A bad debt reserve is money which is set aside as a reserve to cover bad debts. It is sometimes known as 'provision for bad or doubtful debt'. Most businesses will attempt to make an estimate of bad debt expenses which may be incurred during the current time period. These calculations are based on past records and are an integral part of estimating the earnings of a business. Many businesses will ensure that they have a bad debt reserve in order to offset the possibility that a small proportion of their creditors may not pay them in full. Assuming that a business's bad debt reserve has been correctly estimated, its net income will not be reduced should the debts have to be written off as a result of them being uncollectible.

Balance

The balance is the amount of money held in an account which is equal to the net amount of any credits or debits relevant to that account at that particular time. The balance is also known as an account balance.

An alternative definition of 'balance' can refer to any outstanding debt which may be payable on a loan. The balance represents the part of the loan which has yet to be paid.

Balance of payments

Balances of payments are statistical summaries of international transactions – transactions being defined as the transfer of ownership of something which has economic value measurable in monetary terms, from one country to another. These may, of course, include tangible or visible products, services (which are considered intangible), income on investments and financial claims or liabilities. A transaction is an exchange of one asset for another and as far as international transactions are concerned they are recorded on the balance of payments on the basis of **double entry**. Each transaction gives rise to two offsetting entries of equal value, resulting in the credit and debit entries always balancing. Transactions are valued at market prices and are recorded when the ownership changes.

The **International Monetary Fund** defines 'balance of payments' as a statistical statement which shows the transactions in goods and services and income between one economy and the rest of the world. It also goes on to include changes in ownership of an economy's monetary gold, claims on and liabilities to the rest of the world, and transactions which are not mutually offsetting. The US, for example, produces seven quarterly balances, as can be seen in Table 1.

Table 1 US balances of payments

Balance	Description
Balance on merchandised trade	The net transfer of merchandised exports and imports.
Balance on services	The net transfer of services, including travel, business and professional services. From 1990 this excludes investment income.
Balance on goods and services	The sum of the balance on merchandised trade and the balance on services.
Balance on investment income	Net transfer of income from both direct and portfolio investments.
Balance on goods, services and income	The net transfer of merchandise plus services and income on direct and portfolio investment (comparable to net exports of goods and services, which are included in **gross national product**).
Balance on unilateral transfers	The net value of gifts, government grants and other contributions.
Balance on current account	These include transactions in products and services, income and unilateral transfers.

In the US, merchandise is deemed to be visible trade, which is the value of exports and imports of physical goods. Invisible trade is the receipts and payments for various services and other intangible goods (including copyrights, dividends and interest payments).

Clearly, as any money outstanding needs to be paid, theoretically a country's accounts must balance. But in reality the balances are often fudged because balancing is never quite as neat as one might wish and there will inevitably be inconsistencies. In situations where a country cannot pay interest on foreign debts, such as the Russian government in 1988, the country will find it impossible to borrow more money in the International Finance Market. Russia was not able to increase taxes because its economy was collapsing and there were few sources within Russia itself to lend the government money. Situations such as these are known as balance of payments crises.

Miller, Norman C., *Balance of Payments and Exchange Rate Theories*. Cheltenham: Edward Elgar, 2002.

Balance of payments accounts

Balance of payments accounts are the records of international transfers undertaken over a particular period. Normally the accounts are divided into several sub-accounts, the most important being the **current account** and the **capital account**.

The current account is a record of all international transfers, products and services and combines the transactions of the trade account and the services account. The merchandise (product) trade account records the international transactions for goods only, such as cars, food and steel. The services account covers the international transactions for services such as transport, insurance and brokering. The capital account is a record of all international transactions related to assets, including bonds, treasury bills, stocks, currency, real estate and bank deposits.

B

Balance sheet

A balance sheet is one of the primary statements which make up a set of accounts. A balance sheet is a quantitative summary which shows the financial state or condition of a business on a given date or point in time. The point in time or date is usually the last day of a particular accounting period. The balance sheet shows a business's **assets**, **liabilities** and **capital**.

A balance sheet can be used to show how wealthy a particular organization is, as it details the assets less the liability, the balance of which is equal to the capital, or wealth, that is owned by the **shareholders** or business owners. The balance sheet also shows how any assets have been funded. Assets as shown on the balance sheet will have been funded either by borrowing (liabilities) or by the proprietors themselves (capital).

The balance sheet does indeed balance, since the two primary columns of the sheet refer to the balances from the accounts in the **ledgers** of the business. In the US, for example, a balance sheet is often referred to as a statement of condition.

Hawkins, Anne and Turner, Clive, *The Balance Sheet Pocketbook*. Alresford, Hants: Management Pocketbooks, 1995.

International Labour Office, *How to Read a Balance Sheet: An ILO Programmed Book*. London: International Labour Office/International Labour Organization, 1991.

Balanced budget

A 'balanced budget' is a budget in which the expenditures are actually equal to the income generated. A budget will be considered to be balanced even in cases where the expenditures are, in fact, less than the income.

'Balanced budget' is also a term which refers to the effects on the **gross national product** which can be caused by a change in government expenditure which has simultaneously been offset by an equal change in taxation. This is formally known as the 'balanced budget multiplier', when an increase in government spending puts more money, and hence more demand, into the economy. At the same time the increase in taxation does not have an equally inhibiting effect, as some of the income absorbed by the tax may have been used for savings and therefore does not have an impact upon aggregate demand. In balanced budget multiplier cases, individuals suffer a reduction in their savings and so work harder to retrieve their savings' position. Balanced budget multipliers are not often used explicitly, since any increase in taxation is politically unpopular.

B

Bank Advisory Committee

The Bank Advisory Committee is an informal, unstructured organization which consists of the leading bankers who represent the interests of a debtor country's banking industry. They aim to develop restructuring plans to propose to the government. The debtor country's government then puts forward the plans to the foreign lending governments.

Bank for International Settlements (BIS)

The Bank for International Settlements (BIS) was formed in 1930 and has its headquarters in Basel, Switzerland. The organization seeks to promote cooperation between the **central banks**, specifically related to international financial settlements. Members include Australia, Austria, Belgium, Bulgaria, Canada, Denmark, Finland, France, Germany, Greece, Hungary, Iceland, Ireland, Italy, Japan, Netherlands, Norway, Poland, Portugal, Romania, South Africa, Spain, Sweden, Switzerland, Turkey, the United Kingdom and the United States.

www.bis.org

Bank rate

The bank rate is the minimum rate at which a **central bank** provides loans to commercial banks. It is often referred to as the **discount rate**. Under most circumstances, an increase in the bank rate results in commercial banks increasing their own lending rates. Changes in bank rate have a direct impact on credit creation by altering the costs associated with credit.

Gup, Benton E. and Brooks, Robert, *International Exchange Rate Risk Management*. London: Irwin Professional, 1993.

Bank reconciliation

Bank reconciliation is a process which adjusts an account balance that is reported by a bank in order to reflect transactions which may have occurred since the reporting date.

In any accounting system bank reconciliation is performed in order to explain the differences between the balance on a bank statement and the actual balance of the account. It is used to explain any discrepancies, particularly as there are often differences in balances due to delays between the time the transaction entered a particular account, and the time the transaction shows up in the records. Discrepancies are often explained by outstanding cheques, collection of service charges, or the payment of interest.

B

Banker's draft

A banker's draft is regarded as cash and is payable on demand and drawn by or on behalf of a bank itself. A banker's draft cannot be returned unpaid.

Barometer

Barometers are economic or market data which can be used to indicate overall trends in the economy or the marketplace. Typical barometers include the rates of unemployment, interest rates, property sales or consumer spending.

The term is also applied to barometer stock, which are securities whose price is regarded as good indicator of the state of the market. Stock with stable price records is chosen and fluctuations in their value indicate overall market movement.

Barter

Barter is one of the oldest forms of trade, where there is no financial transfer involved in the transaction. At its simplest, barter is the exchange of a package of either products or services for products and services of an equivalent value. Barters are still much used in international trade and may involve the exchange of products and services over a period of time, with both parties undertaking to make the transfer within a year.

Mirus, Rolf and Yeung, Bernard, *The Economics of Barter and Countertrade*. Cheltenham: Edward Elgar, 2001.

Base interest rate

The base interest rate, in US terms, is the minimum rate which investors are prepared to accept when making an investment in non-treasury securities. It is sometimes also known as the benchmark interest rate.

The more generally accepted definition of the term refers to the rate of interest used by banks to determine the rates they charge businesses and other customers. The base interest rate is used as the foundation interest rate figure to which a premium is then applied in order to determine the rate which is charged to customers. The bank will assess the level of premium charged with due consideration to market pressures and in accordance with the bank's policy on the supply of credit.

See also **bank rate**.

B

Basket

The term 'basket' has several applications. The first is related to the purchasing of several securities created for the purpose of buying and selling. These baskets of securities often form part of a **hedge fund**.

An alternative use of the term 'basket' refers to a set collection of products and services, the prices of which are tracked in order to calculate the consumer price index (CPI) (or cost of living index). The CPI is used as an inflationary indicator which measures the changes in costs of these fixed baskets of consumer products.

The third use of the term 'basket' refers to a fixed group of similar currencies against which the value of another currency can be compared over a period of time. The basket comparison seeks to indicate the comparative change in the currency's **exchange rate** against the basket of currencies.

Beige Book

The Beige Book is published by the US Federal Reserve Board and contains data on the current economic conditions of the country. The Beige Book is released some 2 weeks before each of the Federal Open Market Committee meetings and has a summary of the prevailing economic conditions in the regions in which the Federal Reserve Board operates. The contents of the Beige Book are often taken to be an indicator as to what decisions might have to be made at the following Federal Open Market Committee meeting.

Below the line

Although 'below the line' is most commonly associated with marketing expenditure on sales promotional activities, it has two radically different meanings related to finance and accounts.

'Below the line' may refer to transactions which are concerned with capital, rather than revenue, in national accounts.

The more widespread use of the term, however, is related to a horizontal line on a business's profit and loss account. The line separates the entries which establish the profit or the loss of the business from other entries which illustrate how the profits are distributed (or where the funds have come from to finance a loss).

See also **above the line**.

B

Bid costs

Bid costs are costs incurred by a business during the preparation and delivery of a bid to carry out a project. Any legitimate costs incurred during the bidding process can be included as expenses on a **profit and loss statement**.

In certain cases, notably government contracts, reasonable reimbursement of costs can be paid to the bidders to cover their bid costs. During the bidding process for London Transport's tube lines, reimbursement was made to cover bid costs and it was found by the European Commission that this did not amount to State Aid. In this case, as in many others, the payment of bid costs covers what is known as 'Eligible Costs', which are considered to be part of a commercial bargaining agreement.

Bilateral clearing agreement

Bilateral clearing agreements are reciprocal trade arrangements between governments. Both countries undertake to allow a specified value of trade turnover over a given number of years. The value of this trade is expressed in terms of a major currency, such as the $US or the Swiss Franc. Exporters in each of the countries are paid by specific local banks in domestic currency.

Bill of exchange

A bill of exchange is a signed and written order by one business, which instructs a second business to pay a third business a specified amount of money.

Bill of lading (BOL)

A bill of lading is a contract issued to a transportation company (a shipper), listing the goods shipped, acknowledging their receipt and promising delivery to the person or business named. Bills of lading are also known as manifests or waybills.

In essence there are two different types of bill of lading: a non-negotiable, straight bill of lading or a negotiable (shipper's order) bill of lading, which can be bought, sold or traded while the goods are actually in transit. In both cases, however, the customer will be required to produce an original or copy of the bill of lading to prove ownership before taking possession of the goods.

Bools, Michael, *The Bill of Lading – A Document of Title to Goods*. London: LLP Professional Publishing, 1997.

Bill of materials (BOM)

A bill of materials (BOM) aims to list all of the parts, components and individual items which were used to create or manufacture a specific

B

product. In essence, a bill of materials is rather like a list of parts, but it goes one stage further than this as the components, parts and other items are listed as they were added to the product. In other words, a careful examination of a BOM indicates how a product was assembled. Some organizations refer to a BOM as a formula or recipe. Careful examination of the BOM should indicate to the organization the precise ordering of production units and processes within the premises. Assuming that most products are constructed or assembled in this manner, a BOM should help the organization to identify the most common route taken by the product on the shop floor.

Billing cycle

A billing cycle is the period of time which elapses between the delivery of products or the provision of a service and the time after that date when the customer is invoiced. Normally the billing cycle will roughly approximate to one month or 30 days.

Blind entries

A blind entry is a **book-keeping** entry which records either a debit or a credit, but does not show any other information.

Blocked currency

A blocked currency is a currency which cannot be freely transferred into convertible currencies and expatriated. It is a term usually used to describe foreign-owned funds or other earnings in particular countries whose government exchange regulations prevent the money from being expatriated.

Bond

Bonds are debt instruments which can be bought and sold on the market. A bond pays a specific amount of interest on a regular basis and the issuer of the bond undertakes to repay the debt at a specific time, in full.

Book inventory

The book inventory shows a business, theoretically, what stock it should have to hand, according to its accounting records. In the majority of cases there are discrepancies between the book inventory and any actual stock which may be available. The larger the business, and the larger the range of products and components stocked, the more difficult it is to reconcile the actual stock with the book inventory.

Waters, Donald, *Inventory Control and Management*. New York: John Wiley, 2003.

Book profit

Book profits are profits which have been made by a business but that have not, as yet, been realized as part of a transaction. Book profits are, to all intents and purposes, unrealized gains or profits; these are also known as paper gains or profits. A typical example of book profit would be stock which has risen in value and is still being held by the business, being, as yet, unsold.

Book value

The book value is the written down value of an asset as recorded in the financial records (book of accounts). The book value of an asset is usually taken to mean the **historical cost** of the asset, less the amounts written off as **depreciation**.

In cases where the asset has been re-valued, the book value becomes the re-valued amount, less any amounts which will be written off as depreciation following the re-valuation.

Book-keeping

Book-keeping is the precise and systematic recording of a business's financial transactions. Book-keeping has two different methodologies, known as **single entry** and **double entry.** In effect, book-keeping will record all monies received or spent by an individual business or an organization.

Roche, John, *Bookkeeping: Manual and Computerised*. Dublin: Gill & Macmillan, 2003.

Bottom line

'Bottom line' has several actual meanings, all related to the profit or loss which a business is experiencing. Typically, the bottom line could be calculated as the gross sales less expenses, taxes, interest and **depreciation**. In other words, the bottom line is the net earnings or income of a business, or its **net profit**. The bottom line, therefore, indicates the profit or loss that a business has made at the end of a given period. It can be used to assist in the calculations of earnings per share.

B

More generally, 'bottom line' can also be applied to any work or undertaking that the business is involved in which would ultimately produce a net gain for that business.

Breakeven analysis and the breakeven point

In order to identify an organization's breakeven point, it is necessary to consider the relationships between the various costs and sales in an integrated manner. The breakeven point is defined as being the point at which the level of sales is not great enough for the business to make a profit and yet not low enough for the business to make a loss. In other words, where earnings from sales are just sufficient for the business to cover its total costs. This occurs when total revenue from sales exactly equals the total cost of production.

Breakeven point occurs when total cost = total revenue

From this it can be assumed that if total revenue from sales is greater than total costs, then the organization concerned makes a profit. Conversely, if the opposite is true, and the total revenue is less than total costs, then the organization can make a loss. It is essential that organizations take this very important factor into account.

The organization will find that it is essential to determine how many units of output it must produce and sell before it can reach its breakeven point. The total cost of the unit of production is made up of two factors, the fixed and the variable costs, where:

Total cost = fixed costs + variable costs

And the total revenue is given by the number of products sold, multiplied by the selling price:

Total revenue = price × quantity

The drawing up and labelling of a breakeven chart makes the calculation of the breakeven point easier. The breakeven chart requires a considerable amount of labelling in order to enable the identification of exactly what the chart is describing about the breakeven point.

As can be seen in Figure 3, the breakeven chart will include:

- Units of production – which is considered to be the most completed product and not, importantly, the components which make up that product.
- **Fixed cost (FC)** – which are the costs that do not alter in relation to changes in demand or output. They have to be paid regardless of the business's trading level.

B

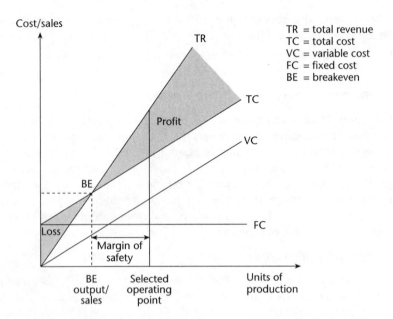

Figure 3 A breakeven chart

- **Variable costs (VC)** – which change in direct proportion to changes in output such as raw materials, components, labour and energy. Breakeven charts require the assumption that some costs vary in direct proportion to changes in output. In fact, it is unlikely that any costs are totally variable as raw materials, for example, are likely to cost less per unit if the organization buys in bulk. In this instance, it cannot be assumed that the cost of raw materials will double if output doubles.
- Total costs (TC) – these are simply the sum of all fixed and variable costs.
- Sales and costs – sales are the income generated from the selling of the units of production to customers. Costs, on the other hand, are expenses incurred by the organization in the purchase of raw materials, other fixed costs, and variable costs.
- Breakeven point (BE) – this is the point at which sales levels are high enough for the organization not to make a loss but not high enough for it to make a profit. In other words, this is the point where total sales equal total costs.
- Profit – in terms of the breakeven chart, and the breakeven point, this is achieved when sales exceed total costs.

- Loss – in terms of the breakeven chart, and the breakeven point, this occurs when revenue from sales has not met the total costs.
- Selected operating point – this is the planned production and sales level, which is assumed to be the same as that in given data.
- Margin of safety – this is the amount by which the selected operating point exceeds the breakeven point. This indicates the amount by which sales could fall from the planned level before the organization ceases to make a profit. The margin of safety is usually expressed in terms of units or a percentage.

Bridging loans

A bridging loan is a loan which is taken out on a short-term basis in order to literally bridge the gap between the purchase of a major asset and the sale of another asset. Bridging loans tend to be used by businesses in the purchasing of larger premises, as well as in the consumer housing market.

Budget deficit/surplus

A budget deficit is usually taken to mean situations where a business's spending exceeds its income over a period of time. It can also be referred to as 'deficit spending'.

Budget surplus is the reverse set of circumstances, in which a business's income exceeds its spending over a period of time.

Budgets themselves tend to be itemized **forecasts** which aim to predict a business's income and expenditure over a period of time. Both budget deficits and budget surpluses indicate that the budget, or the forecast, was imprecise in some way. Factors which contributed to either a deficit or a surplus would normally be included in any subsequent calculations of budgets in order to attempt to ensure that a similar situation does not arise in the future. Clearly, a budget surplus is an advantageous situation and ultimately more desirable than a budget deficit. Budget deficits reflect the fact that a business had not anticipated particular expenditure related to that budget, or had under-estimated associated costs.

B

Burn rate

'Burn rate' refers to the pace at which a new business uses up its **venture capital** or money received from an **angel investor** before it turns a profit. In many new businesses, particularly those at the frontiers of technology, the burn rate is particularly high. In practice, many of these businesses literally burn out of funding long before there is any prospect of them being able to produce a profit for their investors. Increasingly, new businesses wishing to acquire venture capital are rated by an assessment being made of their investment requirement set against time, so that a projection can be made, identifying the point at which they may make a profit.

Business cycle

Businesses need to be aware of the often predictable long-term patterns associated with either economic growth or decline in the economies in which they operate. Business cycles represent fluctuations which have a direct impact on the level of employment, **productivity** and interest rates. During a growth or recovery period, a business would expect to experience a greater demand for its products and services and would also enjoy a low rate of interest. But this interest rate would rise once full recovery of the economy had been achieved. Similarly, during a decline or recession, demand will reduce and, possibly, interest rates will rise on account of the fact that lenders may be less inclined to risk lending money that may not be paid back.

Arnold, Lutz G., *Business Cycle Theory*. Oxford: Oxford University Press, 2002.

Buying power

Buying power is essentially the value of money as expressed in either the quantity or the quality of products a business or a consumer may be able to purchase with that money. Whilst there is a degree of standard-ization in the buying power of businesses that seek to purchase products and services from their own domestic markets, their buying power can be undermined when purchasing abroad, should the comparative value of their own currency be reduced by fluctuations in the **exchange rate**. Equally, when the currency is strong, businesses' buying power in terms of overseas trade is greater and they are able to purchase larger quanti-ties, or better quality products, at comparatively low prices. Buying power is also known as purchasing power.

Cc

Capacity

Simply, capacity is the maximum rate of output for a given process. It is usually measured in output per unit of time. Businesses will tend to use different units of time in order to calculate their capacity, such as per minute, per hour, per day or per shift. In truth, the maximum capacity is much better described as being the demonstrated capacity, as this is the true level of capacity which has been achieved. Some organizations and analysts will attempt to calculate a theoretical capacity, which is largely based on the capacity of the machines involved and rarely takes into account any variables which may affect the capacity. Businesses will attempt to operate at their optimum capacity. This means that they will attempt to reduce costs or loss of capacity associated with waiting time.

McNair, C.G. and Vangermeersch, R. (eds), *Total Capacity Management: Optimizing at the Operational, Tactical and Strategic Levels.* Boca Raton, FL: St Lucie Press, 1998.

Capacity utilization rate (CUR)

CUR is the ratio of actual production, by business sector factories and other productive establishments, in the economy compared with the total potential production of these establishments.

CUR can therefore indicate the productiveness or effectiveness of the factories within a specific sector. CUR is used by analysts and the government to make a judgement as to how close to full employment a sector or the country is, taking into account the fact the CUR fluctuates from day to day, month to month and year to year. Ideally, a CUR of 85% is considered healthy in times of expansion as this is taken as an indication of being as close to full employment as may be possible. When the economy takes a down-turn and there is contraction in demand, the CUR could drop to as low as 70%.

The CUR of the sectors is combined to produce an overall picture of the economy, but this aggregate figure does not illustrate the peculiarities of the different sectors and the mixed fortunes which they may be experiencing.

CUR can also be used to determine a single business's capacity utilization, which is indeed the foundation of the CUR for the sector and ultimately the economy as a whole. CUR is, therefore, the percentage of a company's, industry's or country's production capacity which is actually used, over some period of time – otherwise known as the operating rate.

Capex

Capex is an acronym for '**capital** expense', or 'capital spending'. Capex is, therefore, money which is spent to purchase, or upgrade, **assets**, notably machinery or buildings. 'Capex' is usually a term associated with manufacturing industries that have potentially large expenses related to the purchasing of machinery, buildings and equipment in order to carry out their manufacturing operations. Comparatively speaking, Capex is a much smaller consideration for businesses involved in the service sectors, as primarily their capital expenditure on buildings and machinery is far lower than that of a manufacturer.

Boritz, J. Efrim and Wensley, Anthony K. P., *Capex: An Audit Planning Expert System.* Thousand Oaks, CA: Sage Publications, 1995.

Capital

Using its most simple definition, capital is money which can be invested by a business. It is the value of a business's **assets**, less its **liabilities**.

Capital can also be defined as the interest, in the form of assets, which the proprietors have in an organization, less their liabilities.

Equally the term 'capital' can be applied to any contributions which have been made by the business owners to a particular organization, which allow that business to function. In other words, this is their share capital, which was invested in the business.

Capital can equally be defined as either cash or goods used to generate income. More commonly, however, capital is taken to be the actual net worth of a business, measured by the amount by which the value of its assets exceeds that business's liabilities.

Capital account

The capital account, together with a **current account**, is a measurement of a country's **balance of payments**. Inherently these two accounts must balance. The capital account includes the net foreign lending, investment and changes in currency reserves.

See also **balance of payments**.

Capital appreciation

The most basic definition of capital appreciation is an increase in a business's wealth. Capital appreciation is usually associated with an increase in the market price, or value, of a particular **asset**, thereby making the business, at least on paper, wealthier.

Capital asset

A capital asset is an **asset** owned by a business which is a **tangible asset** that cannot be easily, or immediately, converted into cash. Typical examples of capital assets include land, buildings, or equipment. These assets have a real value to the business, yet the value of those assets cannot be easily realized should the business find itself in a position where it wishes or needs to sell them. Capital assets are often referred to as being **fixed assets**, which businesses tend to use over a considerable period of time. Many capital assets, such as plant and machinery, motor vehicles, and **goodwill**, depreciate over a period of time. Businesses, therefore, tend to make the decision to dispose of depreciating capital assets before they end their useful life. Periodically, on a yearly basis, a business will take account of the depreciation of its capital assets by reducing their **book value**. Theoretically at least, a capital asset which is allowed to depreciate and reach the end of its useful life has a zero value, or at best a scrap value. Other capital assets, given ideal economic conditions, may in fact appreciate. Typical examples of this would be land or buildings in highly sought-after locations. Equally, other capital assets, such as an investment in a subsidiary business, could either appreciate or depreciate according to the trading conditions relevant to that subsidiary.

A business will tend to use a capital asset pricing model which sets a value on those assets to assess the cost of capital, based on the rate of return it receives from its capital assets. An expected return on each of a business's capital assets is anticipated and an assessment can be made as to the risks of continuing to own that capital asset.

Cochran, John H., *Asset Pricing*. Princeton, NJ: Princeton University Press, 2001.

C

Capital efficiency

Capital efficiency is a means by which a business can assess the relationship between its output and its **capital expenditure**. Normally a business will divide its output by its capital expenditure in order to reveal how efficient its capital expenses have been and what impact they have had upon its output. Clearly, the larger the ratio between capital expenditure and output, the more efficient the capital expenditure has been. The capital–efficiency ratio is a somewhat imprecise measure of the effectiveness of capital expenditure, as it does not necessarily take into account any other factors which may have influenced a change in the output of the business. External considerations such as an increase in demand, or internal considerations such as increased proficiency in the business's employees, are not factored into the equation.

Aseerv, Anandarajah and Reid, Atham, *Managing Finance: Setting and Achieving Budgets, Performance, Costs and Efficiency, Operating Capital and Expenditure.* Sydney: Prentice-Hall, 1998.

Capital employed

'Capital employed' is an accounting term for a sum of capital which is equal to the total of the fixed and current **assets** that a business has, less its current **liabilities**. It is a measure of the internal or self-generated investment which the business has provided for itself.

Halpern, Karen, *Understanding Finance: Money, Capital and Investments.* New York: Prentice-Hall, 2003.

Capital expenditure

'Capital expenditure', or 'capital spending' or 'capital expense', refers to the money which a business spends primarily on the **acquisition** or the improvement of physical, tangible **fixed assets**. In other words, capital expenditure is related directly to a business's **capital assets**. In accounting and finance, capital expenditure is not deducted from the profits of the business. The reasoning behind this is that assets have been acquired, rather than a loss being made, in money terms. Ultimately, however, the capital expenditure as a result of acquiring a capital asset is likely to reduce in value, as capital assets tend to depreciate. It is at this point that the **depreciation** of that capital asset is charged against the profits of the business. Not all capital expenditure necessarily means an ultimate depreciation in the value of a capital asset. Some capital assets, such as land or buildings, do not necessarily depreciate, whilst other capital assets, such as plant, machinery and vehicles, do usually depreciate.

Aseerv, Anandarajah and Reid, Atham, *Managing Finance: Setting and Achieving Budgets, Performance, Costs and Efficiency, Operating Capital and Expenditure.* Sydney: Prentice-Hall, 1998.

Capital flight

'Capital flight' is a term used to describe the rapid outflow of **capital** from a country. This usually occurs when a situation has developed, or may potentially develop, which scares investors sufficiently for them to lose their confidence in the economy. The process gathers momentum as there are sharp falls in the exchange rate of the country's currency, which simply speeds the capital flight. This becomes particularly difficult and dangerous to the economy when the capital flight extends to the country's own investors.

Walter, Ingo, *The Secret Money Market: Inside the Dark World of Tax Evasion, Financial Fraud, Insider Trading, Money Laundering and Capital Flight*. New York: Harper-Collins, 1991.

Capital formation

The term 'capital formation' has two distinct definitions, which are inter-related. Capital formation involves the transfer of savings from consumers and government institutions to the business sector. This leads to an increase in output from businesses and a general economic expansion.

'Capital formation' can also be defined as being additions to the stock of a nation's real capital by an increased investment in **fixed assets**. Real capital in this sense means assets that have a distinct monetary value.

Diamond, Walter H. and Diamond, Dorothy B., *Global Guide to Investment Incentives and Capital Formation*. The Hague, Netherlands: Kluwer Law International, 2002.

Capital gain/capital loss

At its simplest, a capital gain is the amount by which a particular **asset**'s final selling price has exceeded the original purchase price of that asset. In order for a business to realize a capital gain, an investment which it has made in an asset needs to be sold at a profit.

Businesses also have unrealized capital gains, if they have made an investment in an asset, but that asset has not yet been sold. When it is ultimately sold, a profit will be made.

The capital gain, therefore, indicates the increase in value of an asset from the time it was acquired by a business to the time it is sold by that business. In the majority of countries there is a tax on such capital gains. Normally this is a different tax from the usual tax made on profits. A capital gains tax seeks to address disposals of assets which are not normally trading stock. Capital gains tax, therefore, assesses the profits which have actually been realized by the sale of a **capital asset**.

A capital loss, on the other hand, indicates a decrease in the value of an investment or an asset. A capital loss may be made by a business by selling an asset for less than it cost in the first place.

Capital growth

Capital growth is in essence **capital appreciation** in as much as it describes an increase in the market price of an asset owned by a business.

Capital investment

Capital investment involves a business purchasing **capital assets**. These capital assets, which may take the form of machinery or plant, are essential in a manufacturing industry, for example, which will rely on them to produce products. Theoretically the overall expenditure on capital investment in a given economy reflects the state of that economy. High expenditure on capital investment indicates a fast growing economy, whereas low capital investment indicates either reluctance on the part of businesses to invest in new plant and machinery, or a general down-turn in the economy itself.

Capital investments' primary goal is for the business to achieve a greater financial return, in terms of either **capital gain** or income. In many respects capital investments can be viewed as being a form of financial investment which leads to savings for the business. In making a capital investment a business is indicating its desire to produce more efficiently and to replace perhaps outdated and inefficient plant and machinery. The aim, in making a capital investment, is to become more profitable. The degree of capital investment is often used as a primary measure by which the government assesses overall business confidence.

Chisholm, Andrew, *An Introduction to Capital Markets: Products, Strategies and Participants*. New York: John Wiley, 2002.

Capital lease

A capital lease is a type of **leasing** which is classified and counted as a purchase by the leasee (and as a sale by the leasor). It must meet the following criteria:

- The leasor transfers the ownership of the **asset** to the leasee at the end of the lease term.
- The lease contains an option to purchase the asset.
- The lease term must be equal to at least 75% of the estimated economic life of the asset.

- The present value of the minimum lease rental payments must be equal to at least 90% of the market value of the leased asset in respect of related investment tax credits.

Capital net worth

The capital net worth of a business can be typically calculated by taking the total value of its **assets** minus the total value of its **liabilities.** For the majority of businesses, when the value of their assets exceeds that of their liabilities, the balance is normally made up of retained earnings (earnings which have not been paid out as dividends but are reinvested in the business), common stock (which consists of securities that represent **equity** ownership) or **net assets**. At its simplest, capital net worth is a measure of the relationship between the **book value** of a business's entire assets against all possible liabilities which that business may have. In many respects capital net worth does not indicate the actual value of a business. The majority of financial statements tend to value the assets and the liabilities at **historical cost**, which is not a reliable indicator of their true value.

Capitalization

Capitalization is, in effect, the amount of invested capital in a business. It is calculated by adding the business's long-term debt (money owed by the business), stock and retained earnings.

Capitalization is also used to calculate the actual market price of a business; this is achieved by multiplying the number of outstanding shares by the price per share. This aspect of capitalization is used when there is a proportional issue of free shares to existing **shareholders**.

The term can also be applied to what is known as a 'capitalization rate', which attempts to measure the current value of any of the business's anticipated earnings. The capitalization ratio measures the proportion of a business's value which is represented by its debt, stock, **assets** and other components.

Parker, D., *Adjusting Comparable Capitalisation Rate Evidence: Guidance for Practitioners.* London: RICS, 1999.

Capitalism

Capitalism is the predominant economic system in existence in the world. In capitalist countries business ownership tends to be in the hands of private individuals. These businesses and private individuals compete to achieve an economic gain. Theoretically, free-market forces determine the prices of products and services.

Capitalism is also typified by a separation between governments and businesses, where governments tend not to interfere in the markets as they are inherently efficient in their own right. The only role a government has in a capitalist economy is to ensure that consumers and businesses are protected from abuse and that the various markets are regulated.

According to the economist Adam Smith, an invisible hand guides free market capitalism. He stated that whilst businesses are concerned with maximizing their profits, the interaction between businesses in the marketplace ensures that both trading partners receive benefits which are in excess of simply producing the products and services themselves. Smith also suggested that as the exchange of goods was mutually beneficial, governments would not have to regulate, as the invisible hand would ensure that businesses which trade with one another only do so if the relationship is mutually beneficial.

Carriage and insurance paid (CIP)

See **carriage paid to (CPT)**.

Carriage paid to (CPT)

Both 'carriage paid to (CPT)' and 'carriage and insurance paid (CIP)' are used to describe the exact terms of the transaction which undertakes to pay carriage to a specific named destination. They are used as an alternative to the term 'CIF', which is a commercial acronym meaning **cost, insurance and freight**.

Cash against documents

Cash against documents is a method of paying for products and services in which the documents which transfer the ownership of those products and services are given to the buyers once they have paid cash to an intermediary (often a commission house) who is acting on behalf of the seller.

Cash basis

Cash basis is a **book-keeping** practice in which sales and expenses are only recorded when cash is either received or paid. This is an alternative to **accrual basis accounting**. Businesses which use cash basis book-keeping do so on the grounds that it is a more simplistic form of book-keeping than using the accrual basis. It does, however, make it more difficult for businesses to secure finance.

An associated term is **modified cash basis**.

Cash budget

A cash budget is simply a budget which seeks to estimate, or **forecast**, a business's receipts and expenditures over a specific period of time.

Cash cycle/cash conversion cycle

The term 'cash cycle' is a description interchangeable with 'cash conversion cycle', as it indicates the time that elapses between the **acquisition** of raw materials (primarily) and the receipt, on **accounts receivable**, of payment which has been generated as a result of the sale of the finished product.

Cash flow/cash flow statement

'Cash flow' is a term used to describe the net funds which have flowed through an organization over a period of time. Traditionally, cash flow is usually defined as earnings. The identification of when those earnings were received and when payments had to be made defines the parameters of cash flow. Cash flow is often complicated by the actual value of the cash received in a given period. Cash flow does not take into account expenses which may have been incurred by the organization prior to the period the cash flow covers, yet during this period the organization is benefiting from those costs in the past. Equally, the reverse is true; payments may now be due over the cash flow period on equipment or stock from which the organization has already profited, and which has been noted on a previous cash flow statement.

Cash flow also has a difficulty in dealing with outstanding debts and money owed by creditors. These do not appear on the cash flow as neither has been paid, yet they are important considerations, as they may have a negative or positive effect on the available working capital of the organization. The available funds which are calculated and identified within the cash flow have enormous implications for the business, particularly as the available working capital determines the organization's ability to pay subsequent debts promptly and to make necessary investments.

Walters, David, *Operations Strategy*. Basingstoke: Palgrave Macmillan, 2002.

Cash in advance (CIA)

This is a form of payment for goods which is made in full before the shipment is despatched. This form of payment occurs when products such as specialized machinery have been built to order. Cash in advance offers an exporter in international business the security of knowing that the goods have been paid for and that there will not be any debt-collection issues. Payment is usually made either by direct bank transfer or, perhaps, by cheque. The latter may in fact be at variance with the desire to receive payment before shipment, as overseas cheques may take as long as six weeks to clear. The difficulty arises when buyers are concerned that the goods will not be sent if payment is made in advance. With the internationalization of banking, cash in advance is being used less and less as a means of doing business.

Cash to asset ratio

The cash to asset ratio is often known as the **liquidity ratio**, or cash ratio. It is the actual value of cash or marketable liquid assets, such as securities, divided by the total **liabilities**.

When specifically the cash ratio, this is a measure of the cash reserve which a bank holds in proportion to the deposits of its customers. Given the fact that cash reserves do not earn interest, banks will seek to keep this ratio down to the absolute minimum. This needs to be consistent with their ability to provide cash on customer demand. As such, this ratio is normally set at around 8 per cent. Under the majority of circumstances a **central bank** will determine the cash ratio required.

A cash to asset ratio itself is useful in as much as it allows a measurement indicating the extent to which a business can liquidate its assets in order to cover its short-term liabilities. A business's cash to asset ratio, or liquidity, is therefore of primary interest and concern to short-term creditors of the business.

Central bank

The term 'central bank' is used to describe institutions such as the Federal Reserve in the United States, or the Bank of England in the United Kingdom. The first central bank was created in Sweden in the middle of the seventeenth century. In Europe the powers of the European Central Bank were effectively transferred to the **European Central Bank** in Frankfurt with the adoption of the Euro in 1999. The central bank's function was to set short-term interests and generally oversee the health of the country's financial system. It would act as a lender of last resort to commercial banks should they find themselves in financial difficulties. During the 1990s, notably in the UK, central banks have become increasingly independent from political intervention and now, in the UK, the Bank of England sets the interest rates without government interference.

Independent central banks theoretically concentrate on the long-term needs of the economy, avoiding short-term fixes, which are often adopted by governments. Above all, central banks are concerned with the reduction of inflation, whereas politicians tend to be concerned with both inflation and its impact on employment.

Charge off (bad debt)

Charge offs are **accounts receivable** which are highly unlikely to ever be collected and are, therefore, identified as being income which will have to be written off. Charge offs, or **bad debts**, appear as expenses on a business's income statement as they actually reduce the business's net income. Normally businesses will make an estimate of the charge-off expenses, which they anticipate, based on past records, when estimating their potential earnings. Many businesses will make a charge-off allowance, as historically they may have experienced the fact that not all of their creditors will necessarily pay them in full, and indeed some may not pay at all.

A closely associated term is 'adjustment', which refers to deductions made to effectively charge off a loss, particularly in the case of bad debts.

Clearing house

A 'clearing house' has three associated definitions. Most commonly, a clearing house is an institution which is involved in the settling of accounts between banks.

A clearing house may also be a business which is associated with an exchange. It effectively settles trade and regulates delivery.

Increasingly, the term 'clearing house' has become associated with aspects of e-commerce. Normally a clearing house is referred to as an acquirer, which is usually a bank. The acquirer processes a business's credit card authorizations and payments. They then forward that data to a credit card association, which in turn communicates with the issuer of the card.

Coincidence indicator

Whilst 'coincidence' in statistics refers to the occurrence of events which are related, but that appear to have no obvious common cause, a 'coincidence indicator' is taken to be an economic indicator. This economic indicator varies with another related economic trend which can assist a business or a government in assembling information about the current state of the nation's economy.

Commercial invoice

A commercial invoice is essentially a bill for goods sent to a buyer by a seller. Commercial invoices are also essential for customs, in order to determine the value of the goods while calculating any relevant duties or taxes. There is no single standard for a commercial invoice, but they tend to have some or all of the following features:

- the seller's contact information;
- the buyer's contact information;
- the consignee's contact information (assuming this is different from that of the buyer);
- the invoice date;
- a unique invoice number;
- sales terms;
- payment terms;
- currency of sale;
- quantities and descriptions of the merchandise;
- a statement of certification that the invoice is correct.

Compensatory and contingency financing facility (CCFF)

The compensatory and contingency financing facility was introduced by the **International Monetary Fund** in 1963 and provides aid to its members who are experiencing **balance of payments** problems. Originally it would fund shortfalls in export earnings or increases in serial import costs. It is now applied more broadly to fluctuations in commodity prices, shortfalls in tourism receipts and other situations. Changes in international interest rates or prices and the impact on primary imports and exports can usually trigger a CCFF payment.

www.imf.org

Compound annual growth rate (CAGR)

Compound annual growth rate is a year-on-year growth rate which is used to assess increases in the value of investments, or increases in other parts of a business's activity over a number of years. In other words it measures the rate of return on investment.

The compound annual growth rate does not represent reality as it describes the rate at which an investment grows as though it had grown at a steady rate. In reality, of course, investments can produce either a positive or a negative return in any given year. Supposing a business invests £100,000, which grows to a value of £300,000 in the first year, this is a growth rate of some 200%. However, in the second year the value of the investment drops to £150,000. By the end of this second year the business has still made £50,000 on the investment. This now means that the total return over the two years is 50%. The CAGR allows the business to illustrate a consistent yearly return which has taken them from the original £100,000 investment to the £150,000 value of the investment at the end of the second year.

Consumer Price Index (CPI) (US)

The CPI measures the current cost of purchasing a fixed set of goods and services and compares this with the cost of the same set at a specific base year. In effect, this is a very similar technique (with an identical purpose) to the **Retail Price Index (RPI)** as used in the UK. The measurement is a broad indication of the degree of **inflation** on basic goods. A standard **basket** of essentials is usually chosen to reflect the real changing costs to the average customer.

C

Contagion

'Contagion', as the term implies, is likened to a transmittable disease which spreads through economies, precipitating an economic crisis. Contagion often occurs when an economic crisis in one country spreads to other countries which then experience the same problems. Businesses increasingly pay heed to economic problems in either neighbouring countries or countries in which they trade. By being constantly aware of the effects of economic crises and the possibility of an economic crisis spreading to either their home market, or other markets in which they trade, they can attempt to prepare themselves for the inevitable economic impacts which may affect their business.

Contra account

A contra account is an account which offsets another account. If a contra **asset** account has a credit **balance**, it will offset the debit balance of a corresponding asset account.

A variation on this is a contra **liability** account, which may have a debit balance which offsets a credit balance of a corresponding liability.

Contraction

A contraction is most closely associated with part of a **business cycle**. It is a period of economic decline. Normally the contraction period will occur following an expansion phase, but before a recession. The business or economic cycle itself traditionally has four stages. These are known by a variety of names, but in essence they are:

- expansion;
- prosperity;
- contraction;
- recession.

Under the majority of circumstances, once a recession phase is over, a new expansion phase can begin. The period over which these pattern changes occur depends on many different factors. Increasingly the business cycles are affected by general cycles or changes in the worldwide economy, and indeed the economic cycle of any particular country may be affected by the economic conditions in other countries. In these cases, **contagion** may speed up or otherwise influence the economic cycle in another country. It is strongly believed that the prices of stocks (shares) and the trends which are being experienced often predict a change in the business cycle.

Contribution/contribution margin

Contribution is equal to total revenue less total **variable costs**. In other words, contribution minus **fixed costs** is equal to the profit made by the business. Contribution is used as a means by which a business can calculate the part played by each product, service or department in the **overheads** of the business. Once the overheads have been covered by the constituent elements, any further contribution is profit. Contribution is used to give a clearer indication of the situation of the business by effectively removing overheads, or other fixed costs, which are otherwise difficult to allocate, from the calculations.

Each product or service provides a unit contribution, which is taken to mean the selling price less the variable costs of producing it. From this excess the fixed overheads are removed. It is therefore possible to calculate the total contribution by summing the unit contribution and the number of units produced. The assumptions are that any marginal costs and the final selling price will remain constant.

Convertible loan stock

Convertible loan stock is broadly equivalent to a **bond** plus a stock option. A convertible, in this sense, means a security, which is invariably a bond or a **debenture** which can be converted into **ordinary shares** or **preference shares** at a fixed point or points in the future at a definite price. 'Convertible loan stock' can also be applied to a government security. In this case the holders have the opportunity to convert their holding into new stock, rather than obtaining repayment from the government.

Corporation tax

Corporation tax is a levy exacted by the government on the trading profits of a business. It also applies to chargeable gains or other income of businesses. In the UK, for example, the level of corporation tax is set by the Chancellor of the Exchequer in a budget statement. Normally corporation tax is paid in two parts, these are:

- advance corporation tax;
- mainstream corporation tax.

In effect, a business will pay corporation tax and then part of its net profit will be paid as **dividends** to its **shareholders.** The shareholders are again taxed for their earnings via the dividends. In the UK, for example, part of a business's corporation tax is treated as payment on account of shareholders' income tax, which they would normally pay on their dividends.

A business may choose to create what is known as a corporation tax company. This company operates to all intents and purposes in an over-

C

seas location which has significantly lower corporation tax than would otherwise be levied in countries in which it actually operates.

Saunders, Glyn and Antczak, Gina, *Tolley's Corporation Tax, 2003–2004: Main Annual.* Oxford: Tolley Publishing, 2003.

Cost accounting

The role of a cost accountant is to gather and manipulate data which is directly related to the costs and the efficiency of a business's manufacturing processes. Cost accountants would normally control budgets which are assigned to particular departments. They will also estimate the unit cost.

Cost accounting, therefore, involves making a detailed breakdown of any costs which are directly related to production or manufacturing and, indeed, providing a service. This information is required primarily for costing purposes. In other words, this is a determination of the total cost of a particular product or service, taking into account the purchase of any raw materials, inputs, **value added** activities and eventual delivery to the customer.

Cost accounting attempts, therefore, to identify all the costs associated with output. As such, this information is vital in establishing the selling price of products and services, the controlling of any manufacturing or service processes, materials planning, manpower planning and general budgeting issues.

Anthony, Robert N. and Govindarajan, Vijay, *Management Control Systems.* New York: McGraw-Hill Education, 2003.
Drury, Colin, *Cost and Management Accounting: An Introduction.* London: Thomson Learning, 2003.

Cost and freight (CFR)

Under the terms of cost and freight, the seller quotes a price to the buyer which includes the cost of goods and the cost of transportation to a particular point of debarkation. Insurance is left to the buyer. This is a typical form used for ocean shipments.

Cost, insurance and freight (CIF)

Cost, insurance and freight is a means by which the seller can quote for the cost of the goods, including the insurance and transportation to a given debarkation point. It is typically used for ocean shipments. Otherwise **carriage and insurance paid** would be used.

Cost of capital

Cost of capital is a means by which an investor who supplies capital can expect a return that is commensurate with the risk to which that capital is exposed. The term can also be used to describe the cost of raising money.

Typically, as far as a business raising capital is concerned, it would include the returns which the investor demands for lending or investing the money, the potential risks of the project, and the returns that would be provided by alternative investments at a similar risk.

Cost of goods sold (COGS)

The cost of goods sold is equal to a business's beginning inventory or stock, plus the cost of goods purchased during a specified period, minus the ending inventory or stock. 'Cost of goods sold' appears on a business's income statement and is associated with the cost of purchasing primarily raw materials and manufacturing finished products. The term 'cost of goods sold' is also known as '**cost of sales**'.

Martin, Christopher, *Logistics and Supply Chain Management*. London: Financial Times, Prentice-Hall. 1999.

Cost of sales

See **cost of goods sold (COGS)**.

Costing systems

There are a number of different costing systems which may be adopted by a business. Typically these could include a manufacturing costing system, a job or contract costing system, or a process and batch/operation costing system. Businesses take the decision as to which system to use. They may do this as a result of particular process-costing complications or difficulties in charting work in progress at the beginning and at the end of each period. Additional complications include calculating and costing equivalent units of finished goods, work in progress and any losses. They may also use weighted averages, or **first in, first out** methods of stock valuation. Both of these methodologies have implications with regard to the costing system adopted by the business.

Nair, Mohan, *Activity-based Information Systems: An Executive's Guide to Implementation*. New York: John Wiley, 1999.

Cost-plus pricing

The cost-plus pricing methodology is one of the most common forms of pricing policy, and it is also one of the more straightforward. The pricing method simply involves adding a predetermined percentage or gross figure to the costs of production or purchase, thereby creating a price point for the product or the service.

This basic form of pricing does not take into account individual current market conditions and is in many cases considered to be too prescriptive in its structure for standard use. Despite this, many base prices are calculated on this cost-plus assumption.

Credit reference

A credit reference provides a business with an indication of a borrower's previous borrowing habits and records. Banks or other lenders can often provide the information when a borrower wishes to extend or open a new line of credit with another business. An assessment is made of the credit worthiness of the borrower (an individual or a business) which aims to state whether they can be safely given credit. In the past, the majority of credit references or credit ratings were indeed provided by banks, but increasingly this information is provided by credit reference agencies (or rating agencies). These organizations gather credit-related information from a variety of sources (e.g. bankruptcy hearings, debt collectors or hire purchase businesses). This information is then available, for a fee, to businesses which have had a credit request from a business or an individual. Some agencies operate exclusively with and for corporate clients. They provide information regarding a business's short-term and long-term debt.

Credit risk insurance

Credit risk insurance is simply a form of insurance which is designed to cover the risk of non-payment for goods which have been delivered.

Schaeffer, Hal, *Credit Risk Management: A Guide to Sound Management Decisions*. New York: John Wiley, 2000.

Credit squeeze

Credit squeeze is a factor which may well have a direct effect upon the accuracy of a business's predictions related to future income. As such, it will have a major impact on the budget allocations and expected returns on investment.

A credit squeeze is generally taken to mean a government measure, or package of measures, which are aimed at reducing or restricting the money supply. Typically, a government will consider one or more of the following:

- an increase in interest rates (to arrest borrowing);
- the control of money lending by banks;
- an increase in hire purchase regulations.

Effectively, a credit squeeze seeks to curb the pressures of **inflation** before they become a serious concern, by aiming to reduce the available amount of credit in the economy.

Credit tranche

A credit tranche is an instalment or portion of an **International Monetary Fund** loan. The loans are invariably made for periods of between eighteen months and three years and disbursed in tranches. There are certain conditions which must be met in order to secure the release of any of the subsequent tranches.

Creditor

A creditor is an individual or a business to which another individual or business owes money. In accounting terms there is a distinction between creditors in as much as a **balance sheet** will reveal just the total amount which is owed to creditors. In reality, of course, some of these creditors will be paid during the forthcoming accounting period (short-term debts), whilst others will not be paid until much later (long-term debts).

A creditor can also be described as an individual or a business which has extended credit to another individual or business. The individual or business that owes the creditor money is known as a **debtor**.

Creditor's payment period

Creditor's payment period is also known as payables turnover. It is calculated by dividing the number of creditors by the purchases made by the business on credit terms and then multiplying that figure by 365.

The net result is the average period of days which the business takes to make their credit repayments. It is vital for a business to be aware of how long it takes to pay a creditor, as it may be the case that continued late payments may result in the reduction of credit facilities or difficulties in obtaining credit from other sources.

An alternative formula can also be used to monitor the day-on-day purchases by credit:

$$\frac{Creditors}{Average\ daily\ purchases\ (i.e.\ purchases\ divided\ by\ 365)}$$

Current account

See **balance of payments**.

Current account deficit/surplus

A current account deficit or surplus is shown on a country's **balance of payments**, detailing the relationship between the exports and imports of products and services. A current account deficit occurs when the value of the exports is lower than the value of the imports. A current account surplus occurs when the value of the exports is higher than the value of the imports.

Pitchford, John, *The Current Account and Foreign Debt*. London: Routledge, 1995.

Current assets

Current assets are **balance sheet** items which are broadly equivalent to cash, or 'cash equivalents'. Current assets form the circulating **capital** used by a business and they are constantly being turned over in the normal course of trading. Typical current assets include stock, **debtors** and cash. Essentially, a current asset may be any asset that may be readily (but not necessarily immediately) transformed into cash. The **creditors** of a business will be particularly interested in the value of the business's current assets. It is those assets that can be quickly liquidated in cases where the business is short of ready cash to pay creditors. Above all, current assets are vital to the business itself as they determine its ability to find funds for day-to-day operations.

Current cost accounting

Current **cost accounting** is a valuation methodology. The methodology states that assets and goods which are used in production are valued at either their estimated or their actual current market prices at the point when production takes place. Current cost accounting is also known as replacement cost accounting as it shows the true current value of assets and stock.

Horngren, Charles T., Bhimani, Alnoor, Datar, Srikant M. and Foster, George, *Management and Cost Accounting*. London: Financial Times, Prentice-Hall, 2001.

Current liabilities

Current liabilities are usually taken to mean amounts which are due to **creditors** and are to be paid within 12 months.

Current liabilities appear on a business's **balance sheet** and are equal to the sum of all money owed to creditors. Current liabilities are also known as payables or current debts.

Current ratio

The current ratio is used as an indicator as to whether a business has the ability to meet its short-term debt obligations. Typically, it is calculated by dividing the **current assets** by the **current liabilities**.

The current assets include all cash or assets which can be easily converted into cash (**stock**, money owed by debtors, etc.). By dividing the current assets by the current liabilities, a business will be able to assess the amount of coverage it may have available to meet its short-term debts.

For example, a business may have current assets valued at £950,000 and its current liabilities may run to £450,000. Using the current ratio, the business can then calculate the following:

$$\frac{950,000}{450,000} = 2.11$$

This figure is often expressed as 2.11:1. The ratio shows that the business has £2.11 of current assets for every £1.00 of current liabilities. If the industry standard current ratio was, for example, 2:2, then this business would be considered to have a satisfactory current ratio.

Fridson, Martin and Alvarez, Fernando, *Financial Statement Analysis: A Practitioner's Guide*. New York: John Wiley, 2002.
Temple, Peter, *Magic Numbers: The 33 Key Ratios that Every Investor Should Know*. New York: John Wiley, 2001.

Current yield

Current yield is equal to the annual rate of return which is being received on an investment. The calculation is made by dividing the interest being paid on a **bond**, for example, by its current market price. This figure is expressed as a percentage. The current yield is differentiated from the nominal yield, which simply states the yield in terms of the interest paid, as a percentage of its par value (the nominal price of the share or security).

In order to calculate the current yield, the following information is required:

- the original (nominal) price of the **stock**;
- the market price of the stock (current price);
- the interest rate paid on the stock.

Therefore, if a business has invested £10,000 in 8% stock which is now valued at £9,000, then the current yield is:

10,000 ÷ 9,000 × 8 = 8.9%

It is normally the case that when interest rates rise, the market value of fixed interest stock falls in order to provide a competitive current yield.

Cyclical stock

Cyclical stock is typically stock whose value may either rise or fall in line with seasonal factors, or indeed economic cycles (or **business cycles**). Normally cyclical stock is stock which is closely tied to, or sensitive to, the economic cycle; many such stocks are dependent upon the overall current performance of the economy.

Cyclical stock may be produced by what are known as cyclical businesses, which make products or services at a lower output to match the lower demand when the economy is suffering a down-turn. Examples of these types of businesses include vehicle manufacturers and the housing/building industry.

Investors will look for increases in the value of the stock of cyclical businesses as an indication that the economy is about to experience an upturn in fortunes. An investor may, typically, invest in a cyclical business at the bottom point of an economic cycle or just before the value of that stock rises. This will enable the investor to make the maximum profit by selling the **stock** at the high point of the economic cycle.

Dd

Date of payment

The date of payment is also known as a 'payment date' and is related to the schedule of the payments of **dividends**, **bond** interest payments or mutual fund distributions. Quite literally, the date of payment is the expected date on which a payment of this type is likely (or contracted) to be made.

Date of record

A date of record, or 'record date', is related to the timing of the ownership of **shares**. A date of record is specified by the issuing business as a means by which the owners of shares become eligible to receive their **dividends**. In other words, if shareowners are in possession of the share(s) on or before the date of record, then they are entitled to the dividend. Should they purchase the shares after the date of record, then they are not entitled to that dividend payment.

Days payable

Days payable is a way in which a business can estimate the average time it takes to pay a **creditor**. It can also be used by potential creditors as a means of calculating the expected period of time they will have to wait to be paid by the **debtor**.

Days payable is usually calculated by dividing **accounts payable** by the annual credit purchases, and multiplying that figure by 365.

Days receivable

In essence, days receivable is precisely the same as **days payable** in as much as it is a calculation of the average time customers take to pay for purchases. In this case, the days receivable is equal to the **accounts receivable**, divided by the annual sales (on credit) and multiplied by 365.

Day's sales outstanding (DSO)

Day's sales outstanding is calculated by dividing the total amount owed to a business by the sales achieved per day. Businesses simply calculate the daily sales by dividing their annual sales (on credit) by 365.

If a business has a yearly turnover of £1,000,000 then the daily sales figure is £2,739.7. If the business is currently owed some £10,000 then the calculation is:

$$\frac{10,000}{2,739.7} = 3.65$$

Should the business improve this DSO then it simply multiplies the amount still owed, by the percentage improvement in the collections. It would then subtract the resulting figure from the amount still owed before repeating the DSO calculation.

In the US, for example, DSO is calculated per quarter in which case the formula is: the **accounts receivable** divided by the sales and then divided by 91.

Debenture

A debenture is a document which either creates or evidences a debt owed by a business. In many cases debentures are secured, giving the creditor a priority in terms of repayment compared with unsecured creditors.

Debit

A debit is an accounting entry. It refers to either an increase in **assets** or a decrease in **liabilities**.

Debit note

A debit note serves to indicate that a business or an individual owes money to another business or individual. In effect, a debit note is not dissimilar to an invoice.

Debt ratio

See **debt to equity ratio** and **debt to total assets ratio**.

Debt service coverage

'Debt service' refers to a business's ability to provide sufficient funds to repay its outstanding debts and interest payments. Typically, the business may have to find periodic payments (monthly, quarterly, yearly, etc.).

Debt service coverage is therefore a ratio of the cash flow available to pay for debt, to the total amount of debt payments which must be made. The typical ratio used is:

$$Debt\ service\ coverage\ ratio\ = \frac{earnings\ (before\ interest\ \&\ tax)\ +\ non\text{-}cash\ charges}{interest\ outstanding\ \&\ loan\ repayment\ instalments}$$

The ideal debt service coverage ratio (DSCR) is 2:1.

Debt to equity ratio

The debt to equity ratio is primarily concerned with the relative contribution of debts and equities (for ordinary shareholders) in financing the operations of a business. The ratio is:

$$Debt\ to\ equity\ ratio\ = \frac{total\ debt\ (long\text{-}term\ and\ short\text{-}term\ liabilities)}{total\ equity\ (ordinary\ share\ capital\ plus\ reserves)}$$

If a business had a total debt of some £2,100,000 and a total equity of £3,600,000 then the ratio would be:

$$Debt\ to\ equity\ ratio\ = \frac{2,100,000}{3,600,000}\ =\ 0.58$$

This means that for every £1 which has been contributed by equity shareholders, the lenders and creditors have contributed £0.58. The higher the ratio, the less protected the lenders.

Fridson, Martin and Alvarez, Fernando, *Financial Statement Analysis: A Practitioner's Guide*. New York: John Wiley, 2002.

Temple, Peter, *Magic Numbers: The 33 Key Ratios that Every Investor Should Know*. New York: John Wiley, 2001.

D

Debt to total assets ratio

The debt to total assets ratio seeks to measure the extent to which lenders and **creditors** are contributing to the financing (of the assets) of a business. The debt to total assets ratio is:

$$Debt\ to\ total\ assets\ = \frac{total\ debt\ (long\text{-}/short\text{-}term)}{total\ assets\ (fixed\ and\ current)}\ \times\ 100$$

A business may have a total debt of some £2,100,000 and fixed and current assets currently valued at £5,700,000. Its ratio will look like this:

$$\frac{2,100,000}{5,700,000} \times 100 = 36.84\%$$

This particular ratio reveals that lenders and creditors are contributing nearly 37% of the total funds which the business has used to finance the purchase of its assets.

Fridson, Martin and Alvarez, Fernando, *Financial Statement Analysis: A Practitioner's Guide*. New York: John Wiley, 2002.
Temple, Peter, *Magic Numbers: The 33 Key Ratios that Every Investor Should Know*. New York: John Wiley, 2001.

Debtor

A debtor is either an individual or a business which owes a debt to another individual or business, known as the **creditor**. On a **balance sheet** debtors are denoted as those who owe money to the business and there is a distinction made between those debtors who are expected to pay their debts during the next accounting period and those debtors who will not pay until after that period.

Debtor's collection period

The debtor's collection period is also known as the receivables turnover. A simple calculation is made which divides the debtors (accounts receivable) by sales on credit and then multiplies that figure by 365.

The resulting figure is the average period, in days, that it takes for debtors to make a payment to the business.

See also **debtor's turnover**.

D

Debtor's turnover

A debtor's turnover calculation is made using the following formula:

$$Debtor's\ turnover = \frac{credit\ sales}{trade\ debtors}$$

Alternatively, it can be expressed as:

$$Debtor's\ turnover = \frac{average\ debtors}{credit\ sales \div 365}$$

In this second and more precise measure, a business could make calculations assuming the following:

- Its credit sales are £2,221,356.
- Its debtors, who are due to pay within a year, owe £298,400.

Therefore the calculation is:

$$\frac{298,400}{2,221,356 \div 365} = \frac{298,400}{6,085.9} = 49.03 \; days$$

The business would then attempt to assess the industry average of debtor turnover to see whether its current debtor turnover was satisfactory.

Declaration date

A declaration date, or declaration day, is the date on which a business's directors meet to announce the date when the next **dividend** payment will be made. They also state the amount of the dividend payment. As soon as the payment has been authorized, it becomes known as a declared dividend. The declaration day in the UK is taken to be the last-but-one day before options must be declared to the Stock Exchange. In other words the owners of an option must decide, and make a statement to that effect, as to whether they intend to purchase or sell the securities.

Declining balance method

'Declining balance method' is a term associated with **depreciation**. Using the declining balance method a high charge is made to **fixed assets** in their first year, but reducing amounts are applied in the following years. In each successive year the depreciation is calculated as a set percentage of the **book value** of the asset, as noted in the previous year.

The business would calculate the periodic, or yearly, depreciation rate using the following formula:

$$Percentage \; periodic \; depreciation \; rate = \frac{100\%}{the \; lifespan \; of \; the \; asset}$$

If the asset has an estimated lifespan of ten years, then the periodic or yearly depreciation rate would be 10%. This 10% is cumulatively deducted on a periodic or yearly basis from the initial value of the asset, or the depreciated value of the asset in the preceding year.

D

There are variations on this theme which include the **double-declining balance depreciation method**, which simply replaces the 100% in the equation by 200% (or any other percentage, such as 125%, 150% or 175%, can also be applied to the equation).

Defensive interval

A defensive interval is a means by which an assessment can be made of a business's ability to satisfy its debts. The defensive interval is calculated by assessing how long the business could operate using its current liquid **assets** without any additional revenues and still be able to satisfy its debts.

Deferred charge

'Deferred charge' is the opposite of **deferred revenue**. A deferred charge, such as pre-paid rental, is an expenditure which is considered an asset until the payment is actually due. In the case of pre-paid rent, it is an asset in as much as the expenditure has already been made, but is no longer an asset once the rent relevant to that payment falls due.

Deferred credit

Deferred credit is revenue which has been received by a business but which has not yet been reported as income.

Deferred revenue

Deferred revenue is the opposite of a **deferred charge**. This is revenue which is considered to be a liability until it becomes relevant. A typical example would be payment which has already been received for work, products or services, when the business has not yet carried out that work or supplied those products or services. The term is directly related to pre-payment, which is the payment in part, or whole, of a debt before its due date.

Deferred tax

'Deferred tax' refers to liabilities derived from income which has been earned for accounting purposes, but not for tax purposes. Normally a business would set aside an amount of money for tax that will become due in a period other than the period in which the accounts are being reviewed. Deferred tax, or deferred taxation, normally arises because of the timing differences between various accounting conventions and prevailing tax regulations. Deferred tax accounting, therefore, seeks to re-allocate tax payments to the same period in which the relevant amount of income or expenditure is actually shown. Normally timing differences between accounting conventions and tax rules arise as a result of the percentages which are being used to calculate capital allowances and the fact that they have differed from calculations used for **depreciation**.

Deficit

A deficit, in the general sense, is a situation where the sum of the debts exceeds the sum of the credits. It is usually applied to the **balance of payments** or indeed any international transactions, and is clearly the reverse of a **surplus**.

Deficit financing

Deficit financing occurs when a business needs to secure additional finance as a result of its expenditure exceeding its receipts. Normally a business will seek to secure deficit financing if the forecasted projections of expenditures and sales revenue are unbalanced in the sense that for a period of time its **liabilities** will exceed the receipts from sales.

Deficit net worth

Deficit net worth, or negative net worth, normally represents an operating loss for a business. On a business's **balance sheet** this would be typified by greater **liabilities** than **assets** or stock/share value. In other words, on paper the business has a negative value as its liabilities are in excess of the sum of its assets and available **capital**.

See also **net worth**.

D

Deficit spending

Deficit spending occurs when a business's expenditure exceeds its income over a given period of time. The deficit spending is usually financed by borrowing, in the form of either a loan or an extended overdraft facility. When governments face deficit spending situations they, too, borrow rather than increase the tax burden on businesses or individuals.

De-gearing

De-gearing is a tactic adopted by businesses to convert some of their fixed interest loan stock with **ordinary share** capital. This effectively reduces the business's dependence upon borrowing, replacing loans with investment in the form of **equity** shares.

Deposit multiplier

A deposit multiplier is the value which represents the ratio of bank reserves to bank deposits. Changes in the reserves are reflected in a magnified change in deposits. The deposit multiplier is the inverse of the required reserves ratio; in other words, if a bank chooses to keep 10% of its deposits in reserve, then the deposit multiplier is the inverse of that 10%, which is 10.

The reserve ratio of most banks ranges between 1% and 3%. As noted, the reserve ratio plays an important role in the deposit multiplier; as the reserve ratio increases then the deposit multiplier increases in proportion.

Depreciation

Depreciation is a systematic reduction of the **acquisition costs** of **fixed assets**, such as machinery, over the period during which those assets are of benefit to the organization. Depreciation is, in effect, a paper-based accountancy exercise which seeks to take account of the fact that the value of fixed assets gradually decreases over a period of time and that those attendant losses should be written off against the expense accounts of the organization.

In the US this process is known as **amortization**, which is the systematic reduction of the value of primarily **intangible assets**, such as **goodwill** or intellectual property (although, of course, tangible assets can be similarly reduced in value in this way). The value of these intangible assets, such as a breakthrough in manufacturing processes, reduces in value over a period of time as the asset is either replaced or copied by competitors.

'Depreciation' can also be used to describe a fall in the value of a country's currency. When the currency relative to other currencies, or to a weighted average of other currencies, falls on the exchange market, this process is known as depreciation.

See also **reducing balance depreciation**.

Devaluation

'Devaluation' has three different meanings. Firstly, it may be used as an alternative description for **depreciation**.

'Devaluation' can also be used to denote a fall in the value of a currency which had been pegged at a particular value.

It can also be used to describe a fall in the value of currency in terms of gold or silver, or indeed a sudden fall in the value of one currency compared with other currencies.

Devaluation usually occurs when there is a sharp fall in a currency which is part of a **fixed exchange rate** system. There have been cases where devaluation was a part of government policy, and on many occasions devaluation has taken place as a result of investors speculating in the currency.

Devaluation can have short-term competitive benefits, but in the longer term higher prices erode these benefits.

See also **J curve**.

Edwards, Sebastian, *Real Exchange Rates, Devaluation and Adjustment: Exchange Rate Policy in Developing Countries*. Cambridge, MA: MIT Press, 1989.

Development bank

Development banks may be involved in activities worldwide, nationally or regionally and aim to encourage economic development by lending or investing money in businesses in a specific region.

Diminishing balance method

See **reducing balance depreciation**.

Diminishing return

Diminishing return is said to be the point which a business may reach where the use of any additional resources results in a less than proportional increase in output. An associated term is 'diminishing marginal returns', which is a theory suggesting that if the amount of one input is increased and all other inputs remain constant, the amount by which output increases for each additional unit will generally decrease.

Direct cost

Direct costs are expenditures which can be solely allocated to a specific product or project. They are differentiated from **indirect costs** as these include unavoidable overheads which, in themselves, are not specifically related to the product or the project in question.

Directly unproductive profit-seeking activities

Directly unproductive profit-seeking activities are those activities which have no directly productive purpose. They do not increase the utility of a product or service as far as a consumer is concerned and are wholly designed to increase profits. Typically, they would include attempts to distort the market in order to achieve a higher profit, without adding value.

Dirty float system

A dirty float system involves a currency which floats in terms of its value compared with other currencies and which is prone to government intervention. Governments adopting this system will attempt to manage the fluctuations in the currency's value in order to maintain desired exchange rates.

Disbursement

Disbursement has two definitions, the simplest of which is 'paying or discharging a debt or expense'.

More generally, however, the term is associated with payments which are made by professional individuals, such as bankers or lawyers, on behalf of their client. The professional is reimbursed for the expenses which have been incurred on behalf of the client when the professional tenders the bill for his or her services.

Disbursing agent

A disbursing agent is either an individual or an organization which deals with **dividend** or interest payments on behalf of a business. In effect the disbursing agent undertakes the function of paying out these dividends or interest payments on behalf of the business, which is in itself rather like outsourcing this activity.

Discount rate

Discount rates are the rates at which future values are diminished each year to make them comparable to present values. Discount rates are used as an integral part of investment appraisal for **discounted cash flow** technique. Discount rates are also the rates at which **central banks** charge commercial banks for short-term loans of reserves. They are an essential tool of monetary policy.

Discounted cash flow

Discounted cash flow is an **investment appraisal** methodology which seeks to investigate **capital investment** projects and compare their income as depicted in forecasted **cash flows**, together with their present and future costs in comparison with other equivalents. These other equivalents, or current equivalents, aim to take into account the fact that any future incomes are less valuable than current receipts. This is because the interest which could be earned on current receipts could be used to offset any current payments. The two standard forms of discounted cash flow types are **net present value (NPV)** and **average rate of return**. Discounted cash flow seeks to discover whether capital outlays will generate positive cash inflows in the future. Each of the cash inflows is multiplied by a discount factor, which is set between 0 and 1 (because money at a future date is worth less to the business than the same sum of money should they have it to hand now). The business may have to wait a considerable time for any future inflows of capital, which inevitably means that these future sums are worth less than the equivalent amount of money at the present day.

Once the business has discounted these figures the future cash flows can be totalled. This gives the business the opportunity to assess the capital outlay by deducting this figure to give the net present value of the project. If the figure arrived at is positive, then comparatively speaking the project is a viable one. If it is a negative figure, then the business should seriously consider whether the project is worth pursuing.

The following assumptions can be made in an example which incorporates both the discount factor and the discounted cash flow:

- A new printing press has cost the business £2m.
- It has been estimated that the printing press will be a viable **asset** for 4 years.
- In each year the printing press will cost £200,000 to run, but will save the business £800,000 in labour costs.
- The business has assessed that the rate of interest and therefore the discount factors run at 10%.

A table can therefore be assembled in order to complete the calculations (see Table 2).

D

Table 2 Calculating discount factors

Year	Cash in (£)	Cash out (£)	Net cash (£)	Discount factor	Net present value (£)
Current	–	2,000,000	(2,000,000)	1.00	(2,000,000)
1	800,000	200,000	600,000	0.91	546,000
2	800,000	200,000	600,000	0.83	498,000
3	800,000	200,000	600,000	0.75	450,000
4	800,000	200,000	600,000	0.68	408,000
					(98,000)

In this case, the business having made calculations as to the possible income and expenditure and adjusted these figures to take account of discounted cash flow, it is shown that the project over the four-year period entailing the purchase of the new printing equipment would represent a loss of £98,000. This would make the purchase of the printing machinery somewhat difficult to justify.

Wright, Maurice Gordon, *Using Discounted Cash Flow in Investment Appraisal*. London: McGraw-Hill Education Europe, 1990.

Discretionary expense

A discretionary expense can be either a recurring or a non-recurring expense for products and services. Typically, discretionary expenses are either non-essential items or items which are more expensive than may be reasonably justified. Examples would include entertainment expenses, such as the **leasing** of a corporate box at a sports venue.

Disposable income

This is the amount of income left to an individual after taxes have been paid, with this remainder being available for spending and saving. Disposable income should also take into account necessary deductions prior to the individual receiving the wage or salary. So, in this respect, disposable income should also include pension, insurance and tax contributions. In other words, disposable income can be likened to net pay.

Distribution

Distribution is the physical movement of products and services from the producer to the end-user and often involves the transfer of ownership through intermediaries between the producer and the end-user. A distribution channel ends when an individual or a business buys a product or service without the intention of immediate resale.

Part of the distribution channel consists of organizations such as storage and transport companies and banks. They are integral parts of the distribution process, but they are outside of it in the sense that they never take ownership of the product or service; they merely aid the channel.

A business faces several different options when setting up the distribution system for its products and services. The key determinants of how this distribution channel is organized usually depend on the following:

- A determination of the role of distribution and how it will help achieve the marketing objectives.
- The selection of the type of channel and whether intermediaries are required.
- An assessment of the intensity of the distribution, which allows the business to assess how many intermediaries will be needed at each level and in each area.
- The choosing of specific channel members which most closely match criteria set by the business.

In terms of accounting and finance, distribution has three further definitions. The first is related to the distribution of profits to **shareholders** by means of a **dividend**.

Distribution also refers to a dividend on which advance **corporation tax** may be payable. In the UK, for example, distribution includes any payment out of the **assets** of a business in respect of **shares** with the exception of repayments of **capital**.

The final accounting and finance-related definition refers to the division of assets, according to the law of particular countries, in the case of the owner of a business dying, or a business being declared bankrupt. In these cases various formulas, precedents and priorities are established as to how the distribution of any remaining assets, of whatever nature, is carried out.

Distribution date

Essentially a distribution date is the same as the **date of payment** in as much as it is the date on which a **bond** interest payment, **dividend** or mutual fund payment is scheduled to be made.

Distribution period

The distribution period is the time between the **declaration date** and the **record date** or **date of record**. In other words, this period, which is usually just a few days, is the difference between the date upon which an announcement is made regarding a **dividend** payment and the date upon which an individual needs to own shares in order to be eligible for that dividend.

Dividend

A dividend is a taxable **distribution** of a proportion of the profits, after tax, which a business's directors undertake to pay to **shareholders**, usually in the form of an annual payment, but in some cases, such as in the US, on a quarterly basis. Dividends need not necessarily take the form of cash; they can also involve a **stock dividend**.

Although businesses have no legal obligation to pay a dividend, dividends provide an incentive for investors to invest money in a business. There is a distinction between different forms of shares and precisely how the dividends are paid. Owners of **preference shares** are paid a fixed dividend, whilst **ordinary share** owners are paid a variable dividend, which reflects the fortunes of the business in the preceding economic period. Ordinary share dividends, therefore, can fluctuate, with a higher dividend being paid in times when the business is trading successfully and a lower dividend in times of difficulty and, indeed, no dividend if the business is not recording a profit at all.

Businesses in the UK, for example, tend to pay their dividends every six months. The lion's share of the dividend is paid after the business's Annual General Meeting (AGM) and is known as the final dividend. A smaller dividend is usually paid some six months before the AGM and is known as an interim dividend. It is common practice in the US for businesses to pay their dividends on a quarterly basis.

The shareholders are asked to validate any dividend payments at the AGM. This is particularly important if the business has decided to reduce the dividend payment as a result of deciding to retain some of the profits they made in the financial year in order to reinvest the money.

Frankfurter, George M., Wood, Bob G., and Wansley, James, *Dividend Policy: Theory and Practice*. Oxford: Academic Press, 2003.

Dividend capture

Dividend capture is a policy adopted by some businesses which involves the buying and selling of other businesses' stocks or shares in order to collect **dividends** as a means of income. In many respects dividend capture is a tax-efficient way of receiving income for businesses as, comparatively speaking, they pay very little tax on the income derived from dividend capture. This form of policy is also known as trading dividends.

Dividend claw-back

Dividend claw-back involves an arrangement between investors and a business, with the **shareholders** agreeing that any **dividends** they receive will be reinvested in the business itself. The investors make these dividends available to the business, particularly in the case of businesses which are rapidly expanding, in order to help cover any possible cash deficiencies, notably in their **working capital** or ability to repay loans.

Dividend discount model

The dividend discount model, or discounted dividend model, is a means by which the value of stock can be calculated by effectively reducing future **dividends** to their present value. In effect this is an application of the same technique used in **discounted cash flow** but applied on this occasion to future dividend payments.

Dividend in arrears

The term 'dividend in arrears' refers to unpaid **dividends** on **preference shares** or **preferred stock**. Normally businesses or individuals who hold these forms of shares would be entitled to a specific dividend at a specific rate of interest before any dividends are paid to common stockholders or **ordinary shareholders**. In other words, these payments would take precedence over other payments made to shareholders. In this case, however, the business undertakes to defer the payment of the dividend to a future date, with the approval of the owners preferred stock, or preference shareholders.

D

Dividend payout ratio

The dividend payout ratio is a means by which the percentage payout in the form of **dividends** from a business's earnings can be calculated. Normally the amount which has been paid in dividends is divided by the business's earnings over a specific time, and then expressed as a percentage. Dividend payout ratio is also known as 'payout ratio'.

Dividend rate

The dividend rate is simply either the fixed rate which is paid on **preferred stock** or **preferences shares** or the adjustable rate which is paid on common stock or **ordinary shares**. In the case of preferred stock or preference shares, investors will already be aware of the **dividend** rate and will have agreed that this is a reasonable rate of return at the time that they decided that the investment was a worthwhile consideration. Owners of common stock or ordinary shares may not necessarily be able to anticipate the dividend rate in any given year until such a time as the business releases an interim report, or holds an Annual General Meeting (AGM) to confirm the dividend rate for that year. Common stockholders in the US are made aware of the dividend rate on a more frequent basis as they are paid quarterly.

In the UK, however, the ordinary shareholders may be able to anticipate the dividend rate when they receive information about an interim payment, and may then be able to assess, on past experience, what the final dividend rate to be announced at the AGM may be worth.

Dividend reinvestment plan (DRIP)

A dividend reinvestment plan, or DRIP, is an investment opportunity offered by some businesses to enable their **shareholders** to reinvest their **dividends** or **capital gains** in more stocks or shares, without the necessity of paying commission for brokerage. Normally the investors will have purchased their first shares in the normal manner through a broker. Once this transaction has taken place, dividends would normally be sent to the investor in the form of a cheque. Instead of doing this the business enters into an arrangement with the investor to purchase more shares on their behalf from the proceeds of the dividend, and does not charge them a commission to do so. Some investors are unhappy with this arrangement as they have no control over when the new stocks or shares are purchased, which may mean that their dividend is being spent on new shares at the least optimal time in terms of the share price. Had they been given the opportunity to choose when the purchases of new stocks or shares were made, they might have been able to obtain more stocks or shares for the same amount of money.

Fisher, George, *All About DRIPs and DSPs: The Easy Way to Get Started*. London: McGraw-Hill Education Europe, 2001.

D

Dividend requirement

Whilst a dividend requirement is not applicable to investors who hold common stock or **ordinary shares**, it is applicable to those who own either **preferred stock** or **preference shares**. A business needs to ensure that a proportion of its annual income is made available to pay the specified **dividends** of its preferred stock or preference share investors. This fund represents the total dividend requirement for that business.

Dividend rollover plan

A dividend rollover plan is a strategy often employed by investors who seek to ensure that they purchase stocks or shares before what is known as an **ex-dividend date**. If the shares are purchased after the ex-dividend date the investor will not be eligible for **dividends payable**. In other words a dividend rollover plan seeks to identify the appropriate ex-dividend dates for specific stocks or shares and then purchases them before that date, selling them shortly after, thus ensuring that the investor collects the dividend.

Fisher, George, *All About DRIPs and DSPs: The Easy Way to Get Started.* London: McGraw-Hill Education Europe, 2001.

Dividend yield

The dividend yield is, in effect, the annual **dividend** per share, but expressed as a percentage of the current market price of that share. Given the fact that the share price fluctuates in the marketplace, a share which increases in value will see a proportionate fall in the yield. Dividend yields are an important consideration for those who seek an income from their shares. The normal formula used is:

Dividend per share ÷ market share price × 100 = dividend yield

D

Using this formula, if a share which has an average value of £20 over a given trading period pays out a dividend of £1, the dividend yield is 5%. However, if the share falls to £10, yet still pays out £1 in dividends, the dividend yield has in fact increased to 10%. Conversely, if the share increases in value to £40, yet still pays out £1 in dividends, the dividend yield has fallen to 2.5%. It is normally the case that more established companies offer higher dividend yields, whilst younger companies that are still growing offer lower dividend yields. It is also true that many smaller, growing businesses do not offer a dividend yield at all as they do not have enough funds to be able to offer dividends to their investors.

Spare, Anthony and Ciotti, Paul, *Relative Dividend Yield: Common Stock Investing for Income and Appreciation*. New York: John Wiley, 1999.

Dividends payable

Dividends payable is equal to the total amount of **dividends** which have been declared by a business's board of directors. This total amount incorporates both the **preferred stock** or **preference shares** and the common stock or **ordinary shares**. Once the **dividend rate** has been established the business is now obligated to pay this total amount collectively to its **shareholders**.

Dividends received deduction

Dividends received deduction is a tax advantage which a business receives on **dividends** from a subsidiary or partly owned other business.

Dollarization

Dollarization takes place when a country adopts a foreign currency to use alongside or instead of its own domestic currency. Panama is an example of a country which has used the dollar as its primary currency, whereas Andorra had two currencies, the French Franc and the Spanish Peseta, prior to the arrival of the Euro.

When a country becomes officially dollarized, it becomes part of a unified currency zone, with the country whose currency it has adopted (the issuing country). In effect, an officially dollarized country relinquishes its independent monetary policy and adopts the monetary policy of the country of the currency it is using. Within the currency zone, **arbitrage** keeps the prices of similar products and services within a narrow band. Inflation rates tend to be similar, as are interest rates. The supply of money is determined by the **balance of payments**. The monetary base is determined by the issuing country. If the country spends less it can acquire more currency.

Countries tend to adopt dollarization when they have had a history of poor monetary performance or when they have established a very close relationship with another country as a major trading partner.

Flowers, Edward B., *The Euro, Capital Markets and Dollarization*. Lanham, MA: Rowman and Littlefield, 2002.

D

Double budget

A double budget is an accounting system which separates **capital expenditure** from **operating costs**. In effect, by adopting a double budget accounting system a business is able to identify expenses related to the **acquisition** of **fixed assets** and the expenses directly related to operating the business. The business can therefore illustrate that, putting aside expenditure on fixed assets, the inherent operating structure is sound, despite the fact that it may be collectively producing a **deficit** or trading currently at a loss as a result of its capital expenditure.

Double entry

See **double-entry book-keeping**.

Double taxation

'Double taxation' refers to the taxation of the same earnings at two different levels. The most common form of double taxation is the levying of **corporation tax** on earnings of the business and then taxing the **dividends** which **shareholders** earn.

Double taxation can equally be applied to the taxation of foreign investment in the country of origin, which is then taxed again when the investment is repatriated. In recent years many trading nations have agreed that this form of double taxation should be prevented in the majority of cases.

Double-declining balance depreciation method

The double-declining balance depreciation method in effect accelerates the **depreciation** of an **asset**. Twice the amount of the **straight-line depreciation** is taken in the first year and this is then applied to the un-depreciated amount in subsequent years.

See also **declining balance method**.

D

Double-entry book-keeping

Double-entry book-keeping is a fundamental accounting system which records each transaction in two accounts. Each transaction will appear as both a credit and a debit. The credit entry effectively represents the source of financing, whilst the debit entry represents how that finance has been used.

The purpose of the system is to establish a balanced **ledger** account by having corresponding debits to each credit. The use of double-entry book-keeping by a business attempts to ensure that the business's **assets** are always equal to its **liabilities**. This is absolutely essential if the business hopes to make its **balance sheet** balance.

See also **single-entry book-keeping**.

Pain, Quentin, *Accounting for Everyone: The Simplest Guide to Debits, Credits and Double-Entry Book-keeping*. Cambridge: Apricote Studios, 1998.

Due diligence

The term 'due diligence' refers to an investigation normally undertaken by investors which involves looking carefully at a potential investment. In their due diligence investigation, investors will be interested in ensuring that both the management and the stated operations of a business can be verified by facts. This is a fundamental measure of whether the business is being run according to required standards and ensures that the business is not hiding any damaging information which could otherwise affect an investor's decision to become involved to any degree with that business.

Due diligence is also associated with accounting professionals, notably **auditors**, who must show due diligence in their assessment of whether the financial information provided to them by the business is, in fact, a true reflection of the business's current financial position and operating policies.

Houghton, G., *Due Diligence*. Milton Keynes: Accountancy Books, 2000.

Dutch disease

The term 'Dutch disease', unsurprisingly, is derived from the Netherlands, where the discovery of natural gas and the exports which the industry generated had a massive impact on the country's other industries. A substantial increase in a particular industry in terms of its exports directly affects the country's finances and causes appreciation to the currency, thus making it more difficult for other industries in that country to compete worldwide.

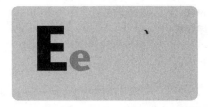

Earning asset

An earning asset is simply any **asset**, fixed or otherwise, which provides the business with earning potential in the form of income.

Earnings per share (EPS)

The concept of earnings per share is a basic investment appraisal ratio. It is used to calculate the profits an investor will receive from each ordinary share which has been issued. The formula used is:

$$Earnings\ per\ share\ =\ \frac{Profit\ available\ to\ equity\ shareholders}{Average\ number\ of\ issued\ equity\ shares}$$

Many analysts believe that this is the most important measure of performance in terms of what the directors and the business are providing as returns for the investors. If a business has made £20 million profit and has some 100 million issued shares, then the earnings per share is 20p.

It is important to remember that in cases when the business discloses a high level of profit at the same time as they issue more shares, the earnings per share will be reduced. If a business was to double its profits, but issue four times as many shares, then in actual fact the earnings per share will have halved.

Earnings report

An 'earnings report' is a US term which is used to describe primarily the financial documents published by a business, which appear either quarterly or annually. The earnings report details the business's earnings, expenses and net profit. In the US an earnings report is also referred to as either an **income statement** or a **profit and loss statement**.

EBIDTA

EBIDTA is a US acronym which stands for 'Earnings Before Interest, Depreciation, Taxes and Amortization'. EBIDTA represents a measure of a business's **operating cash flow**, which is based on the information provided on a business's **income statement**. EBIDTA is calculated by considering the earnings or income of the business before the following have been deducted:

- interest expenses;
- **depreciation**;
- taxes;
- **amortization**.

Businesses that have considerable **fixed assets**, such as manufacturing industries, may be subject to high depreciation costs; others, such as service industries, may have valuable **intangible assets**. These are subject to high amortization charges. These factors do not affect EBIDTA so it is easier for potential investors to compare businesses across different industries. **Creditors** are also interested in EBIDTA as the EBIDTA shows the amount of income which the business has available to pay interest.

EBIDTA tends to be used for large organizations and it is rarely applied to smaller businesses which do not have particularly high loans. EBIDTA, in effect, represents a business's operational cash flow. It is also referred to as EBITDA, which has simply reversed 'tax' and 'depreciation' in the acronym.

A further calculation, known as the 'EBIDTA margin', can also be made. This EBIDTA margin is equal to the EBIDTA divided by the total revenue of the business. The EBIDTA margin effectively measures the extent to which operating expenses use up the business's revenue.

A variation of EBIDTA is known EBITDAR, which is another acronym standing for 'Earnings Before Interest, Taxes, Depreciation, Amortization and Rent'. Again, this is a measure of a business's operating cash flow but in this case incorporates rental charges.

See also **profit before interest and tax (PBIT)**.

E

Economic value added (EVA)

Economic Value Added (EVA) is a measure of surplus value which is created on an investment. It defines the return on capital (ROC) as the true cash flow return on the capital which has been earned from an investment. EVA also defines the cost of capital as a weighted average of the costs of different financing methods used to finance the investment. Typically, the economic value added formula is:

EVA = (return on capital − cost of capital) × (capital invested in project)

EVA is essentially a measurement tool designed to strengthen the return on capital investments. It is a metric which is designed to reduce capital costs and improve gross revenues. A study of best practices in EVA reveals that the metric can help reduce capital costs and improve gross revenues.

Economies of scale

Strictly speaking, the achievement of 'economies of scale' is an economics-related issue. However, it has considerable implications for accounting or finance options. The basic concept revolves around the fact that a business needs to build up a critical mass. In other words, it must be large enough or powerful enough relative to the market to be able to influence it in order to enjoy any degree of success. It is notoriously expensive to establish a presence in anything but the smallest markets. The concept suggests that small businesses are simply too small to register any impact on larger markets. Businesses need to be able to assign a certain percentage of their turnover towards product development and marketing activities. However, in the case of small businesses, this percentage, in real terms, will inevitably be minuscule. Once a business has reached a point where it is a larger trading entity, it can enjoy many of the benefits associated with larger-scale production or distribution. In other words, as the size and scope of the business increases, the generally held view is that the unit costs are driven down. The corollary is that having achieved economies of scale, a business has a greater amount of funds available to further improve its market position. One of the main reasons behind this is that fixed costs and other overheads can be spread over ever-increasing units of output. However, there are inherent difficulties and increased costs, which are known as diseconomies of scale, when increased average costs occur due to the difficulty of managing large operations.

Katrak, Homi and Strange, Roger (eds), *Small Scale Enterprises in Developing and Transitional Economies*. Basingstoke: Palgrave Macmillan, 2001.

Effective debt

'Effective debt' is taken to mean the total debt which is owed by a business. It will include any capitalized values of lease payments which it is required to make. Effective debt is considered to be a more accurate means by which the total debt commitment of a business can be assessed.

Effective par

Effective par is the par value, or nominal amount, of **preferred stock** or **preference shares** that corresponds to a specific **dividend** rate.

Efficiency ratio

The efficiency ratio is another means by which the overall effectiveness and profitability of a business can be assessed. Normally the efficiency ratio is calculated by dividing a business's running costs by any fee income, plus tax equivalent net interest income.

Employer Cost Index (ECI)

The Employer Cost Index (ECI) is a quarterly report issued by the US Department of Labor's Bureau of Labor Statistics. It shows changes in employee compensation in the form of wages received and other benefits. It is a useful measure for many potential investors as it indicates the possibility of **inflation** beginning to take hold of the economy as a result of increases in wage costs.

The ECI, like most other indexes, is calculated on the basis of a fixed **basket** of different occupations.

www.stats.bls.gov

Employment Cost Index

The Employment Cost Index is produced by the Bureau of Labor Statistics, which is part of the US Department of Labor. In essence it provides the same information as the **Employer Cost Index (ECI)** and is released on the last Thursday in January, April, July and November.

www.bls.gov/news.release/eci.toc.htm

Entitlements

Entitlements are simply benefits which are guaranteed to an individual or an institution. A typical example of entitlements would be **dividends**, which **shareholders** are entitled to expect in return for their investment in a business.

Equity

Equity has four associated accounting and finance definitions. The first simply applies to an individual or a business which has a beneficial interest in an **asset**. In this respect a business which has, for instance, purchased factory premises to the value of £1m with a loan of £800,000 has equity equal to the balance between these two figures: that is £200,000 in this example.

Equity also refers to the **net assets** of a business after all **creditors** have received their payments. These include **preference share** or **preferred stock** owners.

The third form of equity is money which is returned to a borrower under a hire purchase or mortgage agreement after an asset has been sold and the full-rate repayment has been made to the lender.

In its fourth definition, 'equity' can simply refer to the common stock or **ordinary share** capital of a business.

In other words, 'equity' can refer to the ownership interest in a business in the form of shares or stock and it can also refer to the total assets of the business minus its total **liabilities**. In these two cases, respectively, equity is referred to as either shareholder equity, in the first case, or **book value**, in the second case.

Coyle, Brian (ed.), *Hybrid Financial Instruments: Risk Management, Debt and Equity Markets*. Canterbury, Kent: Financial World Publishing, 2002.

Equity method

The equity method is an accounting system which aims to identify the income derived from a business's investments in other businesses. These investments in another business usually take the form of a fairly major stock or share holding. Clearly the income derived from these investments contributes to the owning company's own income. Using the equity method, investment income is equal to a share of the net income of the company owned by the original business, proportionate to the size of the equity investment. Businesses' equity investments in other businesses will clearly be identified as income on their **balance sheet**.

Euro

The Euro is the primary currency of the European Union and was officially launched in January 1999, effectively replacing the Ecu. On 1 January 2002 it became legal tender, replacing the currencies of 12 European countries. The adoption of the Euro was seen as an essential step towards full economic and monetary union within Europe.

Euro-12

On 1 January 2002 the **Euro** replaced the national currencies of 12 of the 15 European Union countries. The adoption of the Euro was the largest ever, and most significant, currency change in Europe and indeed the world. The term 'Euro-12' is used to describe the 12 countries which on 1 January 2002 adopted the Euro and jettisoned their old currencies. The Euro-12 are Austria, Belgium, Finland, France, Germany, Greece, Ireland, Italy, Luxembourg, the Netherlands, Portugal and Spain.

Eurobonds

A Eurobond is an international bond which is denominated in a currency that is not native to the country in which it was issued. In other words, a Eurobond can refer to a Japanese bond issued in US dollars, or a US bond issued in Japanese Yen.

Walmsley, Julian, *Global Investing: Eurobonds and Alternatives*. Basingstoke: Palgrave Macmillan, 1991.

Eurocreep

'Eurocreep' is a term used to describe the spread of the use of the **Euro** into countries which have not officially adopted that currency. Eurocreep has become a marked trend, particularly in countries which either intend to adopt the currency at a later date, or have intentions of joining the European Union at some point in the future. For countries already in the European Union, but which have chosen not to adopt the Euro officially, the Euro is technically legal currency and for practical purposes the acceptance of the Euro as legal tender is advantageous.

See also **Euro-12**.

Eurocurrency

A Eurocurrency is currency which is deposited, either by businesses or by governments, in banks outside their own country. The 'Euro' prefix only describes the geographical origins of the first markets in securities. Many Euromarkets are located in Asia and the term 'Eurocurrency' can be transposed as either a **Eurodollar** or Euro sterling. Eurocurrency is a convenient way in which borrowing for international trade and investment can be facilitated. The Eurodollar is the most common form of Eurocurrency.

The Eurocurrency market communicates electronically and deals take place between banks, institutions, businesses and governments. In effect, the Eurocurrency market was the first offshore market.

Gibson, Heather D., *The Eurocurrency Markets: Domestic Financial Policy and International Instability*. Basingstoke: Palgrave Macmillan, 1989.

Eurodollar

Eurodollars are deposits of US $ in financial institutions or banks outside the United States. To all intents and purposes a Eurodollar is identical to a US $. They are often referred to as 'offshore dollars'.

The prefix 'Euro' simply reflects the beginning of the trend of holding deposits offshore. The deposits are often placed abroad to avoid currency-exchange costs and taxation and they have become an important aspect in the creation of credit for international trade.

Burghardt, Galen, *Eurodollar Futures and Options Handbook*. New York: McGraw-Hill Education, 2003.

European Bank for Reconstruction and Development

The bank was established in 1991 in order to support the private sector in the newly democratic central and eastern European countries. The EBRD is involved in some 27 countries in central Europe and central Asia. The EBRD is owned by some 60 countries and two intergovernmental institutions.

The bank finances industries and businesses, mainly privately owned, but it also supports some publicly owned companies. It has been involved in restructuring former state-owned enterprises. Its primary function is not only financial support and business assistance; it is also concerned with moving countries closer to becoming market economies.

The EBRD also promotes co-financing and the direct investment of foreign funds, along with the mobilization of domestic capital.

www.ebrd.com

European Central Bank (ECB)

The first of the ECB's appointments of board members took affect on 1 June 1998. This coincided with the period in which 11 European Union member states agreed to adopt a single currency (the **Euro**). The ECB and the National Central Banks of all the European Union member states form the European System of Central Banks (ESCB). Primarily, they are charged with managing the Euro system by:

- defining and implementing monetary policy within the Euro area;
- conducting foreign exchange operations;
- holding and managing official foreign reserves of the member states;
- promoting smooth operation of payment systems.

E

The ECB is managed by an executive board and a general council comprising the President and Vice-President of the ECB and the governors of the National central banks of all the member states. The ECB's capital amounts to some 5 billion euros and it has reserve assets of 40 billion euros.

www.ecb.int

European Investment Bank (EIB)

The European Investment Bank was established in 1957 as an independent institution under the terms of the Treaty of Rome. It was designed to assist in the steady development of the European Community. The EIB provides loans and guarantees to both public institutions and businesses in order to facilitate regional and structural development as well as achieving cross-border objectives.

www.eib.org

European Monetary and Cooperation Fund (EMCF)

The EMCF was created in 1973 and later revised in 1979 to link it more closely with the **European Monetary System**. It was originally intended to support the Ecu and act as a reserve system for the **central banks**. The fund is used to keep account of short-term borrowings and to support the currencies of member states through intervention in foreign exchange markets.

European Monetary Institute (EMI)

The EMI was established in 1994 under the provisions of the Maastricht Treaty. It manages national currency reserves for the European Union **central banks** and was originally concerned with fostering worldwide acceptance for the Ecu (now the **Euro**). Its other primary functions were to strengthen coordination between the monetary policies of the member states, as well as studying the policies, procedures and infrastructure required for more centralized monetary policies.

www.europa.eu.int/emi/emi.html

European Monetary System (EMS)

The European Monetary System was adopted by the European Community in 1979. Its function was to stabilize the exchange rates between member countries' currencies. The European Monetary System has four major components: the **Euro**, the **Exchange Rate Mechanism**, credit facilities and transfer arrangements. In the run up to the adoption of the Euro, the major tool of the European Monetary System was the Exchange Rate Mechanism, which pegged the currencies of each of the member states to the Euro and only allowed them to fluctuate slightly (2.25% on either side of the Euro value).

Masson, Paul R., Krueger, Thomas H. and Turtelboom, Bart G., *EMU and the International Monetary System*. Washington, DC: International Monetary Fund, 1997.

European System of Central Banks (ESCB)

The primary objective of the European System of Central Banks (ESCB) is to maintain price stability by supporting the economic policies of the community, whilst upholding the concept of an open market, with free competition and an efficient use of resources. The ESCB attempts to control prices by maintaining inflation rates to as close to 2% per year as possible. It achieves this by:

- undertaking economic analysis which looks at current economic developments and how they may affect price stability;
- undertaking monetary analysis of long-term inflation trends and the relationship between the availability of money, and prices over the longer term.

The ESCB offers standing facilities and requires credit institutions to hold minimum reserves with national **central banks**.

www.escb.int

Evidence account

An evidence account is an agreement between an overseas supplier and a government agency in a developing country. Evidence accounts are used to stimulate reciprocal trade. The agreement notes the trade conditions between the exporting foreign business and the jurisdiction the developing countries will have upon that trade. Evidence accounts usually require cumulative payment turnovers for particular goods and not necessarily payments for each individual transaction. The payments need to be balanced, in agreed proportions over a specified period of time, which may be up to three years. The trade flows are then monitored and financial settlements are made through banks which have been designated by both parties.

E

Exchange control

Exchange controls are restrictions or regulations usually imposed by a nation's banking system in order to control the purchase and sale of foreign currencies and gold. In effect, the system regulates both residents and resident businesses in their dealings in foreign currency and gold. Various forms of exchange control operate in different countries. It is notably employed by countries that have shortages of **hard currency**. Over recent years many countries have begun to abandon any form of exchange control, however, as indeed the UK did in 1979.

Exchange rate

An exchange rate is the price of a particular currency as expressed in terms of another currency. In other words, the number of units of one particular currency required to exchange for a unit of another currency. Exchange rates are affected by investor expectations, interest rates, confidence in the currency, the state of a country's **balance of payments**, and many other factors.

Sarno, Lucio, and Taylor, Mark P., *The Economics of Exchange Rates*. Cambridge: Cambridge University Press, 2003.

Exchange Rate Mechanism (ERM)

The Exchange Rate Mechanism came into effect in 1979 and aimed to bring together the currencies of the member states of the European Community (later the European Union). The ERM achieved this by maintaining parity between the exchange rates of the member states' currencies, setting limits to how far the exchange rates could vary between any two currencies. If the exchange rates reached the maximum limit, then the **central banks** of the two countries involved were expected to intervene in the market to bring back the parity which had been previously agreed. Originally the ERM applied to Belgium, France, West Germany, Luxembourg, the Netherlands and Denmark. Italy joined in 1990, Spain in 1989, the UK in 1990 and Portugal in 1992. However, disruptions in 1992 caused the UK to withdraw.

Minikin, Robert, *The ERM Explained: A Straightforward Guide to the Exchange Rate Mechanism and the European Currency Debate*. London: Kogan Page, 1993.

Ex-date

The primary meaning of 'ex-date' is related to **dividends** and denotes the first day of the ex-dividend period. Ex-date serves to allow any

E

ongoing transactions to be completed before the **record date**. If the investors fail to secure ownership of the stocks or shares before the ex-date then they will not be eligible for a dividend payout (**dividends payable**). It is normal practice for exchanges to reduce the price of stocks or shares by the amount of the dividend if the transaction has not been completed by the ex-date. This is because a dividend payout will in effect reduce the value of the business as dividend payments are made from a business's cash reserves. Otherwise the investor would absorb the reduction in the value of the share and in this case neither the buyer nor the seller of the investment would be eligible for the dividend. Hence they are compensated in this way. Ex-date is also known as 'ex-dividend' date.

The second definition of 'ex-date' relates to what is known as stock splits. These are increases in the number of shares in a business's stock, but proportionately each **shareholder**'s **equity** in the business remains the same. Normally this is the case when a business is performing particularly well and may offer extra shares to existing shareholders on the basis of two new shares for each one original share. The new shares in a 2 for 1 swap or split would be worth approximately half of the original share price. Some businesses choose to undertake splits if they believe that the individual price of each of their shares is making it too expensive for normal investors to purchase them. Ex-date, in this respect, denotes the date when the share price has changed in reaction to the stock split.

Ex-dividend date

See **ex-date**.

EXIMBANK

See **Export–Import Bank of the US**.

E

Expansion

Expansion is a part of the **business cycle** or economic cycle. In effect, 'expansion' is an alternative word used to describe the growth period, or period of recovery, of the economy.

Expenditure

'Expenditure' is simply a generic term used to describe any payments which a business may make, or indeed any promises they may make of future payments. Expenditure can naturally be applied to the purchase of **fixed assets**, **stock**, raw materials, wages and salaries, and any other associated **expenses** incurred by the business in the course of its operations.

Expenses

Expenses are usually related to any revenue-generating activity carried out by a business. These costs may include operating expenses, **discretionary expenses** or variable committed expenses (which are unavoidable periodic costs that change in value, such as bills for telephone calls, electricity and other power).

Export credit agency

An export credit agency is invariably a government body which provides subsidies to encourage exports. Loans may be appropriate to foreign buyers who wish to purchase domestic products. Alternatively, guarantees may be made on loans made by banks to domestic businesses in order for them to produce exports which will ultimately pay off the loan. The export credit agency, in effect, insures the producers against non-payment of the loan. For the most part, export credit is offered for political rather than economic reasons, primarily to encourage the country's earnings, to help with the **balance of payments** and, more generally, for employment generation.

See also **Export Credit Guarantee Department**.

Gianturco, Delio E., *Export Credit Agencies: The Unsung Giants of International Trade and Finance.* Westport, CT: Greenwood Press, 2001.

Export Credit Guarantee Department (ECGD)

The British Export Credit Guarantee Department was established in 1919 and is now a part of the Department of Trade and Industry (DTI). It remains the primary source of British export credit. The ECGD aims to assist exporters by providing them with insurance against the risk of not being paid for their exports. It also guarantees banks that have provided finance to British businesses, primarily exporters of capital goods, a facility at a low rate of interest. In effect, the ECGD provides short-term underwriting facilities.

www.ecgd.gov.uk

Export–Import Bank of the US (EXIMBANK)

This independent agency came into existence in 1934 and is charged with the financing of exports from the US in the form of support programmes, guarantees, loans and insurance. The bank underwrites a proportion of the risk associated with the financing of production and the sale of US goods and helps finance overseas customers who wish to purchase US goods, particularly in cases where those customers cannot obtain finance from other lending organizations. Above all, the EXIM-BANK seeks to match other foreign governments' subsidies by helping US businesses obtain credit at lower rates from lenders and providing financial incentives to foreign buyers.

www.exim.gov

Export revolving line of credit (ERLC)

An export revolving line of credit (ERLC) is essentially financial assistance to businesses in the form of guaranteed loans which assist them in bridging the gap in their working capital while production and stock-holding is under way, until the point when they receive payment for what they have produced from an overseas buyer. In the US, for example, ERLC is available via the Small Business Administration (SBA). It will provide up to 85 per cent of the ERLC up to a limit of $750,000. In essence, the ERLC covers the exporter for defaults of their own making and not for defaults by the foreign buyer. The exporters would be expected to have their own export credit insurance or **letters of credit**. In the US, ERLC can be used to finance labour and materials required for manufacturing, or to purchase stock in order to fulfil the requirements of an export order. It can also be used to help develop overseas markets. ERLC cannot be used to purchase fixed assets, but it can be used for advice, business travel, or attendance at trade shows.

Gianturco, Delio E., *Export Credit Agencies: The Unsung Giants of International Trade and Finance.* Westport, CT: Greenwood Press, 2001.

E

Extended Fund Facility (EFF)

The Extended Fund Facility (EFF) is an arrangement by the **International Monetary Fund** to provide assistance to countries in order for them to meet their **balance of payments** requirements. EFF payments are made in larger cash amounts than are available under normal **credit tranche** policy.

www.imf.org

Externalities

Externalities are either costs or benefits which arise out of an economic activity which affects individuals other than those actually engaged in the economic activity itself, but which are not reflected in prices. Pollution, for example, is considered an externality which would have an immediate and long-term impact upon a local population despite the fact that the polluting business is provided much-needed jobs and contributing to the country's **balance of payments**.

Extraordinary item

Extraordinary items are usually one-off events or costs which have a direct impact upon a business's financial position during an accounting period. The exact nature of the extraordinary item and how and why it has made an impact on the business's finances must be explained in either the quarterly or the **annual report** of the business.

E

Factor

The term 'factor' has two applicable definitions. The first refers to a business which is engaged in the purchasing of **accounts receivable** from another business and is engaged in **factoring** activities.

The alternative definition of 'factor' is as a variable which is investigated in a set of statistics.

Factoring

Factoring occurs when an exporter transfers the title of its foreign **accounts receivable** to an independent factoring house. Factoring houses specialize in financial accounts receivable, purchasing them at a discount deducted from the face value of the account. In international trade, factoring is less common than the factoring of domestic receivable accounts.

Salinger, Freddy, *Factoring: The Law and Practice of Invoice Finance.* London: Sweet and Maxwell, 1999.

Factors of production

In international trade, factors of production are significant as they describe the inherent nature of the economic activity of a given country. Typically, factors of production include the available assets in the form of land, labour, capital and enterprise. Each country has its own distinct blend of factors of production, often described as factor endowments (ratio of capital to labour).

Financial Accounting Standards Board (FASB)

FASB, or the Financial Accounting Standards Board, in cooperation with the International Accounting Standards Board (IASB), attempts to set standards in international trade activities which, in terms of quality standards, are broadly comparable to those used in the US and other more developed countries. The FASB attempts to ensure that the quality of information is comparable across national boundaries, and continues to develop the concept of international standards.

www.fasb.org

Financial asset

A financial asset is an **intangible asset**, which may include a bank balance certificate or a security. It is considered to be an asset even though it has no physical presence as such, if it can still provide the business or the owner of that asset with a degree of income. A **non-financial asset** is clearly the opposite of a financial asset.

Constantinides, G. M., Harris, M. and Stulz, R. M., *Handbook of the Economics of Finance: Financial Markets and Asset Pricing*. Oxford: Elsevier, 2003.

Financial capital

The term 'financial capital' refers to funds primarily earmarked to purchase equipment and machinery which will ultimately produce products that can then create what is known as **real capital**.

Walsh, Ciaran, *Key Management Ratios: Master the Management Metrics that Drive and Control Your Business*. London: Financial Times, Prentice-Hall, 2003.

Financial condition

A financial condition is a statement of a business's financial position in terms of its **assets**, **liabilities** and other issues at a particular point in time. Financial conditions tend to be related to either a **financial statement** or an **annual report**.

Financial economies of scale

'Financial **economies of scale**' is simply another way of describing economies of scale. Clearly the main advantage of achieving economies of scale is to save on **expenditure** per unit of production. Therefore 'financial economies of scale' simply refers to those financial advantages which are achieved by a business that is able to manufacture, or otherwise operate, on a large scale.

Financial engineering

Financial engineering involves the swapping of fixed-rate stocks or shares, or other forms of investment, for floating-rate equivalents, or vice versa.

F

Financial statement

'Financial statement' is a generic term which describes any compiled financial data which may be published and released by a business, on either a quarterly or an annual basis. Typically the financial statement would include an **income statement** and a **balance sheet**. In some cases financial statements also incorporate a **cash flow statement** or a **profit and loss statement**. In effect, a financial statement is a quantitative description of the business's current financial position.

Ittelson, Thomas, *Financial Statements: A Step-by-Step Guide to Understanding and Creating Financial Reports*. Franklin Lakes, NJ: Career Press, 1998.

White, Gerald I., Sondhi, Ashwinpaul C. and Fried, Dov, *The Analysis and Use of Financial Statements*. New York: John Wiley, 2002.

Financial structure

The term 'financial structure' refers to the contents of a business's **balance sheet**. The financial structure gives a precise account of how the business's **assets** are being financed. It also includes any issues to do with debt (money owed by the business) or **equity** which may have been used to fund the purchase or **acquisition** of the business's assets.

Harper, Karl, *The Structure of Accounts: A Practical Guide to Financial Reporting and Accounting Standards*. Canterbury, Kent: Financial World Publishing, 2002.

Financial structure and management of foreign projects

The financial structure and management of foreign projects require a considerably different approach to normal investments. Normally a business would use capital budgeting techniques, but here must make a distinction between cash flows to the project and those to the parent company. In many cases the host government may choose to adopt a policy which effectively blocks the repatriation of cash from foreign investment. In order to use capital budgeting techniques, a business will need to assess risks which might arise from its location in an overseas country. These risks could include both political and economic situations. Also, the cost of capital might be cheaper on the global market than in the domestic market and a business may choose to secure finance from the global capital market. Again, this borrowing might be restricted by regulations imposed by the host government. The business may choose to consider local debt financing in countries where the local currency is unstable, particularly if it may depreciate.

Whatever the objectives of the business, it will attempt to utilize the

F

resources in the most efficient manner and may use a variety of different means to transfer funds from one country to another. Dividend remittances are one of the most common methods. The manipulation of transfer prices can also be used, particularly to minimize tax liabilities and to protect against foreign exchange risks. The business may also be able to work around government restrictions, as well as reducing tariff payments. Other businesses choose to use fronting loans, channelling cash from the parent company, via a third party, to a foreign subsidiary. Above all, the financial structure and management of foreign subsidiaries aims to reduce a business's economic exposure and has become a considerable business in itself in moving businesses' assets and distributing them.

Grou, Pierre, *The Financial Structure of Multinational Capitalism*. Basingstoke: Palgrave Macmillan, 1986.

First in, first out (FIFO)

'First in, first out' is used in both stock valuation and stock rotation. When FIFO is applied to stock valuation an assumption is made that the oldest stock will be consumed first, and that stock is valued at the oldest relevant price. When FIFO is applied to stock rotation it is used to ensure that the oldest stock is sold first, or consumed first, in order to make sure that the business is not left with stock which may become obsolete, or, in the case of perishable items, out of date.

See also **last in, first out (LIFO)**.

Fiscal

'Fiscal' is a generic term used to describe money or financial issues. It is particularly used in respect of government **fiscal policy**, which relates to the collection of money, or the regulation of money through government policies. Equally, it applies to the buying and spending policies of either businesses or governments.

Fiscal agent

The term 'fiscal agent' describes a role which is assumed by a third party, and has three distinct connotations. The first is an individual or a business which acts on behalf of a **bond** issuer. The fiscal agent pays subscribers to the issue and generally assists the issuer of the bond.

In the US, the term 'fiscal agent' can mean either an individual or an institution working on behalf of national institutions in the US in the form of an advisor.

F

The term 'fiscal agent' also refers to an agent, normally a trust or a bank, which handles **fiscal** matters for a business. These fiscal agents can collect revenues, taxes and other duties on behalf of the US government (an example being the Federal Reserve Banks in their relationship with the US Treasury).

Fiscal agents can also deal with the **disbursement** of **dividend** payments, bonds and coupons (being a fixed income security).

Fiscal policy

Fiscal policy is the manipulation of government spending and taxation as a means by which the government seeks to ensure stability, high levels of employment, and general economic growth. The fundamental purpose of fiscal policy is to use the taxation rate whilst increasing or decreasing public expenditure, to either stimulate or suppress demand. Theoretically, fiscal policy suggests that a rise in taxation means that consumers have less money (**disposable income**) to spend on products and services. It also means that instead of money passing from consumers to businesses and then a proportion of that amount finding its way to the government, the government can more closely control the movement of money in the economy. Equally, the government can choose to either increase or decrease public spending. By decreasing public spending the government would naturally buy less products and services from private businesses, but in increasing public spending they would buy more products and services from private businesses and, therefore, create more jobs in the private sector. In this way the government can deal with the flow of money in a slightly different manner, as more consumers will have more disposable income as a result of the higher levels of employment. Whichever direction a government chooses, it takes a considerable amount of time for the money to work its way through the economy. As a result, there is often a considerable time difference between the implementation of fiscal policy and its overall impact on the economy.

The use of fiscal policy is at variance with **monetary policy**.

Hansen, F. and Alvin, H., *Fiscal Policy and Business Cycles*. London: Routledge, 2003.

F

Fiscal year

The **fiscal** year is an accounting period which is equivalent to 365 days. In the UK the fiscal year begins on 6 April and ends on 5 April the following year. In some countries the fiscal year literally follows the calendar year in as much as it begins on 1 January and ends on 31 December. In the US the fiscal year begins on 1 July and ends on 30 June the following year.

These accounting periods apply to all income tax, other taxes, annual allowances and other financial deductions. In many cases the fiscal year coincides with the tax year, or the year of assessment, but businesses may choose to have their own financial year, which does not necessarily coincide with the tax year. The only proviso is that it covers 365 days, or in the case of leap years, 366 days.

Fixed asset

The term 'fixed **asset**' is a more common description of what is also known as a **capital asset**. A fixed asset is typified by being a long-term, tangible asset which is unlikely to be traded or sold in the upcoming **fiscal year**. Prime examples of fixed assets include machinery, plant, buildings, land or office furniture.

Fixed asset turnover ratio

The fixed asset turnover ratio measures how effectively the business uses its **fixed assets** in order to generate sales. The ratio is:

$$Fixed\ asset\ turnover\ ratio\ = \frac{Sales}{Fixed\ assets}$$

Normally the end-of-year asset figure is used. In other cases businesses may prefer to use the opening and closing fixed asset figures and take an average (this is useful for an expanding business).

Supposing a business generates £3,200,000 in sales with fixed assets of some £1,900,000, then the calculation is:

$$\frac{3,200,000}{1,900,000} = 1.68\ times$$

The ratio reveals that for every £1 invested in fixed assets, the business generates with those fixed assets £1.68 in sales.

Clearly, assets that have **depreciated** will lead to a higher figure, yet the assets may still be effective and efficient in generating sales potential. It is therefore possible for two identical businesses with identical sales figures to have radically different fixed asset turnover ratios, as one may have ageing and depreciated fixed assets whilst the other is using new fixed assets valued at or near their purchase price of those assets.

Oberuc, Richard, *Dynamic Portfolio Theory and Management: Using Active Asset Allocation to Improve Profits and Reduce Risk*. New York: McGraw-Hill Education, 2003.

F

Fixed budget

In many cases fixed budgets are essential for businesses to be able to successfully plan their financial requirements. Normally a fixed budget is set prior to the beginning of a particular accounting period. Once the budget has been agreed and set, it is not changed as a result of other changes in activity, or changes in costs and revenues. Whilst fixed budgets are rather inflexible, they provide a business with a means by which it can clearly estimate its financial requirements, unlike businesses that use **flexible budgets** which change in response to unexpected occurrences or opportunities.

Fixed cost

Fixed costs incorporate all costs which are attached to a manufacturing process and which do not change, regardless of the volume of production. Typically, fixed costs can be related to overheads, such as the rent of the premises, lease payments on equipment, or other predictable costs which remain static.

Fixed exchange rate

A fixed exchange rate is usually synonymous with a **pegged exchange rate**. The use of the word 'fixed' is somewhat misleading, since it implies that there is a lower chance of change. In reality, however, countries fail ever to have a truly fixed rate of exchange.

Larrain, Felipe and Velasco, Andres, *Exchange-rate Policy in the Emerging-Market Economies: The Case for Floating.* Princeton, NJ: Princeton University Press, 2001.

Fixed-charge coverage ratio

The fixed-charge coverage ratio is another means by which the financial health of a business can be assessed. The calculation for the fixed-charge coverage ratio is:

$$\text{Fixed-charge coverage ratio} = \frac{\text{Profits (before income tax and interest payment)}}{\text{Long-term interest payments}}$$

In many respects this ratio purely determines whether a business is able to meet its long-term interest commitments.

F

Flexible budget

Flexible budgets can be differentiated from **fixed budgets** as they incorporate a mechanism which recognizes and responds to different-costing behaviour patterns. Flexible budgets are designed to change in response to activity changes, such as increased volume or competition.

Floating exchange rate

Floating exchange rates are determined by market forces and occur when one currency's **exchange rate** is free to float in terms of its comparative value with other currencies. The vast majority of currencies have floating exchange rates and are left to fluctuate in comparative value until such a time as either the government or the **central bank** may choose to intervene. Governments and central banks can influence the exchange rate by either buying or selling currency when they feel that the exchange rates have either dropped too low or risen too high. A floating exchange rate is the opposite of a **fixed exchange rate**, in which a government determines the exact exchange rate between its currency and the currencies of other countries.

Forecasts/forecasting

There are a number of associated terms related to forecasting, but forecasting itself is an attempt to predict the future of a variable. Businesses will attempt to forecast the demand for their products or services in order to plan both their stock and manufacturing requirements. The accuracy of a forecast very much depends upon the reliability of the data upon which the forecast has been based and, indeed, the length of time into the future which the forecast is expected to encompass. Generally, a manufacturing organization will seek to forecast demand slightly in excess of its average manufacturing lead time. The further into the future a forecast is projected, the more chance there is of a significant error, as variables become far more unpredictable as a result of other, unknown variables having an influence upon them.

Financial forecasting is essential for all businesses. Banks, for example, or any other providers of finance, including investors, would normally require to see a detailed profit and expenditure forecast. Financial forecasts form the core of any business plan and indeed are at the centre of any proposed project. Financial forecasting remains an integral part of planning and control as it allows budgeting, which can be used to compare actual results with budgeted forecasts. Financial forecasting allows a business to highlight areas where costs require immediate attention.

F

Typically, a business would use a profit and loss forecast to show the relationship between income and **expenditure**, on either a monthly or a quarterly basis. The profit forecast will allow the business to assess its future viability and can be used as an important guide for potential investors. **Cash flow** forecasts are also of vital importance as they show the business's anticipated flows of payments in and out of the business. This forecast differs from a profit forecast as payments are not always received in the same period as the income which has been accounted for in the profit forecast. Cash flow forecasts should highlight where there may be problems in terms of the availability of cash, and allow the business to make plans should that contingency arise.

There is great debate as to how valuable forecasts into the far future are to a business. The further a forecast is made into the future, the less likely it is to be accurate. Most businesses, therefore, produce a profit and loss forecast for no more than a month or a quarter, and a cash flow forecast for around a year (in some cases this is two years).

See also **budget deficit/surplus** *and* **cash flow/cash flow statement**.

Foreign debt crisis

'Foreign debt crisis' refers to situations where countries that have borrowed considerable sums from abroad find it increasingly difficult, if not impossible, to pay even the interest on their debt, let alone addressing the original loan. A prime example of this is Latin America, where in 1985 the combined debt was $300 billion. It now stands at over $750 billion. This is despite the fact that between 1992 and 1999 the region paid some $913 billion in debt-servicing charges. In this example the overseas debt consumes some 56% of the region's income from exports.

The foreign debt crisis has marked impacts upon the poverty levels in affected countries. Again in Latin America, some 44% of the population is considered to be poor, a figure which accounts for some 224 million individuals, of whom 90 million are destitute. The foreign debt crisis also affects infant mortality rates, which, again in Latin America, are 35 for every 1,000 live births.

There have been attempts to assist in the reduction, or the writing off, of these foreign debts, yet there has been little headway and the net outflow of cash from these poorer countries to rich countries continues at an ever greater pace. Mexico, for example, has a current foreign debt of over $163 billion, twice what it owed less than 20 years earlier. The net impact upon Mexico has seen an increase in the price of basic goods, over the same period, at a rate of 560%, while real income has only increased by 135%.

F

Ray, Edward John, *US Protectionism and the World Debt Crisis*. Westport, CT: Greenwood Press, 1989.

Foreign exchange market

The primary function of the foreign exchange market is the conversion of currency. Many international businesses are active in the foreign exchange market in order both to facilitate their international trade and to make investments. They may well invest any available cash in short-term money market accounts, or indeed engage in currency speculation. Foreign exchange markets also provide insurance against foreign exchange risks. Foreign exchange risks can be reduced by using forward exchange rates, or by engaging in currency swaps (the simultaneous purchase and sale of an amount of foreign exchange for two different value dates).

Shamah, S. B., *A Foreign Exchange Primer*. New York: John Wiley, 2003.

Forfaiting

Effectively, forfaiting is a form of supplier credit which requires the exporter to surrender possession of the receivable cash from exports by selling them at a discount to a forfaiter. The transaction is guaranteed by a bank in the importer's country. In some cases there may also be a guarantee by the importer's government and the exporter would approach the forfaiter while formulating the structure of the transaction. Once the forfaiter has committed to the deal a discount rate is set. Forfaiters usually use **bills of exchange** or promissory notes (both of which are unconditional and easily transferable). There is a difference between forfaiting and export **factoring**; forfaiters usually work in the medium to long term as regards receivable cash (180 days to 7 years). Factors tend to work in the short term (up to 180 days). The other major difference is that forfaiters tend to work on a one-off basis, whilst factors prefer to have a longer-term relationship with the exporting business. Equally, forfaiters tend to work on larger projects or deals, mainly with capital goods or commodities, whilst factors tend to operate within the area of consumer goods. Ultimately forfaiters are rather more flexible and are willing to work in the developing areas of the world, whilst factors need reliable, legal, financial and credit frameworks and information.

Ripley, Andy, *Forfait Finance for Exporters*. London: Thomson Learning, 1996.

F

Fractional reserve banking

Fractional reserve banking, as the term implies, is a banking system in which a fraction of the total deposits which are managed by a bank are held as a reserve. In the US, for example, the system is controlled by the Federal Reserve Board. In the majority of countries a similar arrangement is maintained which stipulates that the amount of deposits should be equal to the amount of reserves, multiplied by the **deposit multiplier**.

Fractional share

A fractional share is, as the term implies, part of a single share. Fractional shares are created by **stock splits** or the **distribution** of additional shares in a **stock dividend**. There are clear advantages in creating fractional shares. In the stock dividend case, normal dividends would be taxable, but if fractional shares are created under this system, then there are no tax liabilities (although there will be tax liabilities when the shares are sold).

Free cash flow

Free cash flow is another means by which the general health of a business can be assessed, as it is concerned with the amount of cash which a business has to hand after it has dealt with its **expenses** and made any necessary investments. In many respects free cash flow reveals the actual **working capital** of a business. Free cash flow is used as a financial measurement tool, particularly in the US, where it has an associated ratio:

Operating cash flow (net income + depreciation + amortization) – capital expenditure + dividends = free cash flow

F

Many financial analysts consider free cash flow to be a prime indicator of the way in which a business is being run and of its overall financial condition. Free cash flow, however, can be misleading in some respects since many growing businesses plough back the majority of their earnings directly into new investments. This would obviously reduce their amount of free cash flow. Therefore a negative free cash flow may not be an indication that the business is in trouble, but it may reveal that the business is not earning a sufficiently high rate of return on the investments which it has made. This may indicate that the business is simply spending too much.

Free enterprise

'Free enterprise' is another way in which the **free market** can be described. Free enterprise is typified by a distinct lack of government interference in the form of regulations or subsidies in the marketplace. The fortunes of businesses are purely based on supply and demand, supply meaning the amount of products or services which are available to purchase, and demand being the amount of those products or services which customers or consumers wish to buy. The relationship between these two factors may be determined by price, but in many cases the demand and the supply of those products actually determine the price. In other words, an excess of supply should, theoretically, lead to a depression in the price for those products and services. Equally, a reduction in the level of demand similarly depresses the price. In cases where demand outstrips supply, or supply cannot match demand, the prices rise.

Together supply and demand are the key determinants of what is known as the **free market price**, which is alternatively known as the 'market value'. This means that the price has been determined by the interaction between the buyer and the seller – in other words, the supplier and those who demand the product or service.

Bhagwati, Jagdish, *Free Trade Today*. Princeton, NJ: Princeton University Press, 2003.

Free market

The first definition of 'free market' accords with the familiar understanding of the term **free enterprise**. In terms of finance and accounts, however, free market also has two further definitions. The first refers to a security which is traded on a Stock Exchange, where the quantity available of that stock means that the price is not influenced by its availability. In other words, there is enough of that security available for the price not to be a consideration.

The second definition of 'free market' actually refers to a **foreign exchange market**. This form of exchange market is not influenced or controlled by the government, which has not pegged the rates, thus allowing the rates to rise or fall in line with the normal influences of supply and demand.

Bhagwati, Jagdish, *Free Trade Today*. Princeton, NJ: Princeton University Press, 2003.

Free market price

In order to achieve a free market price, the assumption is made that the markets are efficient, in as much as the prices of products, services, stocks, shares and securities are only determined by the forces of supply and demand. In reality, however, this is rarely the case and there are inevitably influences or interferences from governments and financial institutions which either influence or seek to manipulate the prices.

Free trade

'Free trade' is a general term used to describe the ability of individuals or businesses to take part in economic transactions with other countries, free from restraint or regulation. The scope of free trade is measured as a sum of all imports and exports. The most significant change which has brought about the growth of free trade in the world was the General Agreement on Tariffs and Trade (GATT) and its successor, the World Trade Organization. Indeed, in the 50 years from 1950 to 2000, world trade increased by 1,600%, three times the growth of the world's total output. Exports grew over the same period, in comparison with **gross domestic product**, from 7% to 15%. Free trade has not had a huge impact on traditional trading partners; Canada, for example, is still the largest trading partner with the United States, and the majority of European countries still trade primarily with other European countries. Countries that have particular natural resources, such as oil or agricultural products, trade more freely across the world, whereas many of the lesser developed countries rely on simple manufactured products, such as clothing, for which they find markets across the world.

Bhagwati, Jagdish, *Free Trade Today*. Princeton, NJ: Princeton University Press, 2003.
Gilpin, Robert, *Global Political Economy: Understanding the International Economic Order*. Princeton, NJ: Princeton University Press, 2001.

F

Freely convertible currency

A freely convertible currency is a currency which has no limits on the amount which can be transferred from a country. Typical freely convertible currencies include the US Dollar, the Euro, the British Pound and the Canadian, Australian and New Zealand Dollars.

Fronting loan

A fronting loan is a means by which a domestic parent company can provide a loan to a foreign subsidiary through a financial intermediary.

The loan is usually arranged with an international bank by the parent company on behalf of the foreign subsidiary. In other cases the parent company may deposit sufficient funds with a large international bank, which in turn makes this cash available to the foreign subsidiary. This process often avoids unnecessary complications with regard to the movement of assets across international borders.

Fully depreciated

The term 'fully depreciated' is related to the valuation of **assets**. A fully depreciated asset has reached the maximum allowable amount in terms of **depreciation** and is now at its lowest value possible. This does not necessarily mean that the asset has been used up. Nor does it imply, necessarily, that the asset is obsolete. On the contrary the asset may still be a productive unit, but in terms of market value, it has virtually no value at all. In other words, should the business decide to sell the fully depreciated asset, it would not realize a great deal of its original value. A business may therefore decide to continue to own a fully depreciated asset on the basis that provided there are no excessive maintenance costs related to it, it is still a valuable asset, even though its **book value** may be close to zero.

The term 'fully depreciated' is also associated with the concept of terminal value, which is used to describe the value of an item at the end of a specific period of time. In this case a business may have gradually depreciated the value of the asset over a 10-year period, and in that 10th year the asset reaches its terminal value, as it has become fully depreciated.

Fundamental analysis

Fundamental analysis is an accounting procedure which seeks to investigate a business's balance sheet, income statements and sources and use of working capital. Fundamental analysis evaluates the balance sheet and the other financial documentation in order to assess the following:

- liquidity;
- asset quality;
- earnings quality;
- leverage;
- debt service coverage;
- profitability;
- growth;
- problems and opportunities for improvement.

G-7

The G-7, or 'group of 7', are Canada, France, Germany, Italy, Japan, the United Kingdom and the United States, collectively accounting for around two-thirds of the world's economic output. These seven economic powers, through their finance ministers, seek to promote balanced economic growth and stable **exchange rates**. The first meeting took place in Rambouillet in France in 1975. Canada joined at the 1976 Puerto Rican summit and since then the group has been known as the G-7. Each year a summit is held, the location being rotated amongst the seven countries. Since 1977 the President of the European Commission has been represented. The G-7 finance ministers meet quarterly to review developments both in their own economies and in the world economy, with the purpose of developing international and economic financial policies.

At three of the four meetings each year the G-7 **central bank** governors are present. These are usually the first three meetings of the year, primarily to prepare for the meetings of the **International Monetary Fund** and the **World Bank**, which take place in April and September. At the end of each of the meetings the G-7 ministers issue a joint statement on economic conditions and policies. The G-7 finance ministers also meet before the G-8 summit. When the **Euro** was launched, which would become the common currency of three of the G-7 members, France, Germany and Italy, the presidents of the **European Central Bank** and the Euro group represented the finance ministers of the 12 Euro countries. G-7 does not have a permanent staff or a budget. The government which is hosting the summit in any given year provides facilities and support for that year.

Gearing ratios

Gearing ratios measure the level of debt (money owed) using a business's capital structure, and are a generally accepted indicator of the level of financial risk an investor may face in becoming involved with the business. One of the two most used gearing ratios is the **debt to**

equity ratio, which examines the relationship between the long-term debt and the total equity or **shareholder**s' funds.

The other form of gearing ratio is known as the 'gearing percentage'. This ratio has a slightly different structure:

$$Gearing\ percentage = \frac{Long\text{-}term\ debt}{Shareholder\ funds + debt} \times 100$$

The higher the gearing level, the more speculative the investment may be. In the US, gearing is referred to as 'leverage', which similarly evaluates the relationship between debt and equity in the form of a ratio, and more generally examines the degree to which a business is utilizing borrowed funds. It is considered to be the case that highly geared or leveraged businesses are more likely to fail as they may be unable to continue to make their debt payments. Equally, these highly geared or leveraged businesses may find it difficult to convince new providers of finance to make an investment in the business.

Fridson, Martin and Alvarez, Fernando, *Financial Statement Analysis: A Practitioner's Guide.* New York: John Wiley, 2002.

Temple, Peter, *Magic Numbers: The 33 Key Ratios that Every Investor Should Know.* New York: John Wiley, 2001.

General and administrative overhead

The term 'general and administrative overhead' refers to a business's **fixed costs**, which must be met regardless of the level of operations or output being currently experienced by the business. These general and administrative costs are not directly related to production or the providing of any services. Typically they would include not only the administrative function of the business, but also issues such as insurance and other costs which must be paid for whatever the operating level of the business.

Long, Gary, *313 Ways to Slash Your Business Overheads.* London: McGraw-Hill Education, 2003

General ledger

The general ledger is at the core of a business's financial records. It is sometimes referred to as the 'central books' as every transaction is detailed in the general ledger. It remains as a permanent record of the history of all financial transactions carried out. Most accounting systems will have a series of sub-ledgers and the entries in these sub-ledgers will be placed on the general ledger account. Some items are not put into sub-ledgers, such as capital contributions, loans, loan repayments and proceeds from the sales of **assets**; these are linked to the **balance sheet**. The general ledger provides the information which assists the business in creating its balance sheet and its **profit and loss statement**.

Generally accepted accounting principles/procedures (GAAP)

GAAP is an acronym which means 'generally accepted accounting procedure'. Its use implies that the business uses standardized accounting methodologies, including the relevant checks and balances.

Going concern

The term 'going concern' implies that a given business will continue to operate for the foreseeable future. The inference is that the business is sufficiently established to be able to justifiably claim that it will, under normal circumstances, still be operating for a considerable period of time. Normally the board of directors of a business will make a statement that the business remains a going concern for the next financial period.

The term 'going concern' is also used as a description of a business which may be for sale to a third party. Again, this suggests that rather than simply buying the stock or premises, the third party is actually buying a successful and ongoing business. Clearly the value of a going concern is in excess of the total assets of that business, and this is sometimes referred to as **goodwill**.

Goodwill

'Goodwill' is a term which is often included on a balance sheet, or listed as an asset in the event of an organization being sold. 'Goodwill' implies not only that the business is a **going concern**, but also that there is an additional premium in terms of its value compared with the business's existing and identifiable assets and liabilities. Goodwill therefore implies that the potential purchaser is buying the work which has gone into building up the business over a number of years, and will have access to and will enjoy the benefit of the business's existing customers.

G

Gross domestic product (GDP)

Gross domestic product is the sum of the market value of all goods and services which were produced within the boundaries of a particular nation, regardless of who owns those assets. GDP excludes earnings from business operations in foreign countries and also excludes reinvested earnings in foreign affiliates.

Gross domestic product, therefore, is equal to the private consumption + investment, public spending, change in inventories + the balance between exports and imports.

> Labonte, Marc and Makinen, Gail E., *The Economic Expansion of the 1990s*. Hauppauge, NY: Nova Science Publishers, 2003.

Gross fixed capital formation

Gross fixed capital formation relates primarily to the investment in tangible fixed assets, such as plant, machinery, buildings, transport equipment and other structures. It can also include investment in intangible fixed assets, such as improvement to land and any costs associated with the transfer of assets.

Gross income

The gross income of a business is equal to its pre-tax **net sales** less its **cost of sales**. 'Gross income' is often interchangeable with the term **gross profit**.

> Shaikh, Anwar M. and Tonak, E. Ahmet, *Measuring the Wealth of Nations: The Political Economy of National Accounts*. Cambridge: Cambridge University Press, 1997.

Gross margin

'Gross margin' is normally known as **gross profit margin** and is the percentage of a business's income which is **gross profit**.

Gross national product (GNP)

Gross national product is a measure of the market value of goods and services which are produced by a nation. It includes receipts from the nation's business operations in overseas countries, as well as the share of reinvested earnings in foreign affiliates. It is another prime measure of a country's economic performance. In effect, it is calculated by adding the **gross domestic product** to the income earned by the country's nationals from investments abroad, less the income earned by foreigners from investments made in the country, but sent home.

> Shaikh, Anwar M. and Tonak, E. Ahmet, *Measuring the Wealth of Nations: The Political Economy of National Accounts*. Cambridge: Cambridge University Press, 1997.

Gross profit

'Gross profit' is an accountancy term meaning a calculation of the profitability of a business. The calculation is made by establishing the total turnover of the business, less the cost of sales. Gross profit does not take into account other expenses, such as the purchase of products, any holding costs, or taxes or other overheads which can be attributed to the products or services sold. It is a measure of the total business performed by the organization over a given period of time.

Gross profit margin (ratio)

The gross profit margin ratio is one of several ratios which help to assess the overall operating performance of a business. The ratio itself expresses the gross profit as a percentage of sales. The ratio is:

$$Gross\ profit\ margin\ =\ \frac{Gross\ profit\ \times\ 100}{Sales}$$

If a business generates some £700,000 in gross profit on a total sales revenue of £3,200,000 then the following calculation is made:

$$\frac{700,000\ \times\ 100}{3,200,000}\ =\ 21.87\%$$

This indicates that the business earns £0.218 in gross profit for every £1 of sales.

See also **net profit margin ratio.**

Gross revenue

'Gross revenue' is an alternative term used to describe **gross income**, as it is the revenue of the business less the **cost of goods sold**.

Gross sales

The term 'gross sales' is used to describe the total invoiced value of sales which have been made by a business. The gross sales figure does not take into account any customer discounts or returns of goods. It is a measure of the total amount of business before these deductions, which the business has managed to achieve over a given period of time. Normally gross sales figures are calculated at the end of each week, month or quarter, or on an annual basis.

Group accounts

Group accounts are compiled by business organizations which have a number of subsidiaries. The group of companies or businesses is controlled by what is known as a holding or parent company, which owns 50% or more of those subsidiaries' nominal value in terms of **equity** capital or shares. The parent company also controls the composition of the subsidiaries' boards of directors. These holding companies are required to prepare group accounts. Their financial statements consist of a consolidated **balance sheet** and a consolidated **profit and loss account** for the whole of the group, encompassing all of the subsidiaries.

The precise rules regarding group accounts differ from country to country and some government regulations allow the holding companies not to submit consolidated group accounts, allowing them to prepare and publish separate sets of accounts for each of their subsidiaries. In other cases government regulations allow the holding company to omit particular subsidiaries from the group accounts and therefore not consolidate all the financial details in one set of balance sheets and profit and loss accounts.

Pierce, Aileen and Brennan, Niamh, *Principles and Practices of Group Accounts*. London: Thomson Learning, 2003.

Growth stock

Growth stock can be differentiated from **income stock** in the sense that growth stock offers the investor more potential in the form of capital growth. Growth stock is typified by stocks or shares in businesses whose revenue or earnings are growing faster than other industries (or businesses) in their own market. These businesses with the growth stock tend not to pay **dividends**, and in cases when they do, the dividend payments are relatively low, since they tend to invest the majority of their income in further expansion. Investors, therefore, may choose growth stock in the expectation that the share prices will continue to rise and at some point in the future they will be able to sell them at a considerably higher price than their original investment.

Growth stocks are typified in businesses which are undertaking either research or long-term product development and which have dynamic management teams who seek to maximize their resources.

Peters, Donald J., *A Contrarian Strategy for Growth Stock Investing: Theoretical Foundations and Empirical Evidence*. Westport, CT: Greenwood Press, 1993.

Guarantee

A guarantee is a promise made by a third party to take responsibility if a business or an individual who has the primary responsibility for an obligation does not meet that obligation. It is in effect a promise made by a third party who is not party to a contract between two other parties, yet the party making the guarantee (the **guarantor**) is liable to fulfil the contractual obligations. In many instances providers of finance will require a form of security in the shape of a guarantor before they agree to make a loan or other financial instrument available to a business.

Guaranteed stock

Guaranteed stocks are stocks which have their **dividends** guaranteed by a third party. Guaranteed stock may be either **preferred stock** or **preference shares**, common stock or **ordinary shares**. The stock held will return a guaranteed dividend. This means that potential investors are more likely to consider making an investment in that stock and may indeed be willing to pay a higher price for it. Ultimately, however, the value of the guarantee is only equal to the **guarantor**'s own financial position. In many cases the guarantor is, in fact, a government, such as the situation in the US with regard to railroad construction, or in the relationship between the UK's nationalized industries in the past. In both cases the stocks were guaranteed by the national government and therefore considered to be a relatively safe investment.

Guarantor

A guarantor is an individual or an organization which **guarantees** the repayment of a loan should the borrower default or be otherwise unable to pay the loan back.

G

Hard currency

Hard currency is also known as convertible currency. It is a currency which has a sound value and, above all, it is generally accepted internationally on the open market. Hard currency is expected, by its definition, to retain its value to a great degree. As it is a far more reliable currency than most, it has become the currency of choice for many businesses involved in international transactions. Typically, hard currencies include the dollar, sterling and the Swiss franc.

Hedge fund

In financial markets individuals and businesses will seek to maximize their absolute returns and concentrate on generating profits. A hedge fund allows these individuals and businesses to reduce their risks by taking a new risk which offsets an existing one. In the majority of cases hedge funds are used to make an investment on an adverse position to the original investment.

In international business, for example, an organization may choose to hedge its financial risk of financing the construction of a new factory in a particular country by borrowing the currency of that country. This means that should the economic situation in that country deteriorate, the value of the country's currency will also deteriorate, thereby reducing the business's overall economic exposure.

Barham, Sarah and Hallsworth, Ian (eds), *Starting a Hedge Fund: A European Perspective*. Tunbridge Wells, Kent: ISI Publications, 2002.

Hidden asset

A hidden **asset** is an asset which is not immediately obvious on a business's **balance sheet**. Typical hidden assets may include employee skills or brand values.

Historical cost

The historical cost principle is based on the assumption that **asset** and **liability** measurements should be based on the amount which was given or received during an exchange transaction. Historical cost measurement is considered to be an important piece of **cash flow** information as it is verifiable. It is primarily used for accounting for plant assets. In this instance the recorded costs of the plant assets are equal to the cash equivalent price, the value of which does not change unless the asset has suffered impairment. In using the historical cost principle it is possible to value an asset over its lifespan more reliably, on the basis of past transactions. The value of the plant asset is derived through its use and not through its disposal at the end of its useful economic life.

H

Illegal dividend

An illegal **dividend** payment occurs when a business does not have sufficient distributable reserves. In these cases the business has paid the dividend from its **share capital** or non-distributable reserves. In the US, for example, this is in violation of the Companies Act. In extreme cases, when a business is in financial difficulties, the business's **creditors** may make an application to the court to order that the directors who authorized the illegal dividend pay the dividends back to the business, even if they were not the recipients of the dividend itself.

Most illegal dividends, however, occur as a result of the way in which a business has calculated the **dividends payable**. In this case it may be considered to be a simple oversight and the business may be required to rectify the situation.

Immunization

Immunization is a financial technique which seeks to protect an investor or a business from interest rate risks. Given the fact that the value of **bonds** or other securities can be affected by a rise in interest rates, the business or the investor may seek to offset this risk by holding **assets** and **liabilities** which have an equal duration.

Impairment

'Impairment' is a term related to the value of **capital**. A business will state the value of its capital, but this amount may be reduced by **distribution** (the payments of **dividends** or **capital gain**s tax, or other losses).

Associated terms include 'impaired capital' or 'impairment of capital', which effectively mean that a business is actually worth less than the value of its stock.

Imprest

Imprest is a method by which petty cash expenditure can be controlled. Authorized individuals within a business are given a float, or an imprest, which consists of a certain sum of money. Periodically the authorized individual presents the imprest to the accounts department, with a number of vouchers for the amounts which have been spent. The accounts department then reimburses the authorized individual, bringing the float or imprest back up to its original amount. The imprest accounts system means that each authorized individual will have either cash, vouchers or usually a mixture of both, which amount to the original float or imprest total.

Inactive asset

An inactive **asset** is an asset which is not always being utilized by the business. Typically, inactive assets would be backup systems which can be used if the primary systems used by the business malfunction or require repair or replacement. The inactive asset is then brought into use, such as a power generator or a reserve computer system. During this time the inactive asset becomes an active asset, and it is returned to its inactive status once the problem with the primary asset has been resolved.

Incentives

The term 'incentive' covers pay, benefits and other intangible incentives which are part of an overall package offered by an organization in order to attract potential employees. The inducements represent the total benefits or compensations which the employee would expect to receive as a result of accepting a job offer from a particular organization.

The term 'fringe benefit' refers to any incentive given to an employee as a reward in addition to their wage or salary. Fringe benefits can include:

- a company pension scheme;
- employee sick pay scheme;
- subsidized meals;
- company products or services at a discounted price;
- company cars;
- private medical health insurance;
- counselling or mentoring services;
- occupational health screening;
- social and recreational facilities;
- legal and financial service support.

Fringe benefits are not necessarily related to merit, but often increase with employee status and length of service. They do not necessarily benefit all employees but are established and monitored after the initial analysis process. Once they are established, however, it is difficult for the organization to remove them as this could affect employee retention. Fringe benefits are considered important because they improve job satisfaction provided they are consistently and fairly administered.

Income

Income is usually calculated by taking a business's revenues and then subtracting their **cost of sales**, **operating costs** and taxes. Income is the primary driver of business success and growth. It is also a key issue with regard to attracting investors in the business. The revenue, or income, of the business will ultimately determine the **dividends** available to investors and signal the business's growth potential and **capital appreciation**. Smaller companies that are concerned with immediate growth often have a negative income, but they will display the potential for profits in the future. In many cases income is also referred to as 'earnings'.

Income and expenditure account

An income and expenditure account is essentially the same as a **profit and loss account**, but it tends to be used for businesses or organizations that are not necessarily concerned with profit generation. The income and expenditure account details both the **income** and the **expenditure** of the organization and illustrates whether there is an income surplus over the expenditure or whether expenditure has outstripped income. The income and expenditure accounts usually cover a fixed period of time and do not have any direct reference to the organization's reserves of cash, although it may be noted on the income and expenditure account that reserves have been used in order to fund expenditure.

Income coverage

Income coverage is a means by which investors can determine their current income in the form of money received from investments, including **dividends** and interest. The income coverage is calculated using the following formula:

$$\frac{Net\ income\ from\ investment}{Total\ interest\ payments\ and\ preferred\ dividends}$$

Income statement

'Income statement' is primarily a US term which is used to describe the accounting process or system which details a business's sales, **expenditure** and **net profit** over a given period of time.

Income stock

Income stocks are forms of stocks or shares which are purchased by investors as they have a history of providing relatively steady, high income in the form of **dividends**. These income stocks are expected to produce a consistently high level of **dividend payments**. Typically, these will be common stock or **ordinary shares** which have a good **yield** record in the past, or some form of fixed interest investment which offers a comparatively high level of return.

Independent auditor

An independent auditor is an individual, or a business, which is not affiliated or involved with the business in which it is carrying out an **audit**. Independent auditors are professional accountants with certified status who provide an opinion on the authenticity of a business's financial statements.

See also **auditor** and **auditor's report**.

Index-linked

The term 'index-linked' refers to changes in a value as a result of changes in the **Retail Price Index (RPI)**. In Britain the RPI is the standard measure of inflation, and index-linking has been used in the past to determine wage increases. It was considered prudent that wage increases were index-linked in order to ensure that wages did not rise above the current rate of inflation. In practice, however, index-linking proved not to work as wages increased in line with inflation, which left real incomes effectively unchanged. At the same time, industry costs increased, triggering a rise in the price of products and services. This was then picked up in the next RPI, which triggered another wage rise, and so the spiral continued. Index-linking was thus seen as not a solution to combating inflation, but very much a cause of it.

None the less, in Britain and several other countries pensions still remain index-linked, in order to maintain the buying power of the retired.

Indicated dividend

The indicated dividend is a theoretical figure which seeks to estimate the total amount of **dividends** that will be paid on stocks or shares over a given period of time in the future. The indicated dividend makes the assumption that each of the dividends in the future over that period of time will be equal to the dividend payment made most recently by the business. This concept is also known as 'indicated yield'.

Indicated yield

See **indicated dividend.**

Indicator

'Indicator' is a general term which is used to describe any data or information which may assist a business or a government in predicting movements in the economy or the financial markets in the near future. Typical examples of indicators include:

- employment rates;
- interest rates;
- **inflation**;
- industrial output;
- volume of shares, **bonds** or other contracts being traded.

There are, of course, several different forms of indicator in terms of their relevance to particular businesses. Economic indicators, for example, take the form of statistical data showing trends in the economy. To some extent these may be predictive economic indicators, or leading indicators which show the various trends in economic activity in the economy. Alternatively, relevant indicators may include **coincidence indicators**, which vary with related economic trends.

Leading indicators are major economic indicators that occur just before a change in the economy, whereas **lagging indicators** are economic indicators which occur after the economy has changed.

Momentum indicators help to predict future market trends, on the basis of recent prices and volume of activity. In effect they compare the current price with a price in the past in order to illustrate the rate of change and thereby predict the rate of change in the future.

A monetary indicator shows the impact that money supply has on the economy, and is typified in Stock Market prices and credit market conditions.

An overbought/oversold indicator is another form of technical analysis which bases its calculations on moving averages. If the market is overbought, the investors will sell, and if the market is oversold, they will buy.

Indirect costs

Indirect costs are costs which cannot be directly attributed to a specific product line or indeed a particular cost centre. Usually they are **fixed costs**, such as general maintenance in an office or a factory. Using absorption costing, indirect costs are nevertheless allocated to product lines or cost centres.

Inflation

Inflation is a general and sustained increase in an economy's pricing levels. It is usually caused by an excess in demand within the economy and may also lead to a **devaluation** of the country's currency. Inflation is measured in the US by the **Consumer Price Index (CPI)**, and by similar measures in other countries. It can also be measured by inflationary **indicators** such as the Producer Price Index, which is prepared by the US Bureau of Labor Statistics.

Inflation is typified by a persistent rise in both prices and wages. As wages rise, production costs increase, thereby leading to a further rise in prices. If this cycle is not controlled, then the economy can find itself in an inflationary spiral in which the rate of inflation increases at such a speed that it becomes almost impossible to control without significant restrictions on the supply of money and a major devaluation in the currency.

Inflation is believed to be caused by a wide variety of different situations, such as a rapid increase in the money supply. This was a suggestion made by the US economist Milton Friedman. Monetarists such as Friedman believe that inflation can be controlled entirely by a strong grip on the money supply. Other approaches, such as that by John Maynard Keynes, suggest that a rigid incomes policy would maintain low inflation and low unemployment.

Countries such as the US and the UK have experienced a broad range of inflation, from virtually zero to in excess of 23%. It is generally considered, however, that an annual **inflation rate** of between 2% and 3% is both reasonable and controllable.

Inflation accounting

Inflation accounting is a system of accounting which includes **current cost accounting** and seeks to compensate for the deficiencies which normally occur in conventional **historical cost** accounting by taking account of the variable cost of money during an inflationary period. In essence, inflation accounting, which can include current cost accounting and current purchasing power, aims to provide financial comparisons over a period of time in which the value of money has changed. Inflation accounting seeks to make **gearing ratio** and **working capital** adjustments in accordance with changes in the value of money, and it is a **Financial Accounting Standards Board** requirement that larger businesses use inflation accounting on their **financial statements**.

> Whittington, Geoffrey, *Inflation Accounting: An Introduction to the Debate*. Cambridge: Cambridge University Press, 1983.

Inflation rate

The inflation rate is the percentage increase in the price of products and services, usually calculated on an annual basis.

> *See also* **inflation**.

Initial rate

An initial rate is an interest rate paid on a loan which is normally lower than the average variable rate. At the end of the initial period the business which has taken out the loan will pay the normal variable rate of interest.

Intangible asset

An intangible asset is also known as an invisible asset. It is an **asset** which does not have a physical presence. In other words, intangible assets include **goodwill**, brand names, patents, trademarks, copyrights and franchises. Clearly, intangible assets are the opposite of **tangible assets**.

Interestingly, intangible assets can be more or less intangible, since brand names, trademarks or patents, for example, have, to some extent, a presence in the sense that they can be clearly identified as being an asset; other intangible assets are rather more ethereal. Goodwill is probably one of the most intangible assets as it has no supporting documentation and is of variable commercial value. Goodwill, for example, can be a very valuable intangible asset in the sense that it can offer a business, or a potential purchaser of a business, the opportunity to capitalize on future profits based on the work and relationships which have already been established and which constitute the goodwill.

There is, however, a slight distinction between some forms of intangible assets. Goodwill could be described as either an intangible or an invisible asset, whereas insurance policies, for example, are invariably referred to as invisible rather than intangible assets.

Donaldson, T. H., *The Treatment of Intangibles: A Banker's View*. Basingstoke: Palgrave Macmillan, 1992.

Interest coverage ratio

The interest coverage ratio, or 'times interest earned' ratio, is used in order to determine whether a business is capable of meeting regular financial commitments. The ratio is constructed in the following manner:

$$Interest\ coverage\ =\ \frac{Net\ profit\ before\ interest\ and\ tax}{Interest\ charges}$$

Suppose that, in a particular case, the business's net profit is some £340,000 and has interest charges of some £60,000. Therefore:

$$\frac{340,000}{60,000}\ =\ 5.67$$

This figure, expressed in dollar terms, is £5.67, showing that the business generates this amount of profit to cover each £1 in interest charges.

Interim dividend

An interim dividend is a dividend payment which has been declared and distributed ahead of the announcement or calculation of a business's annual earnings. In the US, for example, interim dividends are usually distributed on a quarterly basis.

Interim statement

Technically, an interim statement can be any **financial statement** issued by a business which covers a period of less than one financial year. Under normal circumstances, an interim statement, which is also known as an interim report or quarterly report, is released by a business four times per year. In the interim report the business outlines its financial results for the period in question and highlights significant changes or events which have occurred during that period.

Internal forward rate

The internal forward rate is a forecast generated by a business which suggests the probable exchange rate of currencies at some point in the future. The business will use this internal forward rate to make an estimate as to the true value of a business transaction with a foreign business, as a means of predicting future cash flows.

Andersen, Torben Juul, *Currency and Interest-rate Hedging: A User's Guide to Options, Futures, Swaps and Forward Contracts*. New York: New York Institute of Finance, 1997.

International Accounting Standards Committee (IASC)

The IASC was established in 1973. It was a standard-setting board which aimed to require businesses to produce high-quality, transparent and comparable information in their financial statements and reporting. In 2000 the IASC became the International Accounting Standards Committee Foundation, which appointed the International Accounting Standards Board (IASB) to develop and approve both international accounting standards and international financial reporting standards.

Since 2001 the standards-setting work has been conducted by the IASB, which has sought to bring international businesses into compliance with its standards – 'an enterprise whose financial statements comply with international accounting standards should disclose that fact. Financial statements should not be described as complying with international accounting standards unless they comply with all the requirements of each applicable standard and each applicable interpretation of the Standing Interpretations Committee.'

www.iasc.org.uk

International Bank for Reconstruction and Development

The International Bank for Reconstruction and Development (IBRD) is more commonly referred to as the **World Bank**. The IBRD is, in effect, an inter-governmental financial institution which seeks to promote economic growth in developing countries and raise living standards. Primarily it grants loans to governments of lesser developed countries, with the proviso that the funds are to promote long-term development. The IBRD tends to loan funds for specific development projects, such as infrastructure, agricultural and rural development, or education. Any loans which are granted must be guaranteed by the government of the country concerned. The IBRD is based in Washington, DC, and was established in 1945, initially to help countries reconstruct their economies after the Second World War.

www.worldbank.org

International Banking Act

The International Banking Act is a US Federal framework which was passed in 1978 in order to govern the activities of foreign banks which had previously only been controlled by State law. In essence, the Act established a policy of how the US would treat foreign banks. The key elements are:

- limiting branching activities so that they are more comparable to US banks;
- requiring that the foreign banks have the same reserve requirements as US banks;
- limiting the degree to which foreign banks can be involved in US securities;
- opening Federal deposit insurance to US officers of foreign banks if they are involved in retail banking.

International Finance Corporation

The International Finance Corporation (IFC) is part of the **World Bank**. It was established in 1956 and is based in Washington, DC. It has a similar objective to that of the World Bank in as much as it aims to improve the quality of the lives of individuals in developing member countries. The IFC is the largest multilateral source of loan and equity financing. It primarily focuses on private sector projects in developing nations. It assists private companies in finding finance on the international financial markets and also provides technical assistance and advice to both businesses and governments. The IFC uses its 175 member countries to collectively approve investments and determine their policy. All IFC members are also members of the **International Bank for Reconstruction and Development (IBRD)**. The IFC has an authorized capital of $2.45 billion. It is independent and therefore financially and legally autonomous, with its own share capital and management. The IFC charges market rates for loans and reinvests its profits in new projects.

www.ifc.org

International Monetary Fund (IMF)

The International Monetary Fund was established in 1945 in order to promote international monetary harmony, monitor exchange rates and monetary policies and provide credit for countries that were experiencing problems in the form of deficits in their **balance of payments**. Each member of the IMF has a quota, known as the Special Drawing Rights. This reflects the relative size of its economy, and its relative voting power. The quotas also determine each member's access to financial resources. The IMF itself is funded through quotas paid by members. Currently the IMF has approximately 175 members.

The IMF came into being as a result of the Bretton Woods meeting and together with the **World Bank** it helps supervise the exchange rate system. There was an abrupt change of policy in the early 1970s when it became increasingly difficult to regulate **fixed exchange rates**. As a result, the IMF is now more concerned with its members' economic policies. During the 1980s it became involved in trying to deal with the debt crisis of many of the developing countries. During the 1990s it was engaged in trying to deal with innumerable currency crises.

Many commentators believe that the IMF has outlived its usefulness and should now be abolished, whilst others believe that it should simply become a lender of last resort.

www.imf.org

International monetary system

The International Monetary System used to be based on the concept of pegging currencies to the value of gold. This was known as the 'gold standard' and guaranteed that a currency could be converted into gold. During the 1930s the system of the gold standard broke down and many currencies were devalued. In 1944, however, the Bretton Woods system set fixed exchange rates, with the $US (still pegged to the gold standard) being at the centre of this new system, in as much as every other currency was pegged to its value. Significant changes in exchange rates were only allowed provided the **International Monetary Fund** agreed. At that time the IMF's main purpose was to maintain order in the international monetary system by effectively disallowing the competitive devaluations which had been seen in the 1930s, and to impose monetary discipline on countries in order to control price inflation. Also at that time the IMF provided loans to countries to bail out their currency on the foreign exchange market, primarily in situations where there had been widespread currency speculation. Loans were also available in order to rebalance a fundamentally unbalanced **balance of payments**.

The **fixed exchange rate** system effectively collapsed in 1973; there were two main reasons for this. First there was a huge balance of trade deficit in the US, and secondly, as a result of the rise in inflation in the US, there was enormous speculative pressure on the dollar. Since that time the fixed exchange rate system has been replaced by a **floating exchange rate** regime. As a result, exchange rates fluctuate far more violently. However, the floating exchange rates give many countries more control over their own monetary policy and also help smooth out imbalances in trade. Fixed exchange rates imposed a strong monetary discipline on each of the countries, whereas floating exchange rates are very vulnerable to currency speculation.

The argument with regard to international trade and investment is that the potential volatility of floating exchange rates makes overseas investment far more risky. Most countries have adopted a form of floating exchange rate, whilst others have pegged their currency to what they perceive to be a strong currency, such as the US$. In order to work around the potential volatility of exchange rates, many international businesses have chosen to build into the system their own strategic flexibility by dispersing their production and other operations around the world. This has been an important side effect and has undoubtedly contributed to widespread foreign direct investment in a number of countries which would otherwise have been overlooked.

www.imf.org

Inventory

'Inventory' is another term for 'stock' and is the preferred term used in the US. In essence, an inventory is the sum of all finished goods, raw materials and work in progress held by a business. Typically a business will count its inventory at the end of a financial year in order to confirm that these figures are broadly in accord with what it expects to own.

There are a number of ancillary uses of the word 'inventory', which include the following:

- *Anticipatory inventory* – which refers to stock held by a business in anticipation of a later increase in demand. This usually only occurs when the costs of storage are less than the costs of changing production levels.
- *Buffer inventory* – this is a level of stock which is held to protect the business against variations in supply, demand and lead times. It is, in effect, a stock safety margin.
- *Cycle inventory* – which seeks to minimize inventory and the costs

of setting up production by minimizing these costs using just-in-time (JIT) techniques.

- *Pipeline inventory* – which is stock items that are at various stages in the production process or the business's system. Although they have a monetary value in themselves they have already been earmarked for particular projects or production processes.
- *Uncoupling inventory* – these are stock items which are currently in transit from one machine to another, or perhaps from a manufacturer or raw material supplier to the manufacturer or customer.

The inventory position of a product, part or component is equal to the number of those items which are immediately available, plus those which are expected to be delivered in the very near future. From this combined total it is necessary to deduct those items which are still in stock, but have already been allocated to the production of a product or products to fulfil an existing order for a customer.

Inventory turnover, or stock turnover, is equal to the cost of goods sold divided by the average investment in the inventory. Or, in other words, it is the cost of goods sold divided by stock. The inventory turnover is the inverse of cycle time. Normally the inventory turnover increases in proportion to demand.

Inventory velocity can be measured in one of two ways. It refers either to the speed at which items enter a manufacturing organization and are then processed and subsequently sold on to a customer, or to the general movement of parts, components or products within a supply chain. Manufacturing organizations will seek to ensure that the inventory velocity is as fast as is practicable, as the higher the speed, the shorter the time between paying for parts and components and receiving payments for the finished products.

Investment appraisal

'Investment appraisal' can refer to an internal appraisal of the potential benefits of a project, which is primarily carried out by the management or employees of a business. It can also refer to an investment appraisal made by an external individual, business or investor who is considering becoming involved in some way with a business.

Typical ways in which investment appraisal can be undertaken include **payback**, which can be considered as a fairly simplistic way of calculating the viability of a project. It is one of the most common ways in which investment appraisals are made. The business would normally identify a period within which the investment would be expected to pay for itself. After this period of time the project would be expected to move into profit. It is possible to calculate the relative payback periods for a number of competing projects or investments. A business will bear in mind that all investments which are to be made will be at the expense of other projects. This means that businesses need to know which, potentially, will be the best investment to proceed with.

Essentially this is a question of **opportunity cost**, which is addressed purely in cash terms. Not all investments are made purely to provide a quick cash return; there may be other motivations behind the investment. Whatever the case, payback does allow a business to look at a number of competing projects and, at least in monetary terms, assist them in making a decision.

Average rate of return is a means by which a business's annual profits on a particular investment can be calculated as a percentage of the original amount paid. In using the average rate of return for a particular project the business would be able to see whether it would be more profitable to leave the money in the bank, rather than risk the investment on a project that might not repay at the same level. The average rate of return, when coupled with a close examination of interest rates, enables a business to identify the opportunity costs of an investment and allows it to compare one project against another.

An alternative is the internal rate of return (IRR), which is the discount, when used in **cash flow**, which makes the **net present value** equal zero. The business needs to discover the rate of return when the net present value is zero. This is used in order to compare the market rate of interest with the internal rate of return so that the business can make a decision about the potential investment. As the rate of interest represents the actual cost of the capital, if the internal rate of return is higher, the project is worth considering. However, the organization may set its own discount rate, which may be higher than the interest rate. In these cases, even if the project looks as if it will match the interest rate, it will still not be accepted because it still does not reach the minimum discount rate set by the business.

Another alternative to investment appraisal is consideration of **discounted cash flow**. The interest rate and time will determine the return on a particular project. Clearly, using this concept it is obvious that money which is earned (or paid) in the future is worth less than it is today.

Finally, businesses may consider either a form of **breakeven analysis** or a cost benefit analysis. In the latter case, the business will take a broader view of the potential costs and benefits associated with a decision. This means that the normal considerations with regard to costs and benefits are extended and may include any relevant external costs and benefits, which may be either unavoidable or, in some cases, desirable. Social costs, for example, may be brought into the equation, as may the longer-term impact of a particular project upon the rest of the operations routinely being carried out or provided by the business itself.

Lumby, Steve and Jones, Chris, *Fundamentals of Investment Appraisal*. London: Thomson Learning, 2000.

Pettinger, Richard, *Investment Appraisal: A Managerial Approach*. Basingstoke: Palgrave Macmillan, 2000.

Investment flows

The term 'investment flows' refers to a business's **cash flow**, which is directly associated with the purchasing or the selling of **fixed assets** or other business interests. Investment flows, therefore, chart a business's involvement in the acquisition or disposal of fixed assets and, in some cases, the acquisition or disposal of subsidiaries and overseas businesses with whom they may have a short-term relationship.

Luenberger, David G., *Investment Science*. New York: Oxford University Press, 1997.

Invisible asset

See intangible asset.

Invisibles

'Invisibles' is a generic term which is used to describe non-merchandise trade. Invisibles therefore include the trade in services, investments, freight costs and insurance.

Invoice

An invoice is simply a record of a sale to a customer. Invoices are used by businesses when the payment for products or services are not required or received at the time of delivery. Invoices consist of a detailed list of the items which have been purchased, together with a total for that invoice. The business will clearly state the date by which payment of the invoice is required. Theoretically, at least, a business receiving an invoice should be able to match it against a purchase order (a business document generated by the buying business).

Invoice discounting

Invoice discounting is a method of raising working capital by converting debts into cash. The primary purpose of this is to optimize and make available working capital for the business.

Many organizations use invoice discounting facilities provided by banks, other financial institutions and specialists in factoring to generate cash without having to resort to additional borrowing. The net effect of invoice discounting is to improve the cash flow and to provide much needed working capital.

Typically, the financial institution will advance the business around 70–80% of the amount of their accounts receivable immediately, and the balance (less fee) when the invoices are actually paid.

The main benefits of invoice discounting are:

- Cash is made available to the business as opposed to conventional banking facilities (e.g. loans, or extensions or overdrafts).
- As sales and debtors grow, the money is made available more quickly for reinvestment and growth.
- The cash availability allows the business to take advantage of opportunities as they arise.
- The system improves the organization's liquidity and can help solve cash-flow problems.
- It allows growth, without the dilution of shareholder's equity.
- It allows better supplier discounts (as payment can be made without resorting to credit terms).
- It can provide the available funds for management buy-out, mergers and acquisitions.

See also **factor** *and* **factoring**.

Invoice or bill presentation

Invoice or bill presentation is the stage at which the supplying business requests payment under their normal trading terms from the business or customer it supplied.

J curve

The J curve is a phenomenon related to the **current account**. A current account may initially worsen before it improves in response to a depreciation in exchange rates, as it takes time for the growth of imports to decline in response to higher import prices. This phenomenon is known as the J curve effect as the downward movement is followed by an upward movement which resembles the letter J. It is, in effect, the shape of the trend of a country's trade balance following **devaluation**. Initially the lower exchange rates mean cheaper exports and more expensive imports; this makes the current account worse. After a period of time, however, the volume of exports will start to rise because of their lower price to foreign buyers. Domestic consumers will simultaneously buy fewer of the costlier imports. In due course the trade balance will improve compared with how it was before the devaluation.

In cases where there is a currency appreciation, an inverted J curve effect may be the outcome.

Job costing

The term 'job costing' refers to the process of identifying a specific cost unit and then identifying the costs attributed to that cost unit. This process is imperative as it is the basis upon which a business sets its selling price, whilst ensuring that costs incurred on that job are kept within a fixed price band. It is also useful in identifying labour or machine time. Job costing requires a cost record for each individual job, incorporating time analysis and material usage records. Whilst it is difficult to incorporate individual job accounts into financial books, a separate job cost ledger is usually kept, which is then reconciled with the financial books. Many businesses now use an integrated system, which is a responsibility of the production control department. It deals with five key issues:

- It assesses the costs of materials and direct labour and how these are charged to the job account.

- The job account is also debited with its share of the factory overheads, usually based on the absorption rates.
- The job account is also charged with other overheads, including administration, the cost of sales, and distribution.
- A calculation is made to compare any agreed selling price with the total actual cost of the job, and this is expressed as either a profit or a loss.
- Finally, the costing procedure also requires a statement of how scrap will be treated and to whom it will be debited.

J

Kickback

Kickbacks are illegal payments which are made in return for the successful conclusion of a transaction, or the acquisition of a contract. Obviously, kickbacks do not appear in a business's financial statements.

Kiting

'Kiting' is a US term which describes a process by which a business can fraudulently improve the appearance of its cash position on the last day of an accounting period. Typically, the business will write a high-value cheque from one of its accounts and credit that amount in a second account. The first account will not have been debited on the relevant day but the second account will have been credited. This results in the business's cash position appearing to be far healthier than it really is.

Labour burden

'Labour burden' is a term used to describe the costs of indirect labour in an organization. The costs of indirect labour are considered to be incidental to the production operations of the business. They are, therefore, given the unfortunate description of being a burden rather than an asset to the business.

Lagging indicator

A lagging indicator is an economic **indicator** that confirms but does not predict a change in the economy. Typically, lagging indicators include unemployment rates, the **book value** of **inventories**, labour costs, business spending and outstanding loans.

See also **leading indicator**.

Last in, first out (LIFO)

LIFO is an **inventory** policy in which the last item added to an organization's inventory is the first one that they use. It is of interest for tax purposes in that in a time of rising raw material prices, taxable profits are postponed. Stock rotation is normal. It is, effectively, the price at which goods are issued which makes LIFO different to FIFO.

See also **first in, first out (FIFO)**.

Law of one price

The law of one price is a theory which suggests that in competitive markets which are relatively free of transportation costs and barriers to trade, identical products which are sold in different countries must sell for broadly the same price when that price is expressed in the same currency. The law of one price (LOOP) is also based on the idea of perfect goods **arbitrage**, which takes places when commodity arbitrages exploit price differences to make a risk-less profit.

Jain, Arvind, *Commodity Futures Markets and the Law of One Price*. Ann Arbor, MI: University of Michigan Press. 1980.

Leading indicator

Leading indicators are economic **indicators** which tend to change shortly before an economy is about to change. Leading indicators can include the money supply, stocks or share prices, changes in **inventories**, the number of building permits granted, and a falling level of employment. Governments can seek to react to these leading indicators by making adjustments to the interest rates, although in many cases this is now the reserve of independent **central banks**. Leading indicators are seen as being useful predictive tools in assessing how an economy may change in the near future. They are differentiated in this respect from both **coincidence indicators** and **lagging indicators**.

Lease/leasing

A lease is often a viable alternative for a business in respect of equipment or property, compared with rental or outright purchase. A lease is a legal agreement between a lessor and a lessee in which the lessee obtains the right to use an item or asset owned by the lessor in exchange for periodic payments. Leases are different from rentals in that the lease may in fact be an arrangement by which the lessees can opt to make additional payments which will mean that the **asset**, at the end of a given period, has passed into their ownership.

Ledger

A ledger, or book of final entry, is a record of transactions which are listed in separate accounts. These separate accounts will have been routinely entered into separate ledgers, such as the **general ledger** or **sales ledger**, and then compiled into the ledger, or book of final entry, which contains all of the transactions.

L

Letter of credit

A letter of credit is issued by a buyer's bank in favour of a seller. It undertakes to pay an agreed amount of money on receipt by the bank of confirming documents within a specified period of time. An irrevocable letter of credit is issued in cases where the issuing bank waives the rights to cancel or amend the payment without the consent of the seller. A confirmed irrevocable letter of credit involves the added responsibility of a bank other than the issuing bank. A revocable letter of credit allows the issuing bank to cancel or amend part of the amount owing.

A typical letter of credit transaction, using an irrevocable letter of credit, would be:

- Once the buyer and seller agree on the terms of a sale the buyer arranges for its bank to open a letter of credit which specifies the documents required for payment.
- The buyer's bank issues or opens an irrevocable letter of credit, including all instructions to the seller relating to the shipment.
- The buyer's bank sends its irrevocable letter of credit to the seller's bank and requests confirmation.
- The seller's bank then prepares a letter of confirmation, which is forwarded to the exporter, along with the irrevocable letter of credit.
- The exporter then checks the letter of credit and, if relevant, contacts a freight forwarder and confirms shipping dates. If the exporter has a problem with any of the conditions on the letter of credit at this stage, the buyer is contacted.
- The exporter then arranges for the delivery of the goods to the appropriate port.
- Once the goods are loaded, the freight forwarder completes the necessary documentation.
- The exporter, or the freight forwarder acting for the exporter, presents the documents which prove their compliance with the terms of the letter of credit, to their bank.
- The bank then reviews the documents. If everything is in order these are then sent to the buyer's bank for review.
- The buyer then uses the documents at their end to claim the goods.
- A draft, which would accompany the letter of credit, is then paid by the buyer's bank to the exporter's bank.

Leverage

See **gearing ratios.**

Liability

Liabilities are both the current and the long-term debts of a business. Debts which have to be paid within 12 months are classed as current liabilities, whilst those payable after 12 months are known as long-term liabilities. Other liabilities include shareholders' funds, for which there is no specified repayment time or period. Liabilities are usually acquired as the result of a purchase of assets.

Like-for-like

Like-for-like is a sales valuation method which seeks to identify the proportion of current sales or business activity which has been achieved through activities comparable to the previous year.

This method of valuation excludes sales or additional activity related to other activities of the business such as expansion or acquisition. Using this approach, these figures are excluded on the grounds that they artificially enlarge the sales figures. In other words, like-for-like identifies and separates the underlying trends from the gross figures which are considered to hide the primary performance improvements of regular activities.

A performance measure, like-for-like is often used in the retail trade. It illustrates the underlying growth by excluding sales figures or savings which have arisen from the opening of new retail outlets or the closure of loss-making outlets.

Liquidation

Liquidation literally means turning a business's **assets** into readily available cash. This process normally begins when the business ceases to trade in its current form as a result of insolvency. Liquidation is often described as 'winding-up', usually as a result of a creditor finally taking the business to court for non-payment of debts. In these cases an individual known as a receiver or liquidator will be appointed to raise enough cash to satisfy the creditors. This is achieved by the disposal of the business's assets or the selling of the business as a **going concern**, to a third party.

In many cases businesses will choose to go into voluntary liquidation, deciding to cease trading as they are currently organized. In these cases the business appoints a liquidator, who calls a meeting of creditors to endorse the liquidator's powers. The liquidator then assumes control of the business and collects assets, pays debts and if there is surplus, distributes it to the company's members according to their rights.

Liquidation value

The liquidation value is equal to the current realistic and realizable amount of money which either an asset or a business is worth if it needs to be sold immediately. The liquidation value represents the true market value of any **assets** or businesses, incorporating an evaluation of the business's **liabilities**. Technically, should the liquidation value of a business be less than the cumulative value of its shares, then the business should no longer be trading, and the share price does not accurately reflect the true value of the business itself.

In the majority of cases the liquidation value is only ever a useful measure if a business is on the verge of collapse. In reality, the liquidation value when compared with the current share price may reveal that the business is indeed worth less than the cumulative value of all of the shares available. This is not an uncommon occurrence.

Liquidity ratio

The liquidity ratio, which is also known as the 'acid test ratio', compares the business's liquid or **current assets** with its **current liabilities**. Under the majority of circumstances a business's liquid assets are considered to be cash, trade debts and any other assets which can readily be sold. The ratio is normally configured in the following manner:

$$\frac{Current\ assets}{Current\ liabilities}$$

The ratio seeks to indicate whether the business is capable of paying its debts without having to make further sales. It is a prime measure of a business's solvency. The majority of accountants recommend that the ratio should produce a figure of around 1.5 and that values below 1.0 indicate that there is a severe problem with the business. Equally, values greater than 2.0 indicate that the business has invested too much money in short-term assets.

A variation, known primarily as the acid test ratio, presents a slightly different version of the liquidity ratio. The acid test ratio is:

$$\frac{Current\ assets\ -\ stock}{Current\ liabilities}$$

Again, most accountants would recommend that the figure should be equal to 1, indicating that the business has £1's worth of liquid assets for every £1's short-term debt. If the business has an acid test ratio result of less than 1, then it has a low liquidity and may be unable to find sufficient funds to finance its short-term debt commitments.

Chorafas, Dimitris N., *Liabilities, Liquidity and Cash Management: Balancing Financial Risk*. New York: John Wiley, 2002.

Long-term assets

Long-term assets are technically any **asset**, such as property, equipment or plant, which a business expects to use for a period exceeding a year. Normally long-term assets are **capital assets**, which do not readily lend themselves to easy conversion into cash. Clearly any long-term assets which would appear on a business's **balance sheet** are subject to **depreciation**. The business's long-term assets, in addition to any **short-term assets** and **current assets**, contribute to its **total assets**.

Mm

MACRS (modified ACRS)

The modified ACRS, or modified accelerated cost recovery system, was brought into effect in the US in 1986. It refers to tax provisions which govern the rate of **depreciation** of assets, which essentially allows either a 150% or a 200% declining balance system, depending on the expected useful life of different **assets**.

Management accounting

Management accounting is the collection, collation and appraisal of financial information in order to assist management in the decision making, planning, control and performance appraisal of the business. Management accounting also ensures that **generally accepted accounting procedures (GAAP)** are followed and that the business is creating, preserving and increasing value during the business's operations, in order to deliver that value to the stakeholders. Management accounting is an essential element of management as it identifies, generates, presents and interprets information relevant to the formulation of business strategy. It is essential in all planning and control activities, including various decisions which need to be made. It also provides essential data for the examination of performance improvement, as well as safeguarding both the **tangible** and **intangible assets** of the business. A business will also use the management accounting function as a form of corporate governance and internal control.

Keown, Arthur J., Martin, John W., Petty, William D. and Scott., David F., *Financial Management: Principles and Applications*. New York: Prentice-Hall, 2001.

Manufacturing overhead

The term 'manufacturing overhead' refers to the direct costs of labour and other materials which are involved in the manufacturing operations. These are distinct from **general and administrative overheads** and indeed from the more general term 'overhead', which can refer to expenses which are not directly attributed to the business's manufacturing activities, but are still necessary for the business to function.

Margin

A margin can be applied either to the total business carried out by an organization, or to a specific product, range or service. In its more general use, margin is expressed as the **gross profit** as a percentage of the turnover of the business. When applied to specific products, it refers to the difference between the total costs (including overheads) attributed to the product and the selling price of that product. In this respect 'margin' is not dissimilar to **mark-up**, which may be based on a fixed percentage addition to the costs of a product in order to ensure a sufficient margin.

Market basket

See **basket**.

Margin of safety

See **breakeven analysis and the breakeven point**.

Mark-up

Mark-up is usually expressed as the **gross profit** achieved as a percentage of the costs. More definitively, it is the percentage added to the cost which is used to obtain the selling price. Mark-up is often referred to as a **margin**, which should reflect a reasonable profit on each sale once all necessary costs have been incorporated into the equation.

Master budget

A master budget is a consolidated budget into which all other subsidiary budgets are incorporated. The master budget will normally include the budgeted **profit and loss account**, **balance sheet** and **cash flow statement**. The master budget is essential for a business in order to be able to plan and control its activities in the next financial period.

M

Medium of exchange

The most common medium of exchange is, of course, money or currency of one description or another. A medium of exchange is any particular item which has wide acceptance in the exchange of products and services in a given market. Other mediums of exchange could include products or services, or indeed raw materials. In these cases raw materials could theoretically be swapped for finished goods, or finished goods swapped for other finished goods. These forms of **barter** are not uncommon, assuming of course that what is offered as a replacement for cash is worthwhile to the business. Certainly other mediums of exchange could be considered when the currency of a particular country is difficult to exchange, or where exchange controls prohibit the movement of **hard currency** from one country to another. In these cases the transaction could proceed on the basis that the customer would provide either raw materials or finished goods which could then be exported to the supplying business, who would in turn sell them on the open market in the more conventional way.

Mercantilism

Mercantilism makes the assumption that money will inevitably become scarce, which in turn would impede higher levels of output and have an impact upon employment. Mercantilists believed that low interest rates, which allowed cheaper money to be available to businesses, were the ideal solution. This was an economic viewpoint originally dating back to the seventeenth century and was very much a forerunner to the models suggested by classical economists of the twentieth century. The classical economists believed that in making money cheap, inflation would be created. Mercantilists were against **free trade** and they believed that protectionist policies, which would minimize imports and maximize exports, would create a trade surplus, thereby dealing with the problem of scarce money.

This viewpoint has largely been disproved as mercantilists believed that ultimately a nation's wealth was dependent upon its ownership or stock of precious metals. Later economic theorists undermined this view by stating that rather than precious metals being the most important consideration, it was a country's stocks of productive resources that were crucial. Each country's available land, labour and capital, and how efficiently they used these, would determine a nation's comparative wealth. With the increase in free trade, efficiency has also increased, which has allowed various countries to specialize in the production of products and services in which they have a comparative advantage. In other words, they most efficiently use their land, labour and capital in a particular way.

M

Vaggi, Gianni and Groenewegen, Peter, *A Concise History of Economic Thought: From Mercantilism to Monetarism*. New York: Palgrave Macmillan, 2002.

Merchant services

Merchant services are **outsourced** pay processing systems which are used for ATM card transactions, as well as credit and debit transactions. They also provide cheque guarantees and internet checks for e-commerce. Merchant services allow payments to be made via the internet, electronic cash registers or point of sale terminals. The customer's chosen method of payment is inputted into the vendor's payment system and the merchant service handles the authorization and transfer of funds. The merchant service provides the vendor with monthly billing statements for which the vendor pays a fee or a percentage of sales. Merchant services also provide the vendor with terminals and connection facilities to their services.

Misfeasance

A charge of misfeasance may be brought against directors or other senior officers of a business by a liquidator who feels that they have breached their duties of responsibility towards the business. Misfeasance implies misconduct and suggests that the directors, or others, did not do everything in their power to ensure that the best interests of the stakeholders or **shareholders** were always considered.

Modified ACRS

See MACRS.

Modified book value

See adjusted book value.

Modified cash basis

'Modified cash basis' describes a **book-keeping** practice which aims to account for short-term **assets**, sales and **expenses** on a cash basis and deals with long-term assets on an accrual basis.

Dealing with the short-term assets, sales and expenses on a cash basis means that they are only recorded when cash is either received or paid out, and is a far simpler method than accrual basis book-keeping. It does, however, make it more difficult for the business to secure finance. In dealing with the long-term assets on an accrual basis the items are only reported when either income is earned or expenses are incurred. In other words, businesses have the discretion as to when they recognize income and expenditure.

Monetarism

Monetarism is a strand of economic theory which suggests that if the money supply is controlled in a given economy, the rest of the economy will be capable of balancing or taking care of itself. Monetarism is founded on the basis that inflation occurs when a government prints too much money. Milton Friedman argued his quantity theory of money, which suggested that governments need to keep a steady money supply, only expanding the money supply each year to allow for natural growth of the economy. In following this policy, market forces would control problems arising out of inflation, recession or unemployment.

Monetarism was eagerly grasped during the 1980s, primarily in the US and the UK. **Central banks** set targets for money supply growth and closely controlled the rates of interest. Since the 1980s the linkage between money supply and inflation has proved to be somewhat erroneous. At the time, the money supply was seen as a useful policy target, providing the relationship between money and **gross domestic product**, and therefore **inflation**, remained predictable and stable. It was further believed that the money supply would necessarily affect both output and prices in as much as the money supply would determine how fast cash circulated around an economy. What monetarists had not considered was the speed at which money revolves around an economy, which is known as the 'velocity of circulation', and monetarists failed consistently to predict sudden changes. Monetarists began to realize that the link between money supply and inflation was far more complex than they had believed. As a result, monetary targets set by central banks largely passed out of favour.

The natural alternative and successor to monetarist policy is the setting of inflation targets and manipulating the economy in order to achieve these targets.

See also **monetary policy**.

Vaggi, Gianni and Groenewegen, Peter, *A Concise History of Economic Thought: From Mercantilism to Monetarism.* New York: Palgrave Macmillan, 2002.

Monetary policy

The primary objective of monetary policy is to control inflation. A country sets a target for inflation and attempts to ensure that it does not deviate to any degree from this target. Since the UK left the **Exchange Rate Mechanism (ERM)** in September 1992, UK monetary policy has involved the use of manipulating interest rates to control the level of inflation.

As the term 'monetary policy' suggests, it is a means by which the government controls the money supply. Adopting a monetarist policy relies on the belief that in controlling the money supply, one also controls the price levels. There are close links between interest rates, the money supply and the exchange rate. At times when the UK was tied to a **fixed exchange rate** system, both the rate of interest and the money supply had to be adjusted in order to maintain a steady exchange rate. During the period between 1990 and 1992, when the UK was part of the ERM, the government effectively lost control of interest rates and the supply of money.

Monetarists realize that it is notoriously difficult to control interest rates, money supply and exchange rates simultaneously. In May 1997 the new Labour Chancellor, Gordon Brown, made the Bank of England independent, setting up the Monetary Policy Committee (MPC), and effectively taking the government and the Chancellor out of the decision-making loop with regard to interest rates.

In US terms, monetary policy consists of efforts which are made by the US Federal Reserve (the **central bank** of the US) to influence the conditions of both money and credit in the US economy. They too have objectives in terms of stable prices, the maintenance of high employment and the promotion of maximum sustainable growth within the economy. The Federal Reserve formulates their monetary policy by setting targets for the Federal funds rate, which is the interest rates which banks charge one another for short-term loans. The Federal funds rate is what the banks pay when they borrow and therefore affects the rates they charge when they lend. These rates, in turn, have an impact upon short-term interest rates in the economy and ultimately economic activity and the rate of inflation. In order to achieve this, the Federal Reserve uses open market operations, the purchase and sale of previously issued US Government securities, as a means by which to influence how much banks can lend. This effectively raises or lowers the Federal funds rate. When the Federal Reserve buys securities, funds flood into the banking system; this gives them more money to lend and places a downward pressure on the Federal funds rate. When the Federal Reserve sells securities, the opposite occurs.

Walsh, Carl, *Monetary Theory and Policy*. Cambridge, MA: MIT Press, 2003.

Money supply

The money supply is the amount of currency issued by a nation's **central bank**. In controlling the money supply, the government and the central bank may seek to control **inflation**, on the basis that any increase in the money supply will lead to a rise in price levels. There are several tactics which can be adopted (see Table 3), and usually governments (such as in the UK) will use a range of M0 or M5. The money supply reserves are usually taken to be as listed in Table 3.

Table 3 Control of the money supply

Money supply measure	Description
M0	Notes and coins in circulation, plus money held by banks, and balances in the central bank.
M1	Notes and coins in circulation, plus private sector current accounts and deposits.
M2	Notes and coins in circulation, plus non-interest bank deposits, building society accounts and national savings schemes.
M3	M1 plus private sector bank deposits and certificates of deposit.
M3c	M3 plus foreign current deposits
M4	M1 plus private sector bank deposits and items such as Treasury Bills.
M5	M4 plus building society deposits.

Bordo, Michael D. and Jonung, Lars, *Demand for Money: An Analysis of the Long-Run Behavior of the Velocity of Circulation.* Somerset, NJ: Transaction Publishers, 2003.

Mortgage

M

A mortgage is the transfer of property to a lender on the assumption that the borrower agrees to terms of repayment of the debt, after which time the asset will be transferred to the borrower's ownership. A mortgage is a common form of security for a creditor.

Multiplier effect

The financial implications of the multiplier effect serve to illustrate that a considerable injection of cash into the economy is multiplied in its impact as it flows through the economy.

Whilst major government spending or considerable investment in the form of overseas investment (foreign direct investment) represents additional national income equal to its original value, it will stimulate other parts of the economy.

The original investment provides direct wages, and the purchase of products, services and raw materials, which in turn create more employment in the supplying businesses, leading to increased demand elsewhere for products and services. As employees and **shareholders** earn from the knock-on effects of the original investment, demand will increase, wages will rise and there will be a positive impact on profits. This will eventually filter down to the consumer market.

Arguably, one of the most effective multipliers is investment in the construction industry. These investments tend to have wider multiplier effects on the economy as a whole. Negative multiplier effects can also occur when considerable sums are removed from the economy by a large reduction in government spending, such as the cancellation of a major infrastructure project.

M

National Association of Purchasing Managers index (NAPM index)

The NAPM index is used as a measure of both the US manufacturing sector and the economy itself. Data supplied by purchasing managers includes information regarding orders, production, employment, deliveries and inventories. The index is released on the first business day of each month (thereby representing last month's data). The government and industry are extremely interested in the NAPM index as it is believed to be an inflationary indicator.

It is generally held that a high reading shows that manufacturing is growing, whilst a low reading shows that manufacturing is shrinking.

www.napm.org

Negative net worth

Negative **net worth** is taken to mean situations where a business's **liabilities** are in excess of its **assets**. For younger and growing businesses this is not often an issue, as their liabilities may be high as they seek to expand through the acquisition of loans and other investments.

Negative net worth is also somewhat inapplicable for service-based organizations, whose assets cannot be measured in the same manner as, for example, those of a manufacturing business. Their assets are somewhat intangible, in the form of expertise or knowledge in developing particular services, rather than producing tangible products with tangible fixed assets.

Net assets

There are various interpretations of exactly what constitutes a net asset, but fundamentally it is a measure of the **capital** available to a business. At its simplest, net assets are equal to the business's **assets** less its **current liabilities.** Arguably, long-term liabilities should be factored into the equation, as they are part of the capital and therefore not deducted before arriving at the net asset figure. Conversely, there are those who argue the reverse in as much as long-term liabilities are just that, and should be deducted.

Another take on net assets is that they are equal to the assets employed by the business. In other words, this means the **fixed assets** plus the **net current assets** (or **working capital**). In the majority of cases, in published accounts, a business is likely to deduct its long-term liabilities, which, in effect, makes net assets the same as **net worth**. Therefore, the equations can either be:

Fixed assets + net current assets

or

Fixed assets + net current assets − long-term liabilities

Net book value

'Net book value' refers to the value of an asset which appears in the accounts of a business (notably the last quoted valuation on the **balance sheet**). Effectively, the net book value of an asset is arrived at using the following calculation:

*The **historical cost** of the fixed assets − the accumulated **depreciation***

The net book value can be misleading as it is only the business's own assessment of its worth. Ultimately, the asset is only worth what another party is prepared to pay in the case of the disposal of that asset. Should this asset be sold in excess of its net book value, then the surplus cash from the sale is normally recorded under **shareholder**s' funds.

Parolini, Cinzia, *The Value Net: A Tool for Competitive Strategy*. New York: John Wiley, 1999.

N

Net capital

The term 'net capital' has two different definitions. Perhaps the most common is that net capital is equal to a business's **net worth** less any **assets** which cannot be easily converted into cash.

Alternatively, net capital can be described as the amount by which **net assets** exceed the value of other assets which cannot be readily converted into cash.

An associated term is the 'net capital ratio'. It is generally held that the relationship between debts and liquid assets should not exceed 15:1. This calculation is simply made by summing the total debts of the business and then comparing them with the total liquid assets of the business.

Net cash flow

A business's net cash flow is equal to all of its cash receipts minus its cash payments during a given period of time. In effect, net cash flow is equal to a business's **net profit**, less of course any **depreciation**, depletion or **amortization**. Net cash flow is more commonly known simply as **cash flow**.

Net current assets

Net current assets are equal to a business's **current assets** less its **current liabilities**. The figure represents the actual **working capital** of the business; in effect, the cash which is being used by the business for trading purposes.

See also **net assets.**

Net domestic product

The net domestic product is a measure used in national accounts. Net domestic product is equal to the nation's **gross domestic product (GDP)** less **depreciation** on that nation's capital goods. The net domestic product is seen as a useful measure of how much that nation needs to spend in order to maintain the level of GDP. Clearly, if the nation is not able to replace its depreciated capital stock, then its GDP will fall. Equally it can be seen that if there is a growing gulf between a nation's GDP and net domestic product, then the implication is that their capital goods are becoming obsolete. Conversely, if the two figures are converging, then it is an indication that generally the nation is replacing its capital stock.

Net earnings

The term 'net earnings' is almost interchangeable with the terms **net income** and **bottom line**. Net earnings are generally calculated as being the business's gross sales less other expenses, taxes, interest and **depreciation**. Net earnings can be seen as an important measure of a business's health and overall performance.

See also **net profit.**

Net foreign investment

Net foreign investment can be summed up as the total of a country's exports in products and services, the receipts of factor income and the receipt of capital grants received from the government, less the sum of imported goods, products and services, payments of factor income, and transfer payments to foreign individuals or businesses. More simply, net foreign investment can be viewed as being the total of the **acquisition** of foreign assets by a country's residents, less the acquisition of that country's assets by foreign residents.

Bouchet, Michel Henry, Clark, Ephraim and Groslambert, Bertrand, *Country Risk Assessment: A Guide to Global Investment Strategy.* New York: John Wiley, 2003.

Net income

'Net income' is a term which describes the earnings of a business before expenses have been deducted. In the case of an individual, 'net income' usually describes gross income after the deduction of tax.

Net income multiplier

'Net income multiplier' refers to an asset which ultimately generates income. The calculation is made by dividing the current price of an asset by the net income which it has generated over a given period of time. The net income multiplier is a prime measure of how effectively a particular asset is being used to generate income, and serves as an ideal way of assessing its value to the business rather than merely in terms of its current market price.

Net interest margin

The net interest margin is a means by which investors can assess the relationship between the interest they are receiving from their investments and the associated investment expenses. Normally investors would seek to express the difference between their interest income and their interest expenses as a percentage of their average earning assets.

N

Net investment

Net investment is normally calculated in the following manner:

Additions to capital goods – capital consumption

The calculation looks at the gross investment in an economy, over a period of time, in the stock of capital goods (**fixed assets**), but then deducts the capital consumption (**depreciation**) to give the actual net investment figure.

Net liquid assets

Net liquid assets is a measure of the actual cash which is available to a business. The calculation involves:

*Cash available (including **current assets** in the form of investments) – short-term loans and overdrafts*

Net margin

The net margin of a business is equal to the percentage of its sales revenue which is its **net profit.** The normal equation used is:

$$Net\ margin = \frac{Net\ (operating)\ profit}{Sales\ revenue} \times 100$$

Net margin can be differentiated from the gross margin as this equation takes into account fixed overheads (administration costs, rates, rents, etc.). This margin is therefore considered to be a far more accurate measure of a business's performance.

Net operating income

A business's net operating income can be calculated by the deduction of operating expenses from its income, but before it deducts any taxes or interest. The net operating income should reveal the amount by which a business's income exceeds its expenses.

Net operating margin

The net operating margin should reveal whether a business is operating profitably. The calculation involves dividing the **net operating income** by revenues received, and expressing this total as a percentage.

N

Net present value (NPV)

Net present value is used to help make the decision as to whether or not to make an investment. The 'net' aspect of the term refers to both the costs and benefits of the investment. In order to calculate net present value, a business will sum all of the benefits which are expected from the investment, both currently and in the future. It then sums all of the expected costs on the same basis. In order to work out the future bene-fits and costs, a business will adjust its future cash flow using any appro-priate **discount rates**. It will then subtract these costs from the benefits. If the result is a negative net present value, then in terms of expected returns, the investment would not be a good one and cannot be easily justified by the business; if the net present value proves to be positive then the business will compare the net present values of alternative investment opportunities before finally deciding whether or not to make the investment.

Net profit

'Net profit' is a term which can be applied to a business's receipts, both before and after the deduction of tax. In the first case, net profit is equal to the profits of a business once all receipts and expenses have been accounted for. In some cases, the net profit is arrived at by simply deducting from the **gross profit** all **expenses** not already taken into account when calculating that gross profit.

As an alternative, net profit can also be described as the final profit of the business, in other words after tax has been deducted.

Net profit margin

The net profit margin is often referred to as the **net margin** and is calcu-lated by deploying the **net profit margin ratio**. This divides a busi-ness's **net profit** by its **net revenues** and then expresses this relationship as a percentage. A business's net profit margin serves as a means by which the cost control functions can be assessed. If a business has a high net profit margin then it is seen to be able to convert revenue into profit. Net profit margins are often used to compare businesses in the same industries, since they are under the same pressures and have similar opportunities.

Net profit margins are also useful in the comparison of unlike busi-nesses in unlike markets, as the net profit margin reveals to potential investors the comparative profitability of different types of businesses.

Net profit margin ratio

The net profit margin ratio differs from the **gross profit margin ratio** in as much as it expresses the net profit as a percentage of the sales generated. In effect, it measures the percentage return on sales after expenses such as tax have been taken into account. The ratio is:

N

$$Net\ profit\ margin = \frac{Net\ profit\ after\ tax}{Sales} \times 100$$

Therefore a business with a total sales revenue of some £3,200,000 has a net profit after tax of £200,000. The calculation is:

$$\frac{200,000}{3,200,000} \times 100 = 6.25\%$$

Typically, the business would then compare this figure with the industry standard to assess its overall ability to produce a net profit from its generated sales.

Net quick assets

Net quick assets are often referred to as the quick ratio as the calculation reveals how liquid a business is. The term is interchangeable with the **acid-test ratio**. The net quick asset calculation is equal to the business's cash, **accounts receivable** and marketable securities (securities that can be quickly turned into cash) less the business's **current liabilities**.

See also **acid-test ratio** and **quick ratio**.

Net realizable value

'Net realizable value' refers to asset valuation; specifically it is related to the actual and realistic market value of an asset in the event that the business is forced to sell that asset. The net realizable value incorporates the fact that there may be costs related to the disposal of that asset, and deducts these costs from the value of the asset.

Net revenue

The net revenues of a business are payments made to it after adjustments have been made, particularly in relation to expenses. Revenue figures tend to be net of discounts. By subtracting expenses from revenues a business's real **net income** can be calculated. In financial terms, however, there is always a question of when revenues should be considered to have been received. There is a degree of regulation with regard to this, but businesses may consider revenues to have been received either when the actual money was received, or when an agreement to carry out a transaction was signed, or when the products or services were actually provided or delivered. Theoretically, however, the revenue should be considered to have been received when the owner-

N

ship of products or services is transferred to the customer and when the business can be sure that the revenue will be received.

Net sales

The net sales of a business are taken to be the **gross sales** less any returns, discounts or allowances.

See also **net margin**.

Net surplus

The term 'net surplus' refers to the profits of a business less a number of deductions. Typically net surplus uses the following equation:

Profits – operating expenses, interest, insurance, dividends, taxes =

net surplus

See also **surplus**.

Net tangible assets

The net tangible assets of a business are its **tangible assets** less its **current liabilities**. In many respects the net tangible assets of the business are a better indicator as to the financial strength of that business, in as much as they do not incorporate **intangible assets**, which are notoriously difficult to value accurately.

An associated term is **price to net tangible assets ratio**.

Net worth

In many cases net worth is taken to be the same as net asset value, meaning that it is equal to:

Total assets – current liabilities

Normally this is the calculation and figure as shown on the **balance sheet**. The published net worth of assets is never considered to be particularly reliable. Assets are rarely actually worth what the **book value** places their value at, and it is often the case that this is at variance with the true market value of the asset.

Net worth represents, therefore, the value of the business, less its liabilities, but it does not include **intangible assets**, such as **goodwill**, as it is rare that they even appear on a balance sheet.

See also **net tangible assets**.

Non-cash expense

The term 'non-cash expense' is associated with an **income statement** (which is an account of a business's sales, expenses and net profits over a given period of time). A non-cash expense, therefore, is an expense which did not involve the spending of money. Typical examples include **amortization** and **depreciation**.

Nonconvertible currency

A nonconvertible currency is a currency which both residents and non-residents of a country are prohibited from converting into another currency. This state of affairs can lead to significant problems in international trade in as much as it may be desirable to sell products and services into a country which has a nonconvertible currency. The difficulty arises when payments received for those products and services in the form of a nonconvertible currency are to be moved out of that country. In effect, not only has the currency no value as it cannot be converted, but it also leaves an international business with a potential hole in its balance sheet.

There are, of course, alternative means of dealing with countries with nonconvertible currencies. A British clothing manufacturer, for example, might consider four different alternatives in getting around the problem of dealing with a country with a nonconvertible currency. Its options may include one of the following:

- The British clothing manufacturer may choose to use **barter**, in effect, offering to trade its manufactured clothing for locally manufactured textiles, which it could either use itself or sell in another market to recoup the cash.
- The clothing manufacturer may choose to strike a compensation deal, whereby the local business in the overseas market covers the costs of any business travel and expenses undertaken by the British clothing manufacturer's employees, the balance being paid in the barter system as outlined above.
- The third alternative is to choose a buy-back system. The British clothing manufacturer may choose to fund a small production facility which makes the same items of clothing, of similar quality to the ones produced at home. The British manufacturer would then be paid back over a period of time in finished goods.
- The fourth alternative is to use the 'offsets' method, which means that the British manufacturer receives full payment in the nonconvertible currency. It can then use those funds to purchase products

N

or services in the country, or goods which it can export and then, perhaps, resell.

Non-cumulative preferred share

A non-cumulative preferred share is a share which does not accord the owner the right to receive an additional **dividend** from the profits of a subsequent year, in order to compensate them for the non-payment of a dividend when the business's profit was low.

Non-current assets

The term 'non-current asset' usually refers to **fixed assets** and, in some cases, **intangible assets**, and is considered to be the opposite of a **current asset**. Typically, a non-current asset is described as being an asset, owned by a business, which either cannot be readily converted into a cash equivalent, or is not expected to be converted into cash within the next financial period.

Non-current liabilities

A non-current liability is clearly the opposite of a **current liability**. Broadly speaking, non-current liabilities are debts, loans or other repayments which are not due, or expected, to be paid within the next financial period.

Non-financial asset

Obviously the non-financial asset is the opposite of a **financial asset**. Non-financial assets are therefore **tangible assets**, which include land and buildings.

Non-ledger asset

A non-ledger asset is an asset which does not generally appear in the **general ledger**. Typically, non-ledger assets include uncollected or deferred premiums or accrued dividends. They may also include the difference between the **book value** and the market value of securities.

Non-negotiable instrument

The term 'non-negotiable instrument' refers to any financial instruments which cannot be signed over into the possession of a third party. In other words, they are non-transferable financial instruments.

NOPAT

NOPAT is an acronym for 'Net Operating Profit After Tax'. It is used to estimate what a business would have earned if it did not have debt. It is equal to:

Operating income × *(1 − tax rate)*

NOPAT is often used to calculate a business's EVA (**economic value added**), which is a business's after-tax earnings, less the opportunity cost of capital. The EVA measures the increase in value of a business over a given period of time.

N

Off the books

'Off the books' is a term associated with transactions which do not appear in any of the financial records kept by a business. Strictly speaking, 'off the books' implies cash payments received for **assets** (products and services) which are not officially recorded in the accounting system of the business.

Off balance sheet financing

This is a form of borrowing in which the obligation is not recorded on the borrower's **financial statements**. Off balance sheet financing can employ several different techniques, which include development arrangements, leasing, product financing arrangements or recourse sales of receivables. Off balance sheet financing does raise concerns regarding the lenders' overall risk, but it improves their **debt to equity ratio**, which enhances their borrowing capacity. As a result, loans are often easy to arrange and are given lower interest rates because of the improved debt structure on the **balance sheet**. Off balance sheet financing is a technique often used by multinational businesses in order to secure additional loans on the worldwide loan market.

Ketz, J. Edward, *Hidden Financial Risk: Understanding Off Balance Sheet Accounting*. New York: John Wiley, 2003.

Offshore banking unit

An offshore banking unit is an entity which acts as an intermediary in financial transactions between non-resident borrowers and lenders. Offshore banking units are normally foreign banks which conduct business in the domestic money market. They can deal in foreign exchange settlements and in **Eurocurrencies**, for example. Offshore banking units cannot accept domestic deposits and their activities are unrestricted by domestic authorities. Offshore banking units tend to be located in major financial centres, which are often known as offshore banking centres. Normally these financial centres have fairly liberal tax and capital market requirements.

Typical offshore banking activities include:

- borrowing or lending;
- making guarantees;
- trading;
- contracting;
- investment;
- advisory work;
- hedging.

Schneider, Jerome, *The Complete Guide to Offshore Money Havens*. New York: Prima Lifestyles, 2001.

Omitted dividend

An omitted dividend, as the term implies, is the non-payment of an expected dividend. The dividend is usually unpaid as a result of the business finding itself in financial difficulties. Omitted dividends tend to be regularly scheduled dividends.

One-time charge

One-time charges relate to single, one-off expenses incurred by a business, which it does not expect to have to allow for in a future accounting period. One-time charges could include the payment of additional taxes, redundancy payments, or the acquisition of new assets which were not expected. Typically, the business will seek to assure its **shareholders** that the one-time charge will not be a recurring theme.

Operating asset

An operating asset is seen to be an asset owned by the business which makes a positive contribution to the output and hence the revenue of the business. Typical forms of operating assets could include plant and machinery and, in some cases, assets such as the delivery and transportation fleet which ensures customers' supply.

Operating budget

A business's operating budget is, essentially, a forecast of its future financial needs. The operating budget may cover a range of different time periods into the future, but typically will cover the forthcoming year.

The operating budget will include not only estimates of the financial requirements, but also the expected revenue streaming into the business, which will (ultimately) fund the operations. The operating budget will, therefore, incorporate sales, production and **cash flow**.

It is the function of managers and accountancy personnel to monitor the relationship between the operating budget and the actual figures being produced, as they occur. Changes or divergent figures are monitored, assessed and adjusted as required.

Operating cash flow

The operating cash flow of a business relates to the money moving in and out of the organization which is directly related to its operations, rather than any other form of movement, including financial transactions. Typically, the following formula is used to calculate the operating cash flow for business:

$$\underset{profit}{Net} + \underset{change}{accrual} + \underset{(expenditure)}{\underset{accounts\ payable}{change\ in}} - \underset{(receipts)}{\underset{receivable}{accounts}} - \underset{(stock\ levels)}{\underset{inventory}{changes\ in}}$$

Reider, Rob and Heyler, Peter B., *Managing Cash Flow: An Operational Focus*. New York: John Wiley, 2003.

Operating costs

Typically, operating costs refer to a costing system which is applied to the number of units produced over a period of time. The operating costs are calculated by identifying the costs incurred over the period in relation to the number of units produced. The calculation is:

$$\frac{Total\ operating\ costs}{Number\ of\ units\ produced}$$

This figure reveals the average unit cost for the period of time in question.

Alternatively, operating costs may refer to other costs not directly associated with production. In this case, 'operating costs' refers to the day-by-day expenses of the business in relation to such items as administration, marketing or sales.

Harrop, David and McGladrey, R. S. M., *Controlling Operating Costs*. Arlington, VA: A. S. Pratt & Sons, 1997.

Operating cycle

The 'operating cycle' refers to the following process, typical in many businesses:

- funds are used to purchase raw materials, components or products;
- funds are used to convert, process, distribute or otherwise hold and deliver those items;
- funds are received by the sale of those items.

More specifically, the operating cycle can also refer to the average time taken between the following:

- purchasing/acquiring;
- receiving cash from sale.

Operating income

'Operating income' refers to the amount of funds which a business has received from its operational activities. Operating income is variously known as **operating profit** or EBIT (earnings before interest and tax).

At its simplest, operating income is equal to:

$$\textit{Revenue received (from operations)} - \frac{\textit{cost of goods sold and}}{\textit{operating expenses}}$$

In this case 'operating expenses' refers to the normal expenditure directly attributable to operations.

Operating leverage (gearing)

Operating leverage is a measure which seeks to investigate the relationship between the fixed operating costs and the total operating costs. The normal equation used is:

$$\frac{\textit{Fixed operating costs}}{\textit{Total operating costs}}$$

In this sense total operating costs include both fixed and variable operating costs.

Operating margin

Typically, the operating margin of a business is calculated by:

$$\frac{\textit{Operating income}}{\textit{Revenue}} \times 100$$

o

In effect, the operating margin is another means by which the **profit margin** can be calculated.

Operating profit

An operating profit, or indeed an operating loss, is calculated by looking at the total trading activity of a business. The operating profit is calculated by deducting the operating expenses from the trading profit, or adding operating expenses to a trading loss, excluding any extraordinary or exceptional items which may otherwise distort the appreciation of the business. All calculations are made before interest.

Operating rate

The operating rate of a business is a measure of the percentage of its total production capacity which is currently being used. In other words, the operating rate is a means by which the utilization of the production facilities can be assessed, illustrating whether or not the output is close to an optimum level.

See also **capacity utilization rate**.

Operating ratio

The simplest form of operating ratio addresses the relationship between a business's operating expenses and its operating revenues:

$$Operating\ ratio = \frac{Operating\ expenses}{Operating\ revenue}$$

In reality, however, the operating ratio can be a number of different calculations and comparisons, including:

- sales to **cost of goods sold**;
- **net profits** to gross income;
- **net profits** to **net worth**.

All of these equations offer an insight into the relationships between revenue and expenditure, or profit and perceived market value.

Operational gearing

Operational gearing seeks to measure the relationship between a business's fixed costs and output. In cases where a business has high **fixed costs** as a proportion of its **total costs**, the business is deemed to have a high level of operational gearing. Potentially this could cause the business problems in as much as it is reliant on the fact that demand continues to remain buoyant. If there is a fall in demand, then the revenues of the business will fall, thereby making the proportion of fixed costs to revenue (or output) even greater. In this way, the business can foresee a series of situations which may turn its profits into serious losses.

Normally, businesses cannot themselves do a great deal about the operational gearing, largely on account of the fact that it may be typical and necessary in the industry in which they operate. An industry which continues to suffer from high levels of operational gearing is the airline business. Airlines have extremely high operational gearing costs and are prone to huge losses should demand for flights fall away. This was a particular case after the attacks on New York and Washington in September 2001.

Opportunity cost

'Opportunity cost', although strictly speaking an economics term, can be equally applied to accounting, marketing and advertising. Each time a business chooses to pursue a particular form of activity, it has made that choice after having investigated all of the other options. Given the fact that it is unlikely, even with the largest budget available, that a business can pursue all forms of activities simultaneously, some options have to be discarded. 'Opportunity cost' argues that the potential benefits which could have been enjoyed by choosing a particular activity have to be considered if they are not chosen and an alternative action is preferred. In other words, opportunity cost examines the real cost of an action in terms of the next best alternative that has been forgone.

Buchanan, James M,. *The Cost and Choice: An Inquiry in Economic Theory*. Indianapolis, IN: Liberty Fund, 2000.
Heymann, H. G. and Bloom, Robert, *Opportunity Cost in Finance and Accounting*. Westport, CT: Greenwood Press, 1990.

O

Option

An option is the right to buy or sell a specific quantity of a currency, security or commodity at a specific price on a named date.

The purchaser of the option is not bound to either buy or sell at what is known as the exercise price, which is the price it is traded at. The purchaser may simply decide to allow the option to lapse, in which case any premium that was paid is lost.

The actual option to buy is known as a call option and the option to sell is known as a put option. Call options are usually purchased when an investor predicts that prices will rise, and a put option when prices are expected to fall.

Normally investors will hedge with their investments in order to offset the dangers of wildly fluctuating prices. Therefore, investors take out options on numerous investments to cover potentially exposed positions.

Kaeppel, Jay, *The Four Biggest Mistakes in Option Trading*. Colombia, MD: Traders Library, 1998.

Natenberg, Sheldon, *Option Volatility and Pricing: Advanced Trading Strategies and Techniques*. London: Irwin Professional, 1994.

Optional dividend

An optional dividend offers the **shareholder** the opportunity either to take the regular **dividend** payment in cash (which has tax implications) or to take the dividend payment in the form of additional stocks (or shares), which is a more tax-efficient option. The value of the optional dividend choice is clearly related to the intentions of the investors and whether they are seeking income generation (from cash dividends) or capital growth (in the form of extra shares).

Ordinary share/shareholders

An ordinary share is a fixed unit of share capital of a business which is a publicly quoted organization whose shares are traded on the stock exchange. Ordinary shares yield a dividend on the capital that was invested in the purchase of the share. These dividends represent a proportion of the profits made by the business. Many investors purchase shares for longer-term rewards, taking the gamble that whilst they receive dividends throughout their ownership period, at some point in the future the shares will be worth considerably more than the price they paid for them at the beginning of their investment. Ordinary **shareholders** are the last investors in the business to receive any return in cases where the business goes into **liquidation**. **Preference shareowners**, creditors and government agencies, including the Inland Revenue, all have their outstanding debts settled before ordinary shareholders. This makes ordinary shares a higher risk, yet they enjoy the benefits of the business should it prove to be successful.

Original cost

In accounting terms, original cost refers to all expenses associated with the acquisition of an asset. These total costs may include the disposal of

fully depreciated assets which the new asset will replace, installation, maintenance and support costs, and delivery and training implications.

Other current assets

This is a term associated with the **balance sheet** of a business. Other current assets refer to non-cash assets which are expected to mature within the coming year.

Other long-term liabilities

This is a term associated with the **balance sheet** of a business. 'Other long-term liabilities' refers to financial obligations of the business which do not attract the requirement to pay interest in the coming year. Other long-term liabilities can include:

- value of leases;
- employee benefits;
- deferred taxation.

Outgo

'Outgo' is a shortened version of the term 'out-goings', i.e. expenses.

Outlay

'Outlay' is another term used to describe a business's expenditure.

Outsourcing

Outsourcing is gradually gaining ground as a primary means by which the functions related to employees are handled by a business. There have been significant changes in policy where a shift has been in progress from providing services in-house to using external organizations. In effect, outsourcing is the use of another organization or an agency for some, or all, of the business's functions.

Outsourcing is not only restricted to smaller businesses; for example, a business that has grown significantly over recent years has a greater tendency to consider outsourcing, largely as it prefers to focus on the operations of the core business, and there is a culture of outsourcing which has enhanced the growth. For example, in the USA where there is a strong tradition of outsourcing human resources functions, this industry was worth an estimated $13.9 billion in 1999, and according to research businesses such as Dataquest, it will reach $37.7 billion in 2004.

O

Outsourcing falls into four broad categories:

- Professional Employer Organizations (PEO) take on all of the responsibilities of the human resource administration for a business, including the legal responsibilities and the hiring and dismissal of employees. Typically, the relationship is co-operative, with the PEO handling human resources and the business itself dealing with all other aspects of operations. Not all PEOs take the full responsibility for human resources, some merely handling payroll and benefits systems.
- Business Process Outsourcing (BPO), although a general term used to describe outsourcing in the broadest sense, refers to human resources in respect of supporting the human resource functions with technology and software (including data warehousing and other services).
- Application Service Providers (ASPs) restrict their relationship with a business to providing either web-based or customized software to help manage human resource functions such as payroll and benefits.
- E-services can be either ASPs or BPOs, which again are restricted in the relationship to web-based services such as recruitment, software and data warehousing or other forms of data storage and access provision for human resources departments.

Incomes Data Services, *Outsourcing HR Administration*. London: Income Data Services, 2000.

Vanson, Sally, *The Challenge of Outsourcing Human Resources*. Oxford: Chandos Publishing, 2001.

Overbought

The term 'overbought' has three associated finance and accounting applications. One of the simplest definitions relates to a business purchasing more components, raw materials or finished goods than it actually needs in order to fulfil the orders it has.

The second definition relates to the purchasing of more commodities and securities than are covered by the margins which have been deposited with a dealer or a broker.

The third finance-related definition refers to a market which has rapidly risen due to a high volume of purchases. In reality, the market may be somewhat unstable and may well fall at any time in the near future.

Overcapacity

Overcapacity in a market occurs when the supply (or output or capacity) of the suppliers in that market is in excess of the current, or for that matter, the anticipated demand levels in that market.

The financial implications are that demand may fall beneath the **breakeven point** of certain businesses. This may mean that some or all of the following could occur:

- The weaker producers with a more vulnerable breakeven point may be forced into liquidation.
- The producers may attempt to reduce their overheads and attempt to downsize or rationalize their operations.
- In order to stimulate demand, the producers may reason that a drop in prices might well be the only alternative for the short to medium term.

Overcapitalization

Overcapitalization occurs when a business finds itself in a position of simply having more cash (capital) than it needs in order to operate. Normally an overcapitalized business suffers from one of the following problems:

- It may have a high burden in respect of interest charges;
- It may have to distribute its profits to a great many **shareholders** through dividend payments.

The standard approach to dealing with overcapitalized situations is to either:

- Pay off the long-term loans and other debts to reduce the interest payments.
- Purchase shares back from the shareholders to enable the business to retain its own profits for reinvestment.

O

Overdraft

Technically, this term refers to the amount by which a bank account has seen withdrawals exceed the actual balance of the account.

Overdrafts are designed as a form of short-term credit, allowing a business to temporarily (if frequently) withdraw sums in excess of the balance of cash held in the account. Typically, the level of overdraft is set by mutual consent after the business requests the facility from its bank. Varying rates of interest are paid to the bank for accounts which are overdrawn depending on arrangements.

Overhead

Overheads are costs generated by a business that are not directly related to the production process. Many businesses refer to overheads as either **fixed costs** or **indirect costs** as they include costs related to the ownership and maintenance of the property in which the business operates, for example, heating, lighting, and administrative costs.

Booth, Rupert, *Control your Overheads: A Practical Programme to Improve Performance and Reduce Costs*. London: Financial Times, Prentice-Hall, 1994.

Overhead ratio

The overhead ratio shows the proportion of expenditure, in relation to the business's total income, which cannot be directly attributed to the production or delivery of products or services.

Typically, the overhead ratio is calculated using the following equation:

$$\frac{Operating\ expenses}{Total\ net\ interest\ income + operating\ income}$$

A business's operating expenses include:

- rent or lease payments;
- maintenance;
- **depreciation.**

Overinvestment

Overinvestment implies somewhat too much capital investment. It is a frequent factor which occurs in manufacturing industries. The process usually occurs towards the end of a boom period which has seen a sustained level of demand for products and which had been steeply growing over a period of time. The investment takes place just as the boom is beginning to falter, in the hope that the boom will remain and that demand will continue to increase.

Gradually, or in some cases abruptly, the boom terminates, leaving the manufacturing industry with overproduction. In other words, they are geared up to produce more capacity than the market needs. Investment ends equally as abruptly and employees are laid off, which only serves to deepen the problems of the forthcoming recession period.

Oversubscription

Oversubscription occurs when there is an excess demand for newly issued shares. Under the terms of most businesses, the applications are all scaled down. In other cases, the business may decide to allocate shares by a ballot system (this has to have been announced as the method chosen before the share issue).

Oversubscription usually occurs when the business has set the share price too low; the low value having been decided on to ensure that the shares are taken up. In these cases, there has been a miscalculation in respect of the demand that would be generated by the low price. Clearly, businesses would not wish to be in a position where the shares have not all been sold and the maximum capital injection has not been achieved.

See also **undersubscription**.

Overtrading

Overtrading occurs when a business enters into commitments or trans-actions which are in excess of its available short-term resources. In other words, it has taken on commitments which, under current circum-stances, it will find impossible to complete. Overtrading can occur even when a business is trading profitably, and in most cases overtrading takes place when there are financial strains on the business which are imposed by lengthy production cycles. The net effect of overtrading is to render the business incapable of continuing its operations, as it has overcommitted its resources and will find it impossible to meet those commitments.

Owner's equity

'Owner's equity' is another term used to describe **net worth**, **share-holder's equity** or **net assets**. It is calculated using the following equation:

Total assets – total liabilities

See also **capital net worth**.

Participating dividend

A participating dividend is paid on a **participating preferred stock**. Owners of this participating preferred stock are entitled to receive additional payments over and above the normal dividend rate in certain sets of circumstances. Typically, a specific event would trigger an additional dividend payment. Typical examples would include a take-over or an increase in the normal payout to common stockholders (**ordinary shareholders**). In each case a mathematical calculation is made to link the additional preferred stock payment to any increases in the common stock payout.

Participating preferred stock

Participating preferred stock is stock which attracts a **participating dividend**. This type of stock attracts the normal dividend but also entitles the owner to a participating dividend, which is normally triggered when the common stock (**ordinary shares** dividends) has exceeded a predetermined level.

Partly paid share

A partly paid share, as the term implies, is a share which has not had the par value, or nominal price, fully paid. Traditionally, they were offered on the basis that **shareholders** could be asked to pay the full amount at some point in the future, giving the business additional capital injections if required. In practice, however, shareholders were wary of the offer and did not feel comfortable with the prospect of being asked to find extra funds at some undisclosed point.

During the **privatization** drive in the UK during the 1980s and early 1990s, partly paid shares made something of a comeback. In these cases shareholders paid partly for the shares and were asked to find additional balance payments at specified dates in the future.

Payable date

The term 'payable date' refers to the date upon which dividends are actually paid out to **shareholders**. The payable date is determined on the business's **declaration date**. The payable date is also known as the **distribution date**.

Payables

The word 'payables' can appear on a business's **balance sheet**, and is another word used as an alternative to either **current liabilities** or current debt. Payables are equal to any money which is owed by a business and falls due for payment within a year.

Cooke, Robert A., *Positive Cash Flow: Powerful Tools and Techniques to Collect Your Receivables, Manage Your Payables and Fuel Your Growth*. Franklin Lakes, NJ: Career Press, 2003.

Payback

Payback, or the payback period, is the time required for a project to repay the initial investment which was made by the business. Although the payback period calculations are not very sophisticated, they are often used as a method of investment appraisal. Typically, the formula to work out the payback period is:

$$\frac{Investment\ outlay}{Contribution\ per\ month} = Payback\ period$$

The payback method is particularly useful for businesses which have a somewhat erratic **cash flow** as it helps them to assess how long it will take for an investment in a particular project to repay itself. Unfortunately, the payback method is somewhat short term in the way it approaches the possible return on investments. Should a project take a considerable amount of time to pay back, it becomes increasingly difficult to predict exactly what might happen far into the future. This methodology also ignores profits and focuses on time, which means that this form of **investment appraisal** needs to be coupled with other assessment method.

P

PAYE (Pay As You Earn)

PAYE, or 'Pay As You Earn', in its various incarnations in different countries, is essentially tax collection on behalf of the tax authorities by the employer. The deduction is made from the wages or salaries of employees. In effect, employers operate as unpaid tax collectors and the onus is upon them to ensure that the correct amount of tax is paid by each employee. This represents a considerable accountancy burden for employers, as the amount of tax each employee has to pay is dependent upon a number of factors, which include:

- the wage or salary level;
- marital status;
- allowances;
- additional deductions.

For the most part, the formula to make these deductions on behalf of the tax offices is encapsulated in a tax code. Employers provide a summary to their employees at the end of each tax year, which totals the amount of tax which has been levied on behalf of the revenue services.

Tew, Paul, *PAYE and National Insurance Contributions Handbook*. London: GEE Publishing, 2001.

Payee/payer

These two terms are commonly used in accountancy, 'payee' referring to an individual or a business which receives a payment, whilst 'payer' is the individual or business that makes the payment.

Paying agent

The term 'paying agent' is associated with financial **outsourcing**. Typically, the paying agent operates on behalf of the issuer of stocks (shares) or **bonds**. An agent, whether this is an individual or a business, is empowered on behalf of the issuer to make **dividend** payments to stockholders. The agent may also be engaged by the issuer of bonds to make payments in the form of interest or principle to bond holders. In outsourcing this function a business, or government, can concentrate on the management of the organization and other matters rather than specifically having staff concerned with dividend interest payments. It also means that the paying agent will take responsibility for any communications on behalf of the organization in respect of queries and problems that may arise from payments.

Payment date

The term 'payment date' is an alternative term for **distribution date**. The payment date is taken to mean the date on which payments are made, or scheduled to be made in the cases of **dividends**, distribution of money from mutual funds, or **bond** interest payments.

Payment processing

'Payment processing' refers to the use of third-party processors to assist in dealing with transactions. Typically, this would include banks and other organizations capable of dealing with electronic payment processing, including the use of debit and credit cards, ATMs, corporate purchasing and the payment of wages and salaries (**payroll processing**). For the most part, businesses **outsource** these payment systems, particularly as a result of the payment processors offering hardware, software and support services to allow a fully integrated payment-processing transaction system.

Payment systems

Payment systems can include a variety of hardware and software systems aimed at automating payment transactions. These would include payment systems at point of sale, credit card transactions, and commercial accounts receivable. Internally, payment systems are also used for **payroll processing**.

> Kou W. (ed.), *Payment Technologies for E-commerce*. Berlin and Heidelberg: Springer Verlag, 2003.

Payout

The term 'payout' is usually a word which may be used as an alternative to **dividend**. Payouts, therefore, are dividend payments made to **shareholders** from a business's earnings, which may derive from either their current or **retained earnings**. Payouts do not have to be made in cash, although if they are, then these payouts are taxable. Payouts can be made in the form of additional stock or shares, in which case a **stock dividend** payout is made. It is not a legal obligation for a business to make a payout as either it may argue that it wishes to retain its earnings, or profit, for reinvestment, or indeed the business may not be in a position to pay a dividend, as a result of financial difficulties. In the vast majority of cases payouts are rare in small or growing businesses. Investors in those stocks or shares fully appreciate that the businesses needs to reinvest as much of its profit as possible in order to continue growth. By reinvesting their profits rather than making a payout, businesses can avoid the necessity of having to secure loans, either in the

P

short, medium or long term, which would then attract interest payments as well as the subsequent repayment of the principle.

Investors who accept the fact that payouts will not be made in the early growth period of a business look for other benefits from their investment. Notably, this means that they are hoping for **capital growth** (in other words an increase in the share value), rather than standard dividend payments. In the US, for example, when payouts are being made, this is usually undertaken on a quarterly basis. There does come a point when the business needs to make payouts in order to continue to receive the support and confidence of its investors and to give to the stock or shareholders some form of reward for having made the investment. It is equally the case that payouts are made when a business would not sufficiently benefit from reinvesting the profits, but this usually occurs after the business has progressed beyond the growth phase itself.

Payout period

The term 'payout period' is usually associated with the start-up costs, or any other cumulative operating expenses related to a particular project undertaken by a business, during which there is a negative **cash flow**. Quite literally the business, in order to support the project, is paying out sums in the hope, or the knowledge, that the project will eventually begin to make financial returns. Clearly a business will have attempted to make a forecast of its probable exposure financially during the payout period. It will compare its **liabilities** in terms of payouts during this early stage of a project's life and will seek to control any costs and prevent them from spiralling beyond their forecast.

This payout period has significant financial implications for a business and must either be subsidized by profits from other areas of the business's operations, or may have to be financed by the acquisition of a loan, or perhaps additional share capital.

The payout period also applies in some cases to **dividend** payments. More precisely, the payout period in respect of dividends per share can be calculated by dividing the dividend per share by the earnings per share. This is considered to be a measure by which the value of a given investment can be made over a period of time.

Payout ratio

See **dividend payout ratio**.

Payroll processing

Payroll processing is the business function which deals with employee compensation. As an integral part of payroll processing, the employer needs to maintain records which track employer-paid benefits, deductions, pay and expense details, attendance records and a variety of other payroll-related issues. Payroll processing can be carried out internally using proprietary software programs or, increasingly, the function is **outsourced** to a specialist organization which also provides human resource management and administrative backup.

Pegged exchange rate

A pegged exchange rate occurs when a nation's government or **central bank** officially announces the Gold Par Value of its currency and then seeks to maintain its market rate within a narrow band above or below that official exchange rate. The pegging is achieved by the country's central bank buying and selling its own currency in order to influence its price.

There are inherent dangers in doing this as it may well affect the country's money supply and its monetary stability.

Permanent capital

'Permanent capital' is a term which is used to describe the actual **capital** which is available to a business. It can be calculated using the following formula:

$$\begin{matrix} \text{Common stock} \\ \text{(ordinary shares)} \end{matrix} + \begin{matrix} \text{preferred stock} \\ \text{(preference shares)} \end{matrix} + \begin{matrix} \text{retained} \\ \text{earnings} \end{matrix}$$

This simple equation provides a business with a clear indication as to the actual funds theoretically available to it, and which may also be known simply as 'capital'.

P

Petty cash

Petty cash is distinguishable from other cash at hand to a business in as much as it is literally available in cash, rather than in deposit at a bank. Petty cash is kept on the business's premises and used to pay for low-value items and small incidental expenses.

The common practice in dealing with petty cash is for the individual requesting cash from the float, or reimbursement for an expense, to complete a petty cash voucher in the petty cash book. At all times the sum of the cash and petty cash vouchers should equal the total amount in the petty cash float.

Pioneering costs

The term 'pioneering costs' is associated with the costs and risks facing international businesses entering a new overseas market for the first time. In many respects they are trail-blazing organizations that do not have the benefits of knowing how to deal with that overseas country, either from experience or by learning lessons from other international businesses that have come before. Pioneering costs include the time and effort required to learn how the market operates and how that country's government, rules and regulations can have an impact upon the business's ability to be successful. Pioneering costs are borne alone by the first entrant into the market. Later entrants into the market can benefit from lessons and mistakes learned by the pioneer. However, assuming the pioneer has been successful, later arrivals may find it difficult to establish themselves in the new marketplace.

Plant

Plant or machinery is essentially what is known as **fixed assets**. Plant normally represents a business's manufacturing machinery, but can also be used to describe land holdings and indeed other pieces of machinery, such as computers, which are considered to be **tangible assets** and which will be retained by the business in the long term. Plant, therefore, represents fixed, long-term tangible assets which the business does not predict needing to convert into cash either in the current or the following financial year. Indeed this plant is essential for the business to continue operating and will be used as an integral part of its business activities for the foreseeable future.

Ploughback

Ploughback is an alternative to distributing a business's earnings to its **shareholders** in the form of **dividends**. At a business's Annual General Meeting (AGM) it will declare its intention to retain some or all of its earnings and earmark those earnings for reinvestment into its core activities. Whilst shareholders can challenge this decision, the frequency of ploughback is such that it is an accepted form of reinvestment. Usually the ploughback for established businesses will not be equal to the total sum which would otherwise have been distributed to shareholders in the form of dividends. Instead a proportion of what would have been dividend payments is retained. Ploughback is far more common in new or growing businesses, who seek to use their earnings for reinvestment rather than in making **payouts** to shareholders.

Pooled fund

A pooled fund is a fund such as a unit trust, in which a number of investors contribute to that fund for mutual benefit. In the case of unit trusts, for example, large numbers of investors contribute money, or assets, in order to create a more powerful buying group to purchase stocks, shares, securities and bonds. In pooling their resources they are able to make larger single purchases and avoid individual brokerage charges which would otherwise be payable had the individual investors taken the decision to purchase particular securities on their own. Typically, pooled funds are managed by professional **portfolio** managers.

See also **portfolio.**

Pooling of interests

Pooling of interests is the consolidation of the accounts of two or more businesses which have formed an association, usually by merger. The **balance sheets** of the two businesses are brought together into a consolidated balance sheet, which sums the two businesses' joint assets and liabilities.

See also **purchase acquisition.**

Portfolio

'Portfolio' is a term used to describe an investor's holdings in **securities**. The investor will usually look for a mix of holdings which will offer a balance of income in the form of **dividends**, and **capital growth** in the form of increased share price.

Investors will use a variety of different **investment appraisal** techniques in order to determine exactly what mix of securities to purchase, as well as judging when to buy and sell their securities.

'Portfolios' can also refer to **pooled funds**, in which a number of investors provide the financial resources for portfolio managers to invest on their behalf.

See also **portfolio management.**

Portfolio management

Portfolio management is the process of managing assets, on behalf of either a business or a number of individuals in a **pooled fund**. A dedicated investment manager creates a portfolio of investments, which may focus either on income (in the form of dividends) or on growth (in the form of capital growth). In many cases the portfolio management process aims to strike a balance between the two requirements. The portfolio manager constantly adjusts the degrees of investment in various securities in order to maximize the returns from the portfolio. In effect, portfolio management involves a series of decisions which assist the portfolio manager in making appropriate investments in accordance with the goals of the investor(s). The portfolio manager will use various measures, such as **return on investment** or **net present value**, in order to make appropriate decisions.

Litterman, Bob, *Modern Investment Management: An Equilibrium Approach*. New York: John Wiley, 2003.
Reilly, Frank K. and Brown, Keith C., *Investment Analysis and Portfolio Management*. London: Thomson Learning, 1999.

Portfolio theory

Portfolio theory revolves around the overall investment strategy which seeks to create a **portfolio** that has the ideal balance between risks and returns. Portfolio theory, which is also known as 'modern investment theory', states the following:

- An investment risk should not be considered on an investment-by-investment standalone basis.
- An investment risk should be viewed by comparing how that security's price varies in relation to variations in the price of the market portfolio.
- Dependent upon the investors' views as to the level of risk that they wish to take, portfolios can be created with regard to that level of risk, but which maximize the investors' expected returns.

Elton, Edwin J., Gruber, Martin J., Brown, Stephen J. and Goetzmann, William N., *Modern Portfolio Theory and Investment Analysis*. New York: John Wiley, 2002.

Portfolio tracking

Portfolio tracking is increasingly carried out using computer software or internet applications. As the term implies, portfolio tracking involves the monitoring of a collection of investments. The purpose of the monitoring exercise is to see how the prices of these **securities** move and whether profits are being made. Portfolio tracking can equally apply to either real or modelled **portfolios**. Portfolio tracking can, therefore, offer a potential investor the opportunity to see the performance of a particular portfolio and the effectiveness of the associated **portfolio management** before deciding to become involved with that portfolio.

Campbell, John Y. and Viceira, Luis M., *Strategic Asset Allocation: Portfolio Choice for Long-term Investors.* Oxford: Oxford University Press, 2002.

Portfolio turnover

Portfolio turnover is a means of tracking the trading activities of a particular **portfolio** of investment. The following equation can be used:

$$\frac{\text{The sum of purchases and sales made during a trading period}}{\text{The average total assets held in portfolio during that trading period}}$$

Posting

'Posting' is a term associated with the transferral of entries from an original journal of entry into a **ledger** book.

Pre-acquisition profit

Pre-acquisition profit refers to the **retained profits** of a business before it is the subject of a take-over by another business. The pre-acquisition profits must normally be distributed back to the purchasing business in partial repayment of the capital expenditure incurred when acquiring the share of the business which it has bought. It is not acceptable to simply distribute this cash as a dividend to the shareholders of the acquiring business.

Predatory pricing

Predatory pricing is a pricing strategy adopted by some businesses in order to inflict financial damage on competitors by forcing them to cut their profit margins, and match the unfeasibly low prices the business is offering. This is an extremely aggressive and often short-term policy, used to drive competitors out of a market. Invariably it is adopted by businesses that already have a substantial market share and enjoy considerable **economies of scale**, allowing them to temporarily offer products and services at prices well below the market norm. In recent

P

years predatory pricing has become a feature in a number of areas, particularly with regard to supermarkets, where prices of basic stock items such as bread, baked beans and tinned tomatoes have been offered at virtually cost price. Extreme cases of predatory pricing do in fact aim to drive competitors out of business. If this purpose is revealed and proved, the strategy is deemed illegal.

Pre-depreciation profit

The pre-depreciation profit of a business is calculated by looking at the profits which have been made before taking **non-cash expenses** into account.

See also **depreciation**.

Preference share/shareholders

Preference shares pay a fixed dividend, and compared with **ordinary shares** they offer greater security to the investor, as they are repaid in full before ordinary **shareholders** are paid. Unlike ordinary shares, however, preference shares do not normally have voting rights and neither do the shares entitle the owner to a slice of the business's profits, in as much as even if profits increase, the fixed dividend remains the same.

Preferred debt

Preferred debt is debt which must take precedence, or priority, over other debts owed by the business.

Preferred stock

Preferred stock is the US equivalent of **preference shares**. These are stock which provides the owner with a guaranteed and specific **dividend** prior to any dividends which may subsequently be made to common stockholders. Preferred stockholders, just like preference shareholders, also take precedence in terms of payment should a business be forced into **liquidation**. Technically, of course, a preferred stock owner is a partial owner of the business, but unlike common stockholders, they have no voting rights.

The principal advantage of being a preferred stockholder is that in the majority of cases the business is obliged to pay a dividend, although if the business is suffering from financial difficulties this may not be the case. Preferred stockholders, assuming that the business is not in financial difficulties, will be able to predict a fixed dividend on a particular date in accordance with the agreement made prior to the purchase of the stock. Preferred stockholders; although they have no voting rights and so cannot directly affect the policies of the business, enjoy the first claim on the business's assets compared with common stockholders. In effect there are four main versions of preferred stock:

- *Cumulative preferred stock* – which is preferred stock on which dividends accrue if the issuer does not make dividend payments on time. The vast majority of preferred stock is cumulative preferred stock.
- *Non-cumulative preferred stock* – this form of preferred stock is clearly the opposite of cumulative preferred stock, and unpaid dividends therefore do not apply.
- *Participating preferred stock* – in this version of preferred stock the owner of the stock may be entitled to an additional dividend at times when the dividend paid to common stockholders exceeds a particular level.
- *Convertible preferred stock* – which is a version of preferred stock that has the capacity to be converted into an agreed and specified amount of common stock, should the holder so wish.

There are, of course, other variants of preferred stock, including:

- *First preferred stock* – which is stock that takes precedence over other preferred and common stock, particularly in regard to the payment of dividends, and in payments arising from the sale of liquidated assets.
- *Second preferred stock* – which is subordinate to first preferred stock.
- *Adjustable-rate preferred stock* – which is usually linked to changes in the Treasury Bill rate, and where the dividends are adjustable using a formula. The amount of dividend payable is offset by price changes, therefore stabilizing the actual value of the dividend itself.

Prepaid expense

A prepaid expense is expenditure incurred for items or services which will either be delivered or provided (in whole or in part) in a later financial year.

If the expenses are incurred for an item or a service and these are provided within the same financial year (even at the end of that year), then this is not strictly speaking a prepaid expense.

Payments made in advance for items such as office supplies, rent, insurance and advertising, and which will be used to help generate revenue, are also, technically speaking, considered to be prepaid expenses.

Present value

Present value is a technique which seeks to calculate the actual value of payments, either received by or due to the business, in relation to the current value if that payment was made in the present day. In other words, present value seeks to calculate the impact of **inflation** or changes in the interest rate which have an effect upon the actual value of payments in the future. Clearly, taking inflation into account, for example, the value of a payment which may be made in, say, a year's time, will be subject to **devaluation** in the sense that if the money was paid today it would be worth more than the money being paid in a year's time. This also means that outstanding debts are comparatively less in the future on account of the fact that the value of money will be lower by that time.

Pre-tax profit margin

The pre-tax profit margin is another means by which a business can assess its overall profits. Clearly, in this case, it is the profit before taking taxes into account. The normal formula which is used to calculate this figure is:

$$\frac{Net\ profit\ (before\ taxes)}{Net\ sales}$$

This equation provides the business with a measure of its gross **profit margin** in the sense that although the two figures used are 'net', this is still technically a gross profit margin as taxes have not yet been deducted, and therefore the pre-tax profit margin is not equal to the actual **net profit margin**.

Price elasticity

Price elasticity, or price elasticity of demand, measures the responsiveness of quantity demanded against a change in price. The most commonly used formula takes the proportion of the change in quantity divided by the proportion of the change in price. The effects are summarized in Table 4.

Table 4 Price elasticity

Elasticity	Demand is price elastic: $|\eta_p| > 1.0$	Demand is price inelastic: $|\eta_p| < 1.0$
Price reduction	Expenditure increases	Expenditure decreases
Price increase	Expenditure decreases	Expenditure increases

Tellis, Gerard J., *The Price Elasticity of Selective Demand: A Meta-analysis of Sales Response Models*. Cambridge, MA: Marketing Science Institute, 1988.

Price index

Price indices seek to measure price changes and thereby reveal the underlying trends of **inflation**. In the US, for example, the **Consumer Price Index** and the Producer Price Index are used. In the UK and in several other countries, an alternative, known as the **Retail Price Index**, provides a similar measure by which inflation can be tracked.

Price to book ratio

The price to book ratio is a means by which the market valuation of a business can be compared with the actual value of the business as revealed in its financial statements. Effectively, price to book ratio can be calculated using the following formula:

$$\frac{Stock\ capitalization}{Book\ value}$$

This calculation can be applied either to shares or for the business as a whole. The price to book ratio reveals the difference between the value of the business as far as the market is concerned and the actual value of the business as far as its assets are concerned. A high ratio will reveal that the market sets a high premium in terms of market value compared with assets, whilst a low ratio may indicate that the business, in market terms, is perhaps somewhat undervalued. Calculations which reveal a low ratio may either signal an investment opportunity or prompt another business to attempt to acquire the low-ratio business in the certain knowledge that the assets of that business are in excess of the value which has been placed upon it by the market.

P

The price to book ratio, however, does not incorporate **hidden assets**, which may have a considerable value, but are not incorporated into the **book value** of the business.

Typically, the price to book ratio will be used by investors who are not necessarily concerned with growth investment, but are more interested in assessing the true relationship between the current value of a business's stocks or shares and the actual value of the business in reality.

Price to cash flow ratio

The price to cash flow ratio is another means by which an investor, or the business itself, can compare the value in market terms of its stocks or shares and the amount the business succeeded in turning over in a given financial year. Typically, the equation used is:

$$\frac{Stock\ capitalization}{Cash\ flow}$$

This equation can either be used on a per-share basis or for the business as a whole.

Price to earnings ratio

The price to earnings ratio has the following structure:

$$\frac{Current\ market\ price\ of\ shares}{Earnings\ per\ share}$$

The price to earnings ratio is usually calculated on an annual basis and expresses the relationship between actual share prices, as a multiple of the earnings which each share provides in the form of a dividend. In the following example, a business has a share price of some £10 and has paid a dividend of £0.50. Therefore:

$$\frac{10}{0.50} = 20$$

This reveals that the current market price for the share is 20 times its earnings. Technically, this means that on current earnings performance it would take 20 years to justify the current value of the share price. In actual fact, however, a high multiple suggests that the business is growing at a fast rate as low **yields** are most closely associated with high multiples. Other investors may take the opposite view and consider that high multiples simply reflect the fact that the business's share price is grossly over-inflated.

The price to earnings ratio, therefore, is used as a fundamental **investment appraisal** tool to make a judgement as to whether the shares of a business represent good value in terms of their price compared with the market as a whole.

Price to net tangible assets ratio

The price to net tangible assets ratio is a calculation involving a business's current share price value and its **net tangible assets**. The ratio is:

$$\frac{Current\ market\ value\ of\ share}{Net\ tangible\ assets}$$

The ratio reveals the relationship between the share value and the actual assets of the business. Higher ratios suggest that the business is a better investment proposition.

Prior preferred stock

'Prior preferred stock' is another term which is used to describe first preferred stock. In essence, this form of **preferred stock** has precedence over other forms of preferred stock, and owners will be the first to receive **dividends** or proceeds from the liquidation of assets.

See also **preferred stock.**

Private sector

The private sector represents the part of an economy which is not under the control of the government. In other words, the private sector represents the businesses which are privately owned, perhaps by **shareholders**. Their actions, profit and loss are determined by the interaction between 'supply' and 'demand', which in turn is determined by market forces in a **free market** situation.

In many of the developed countries of the world, the private sector is the dominant sector in the economy, whilst in less developed or developing countries there is a mix of both private sector and **public sector**, the latter more dominant in some.

P

Privatization

Privatization involves the sale of government-owned businesses to private investors. In the UK, privatization was a key policy of the

Conservative government during the 1980s, during which time many public utilities were sold into private hands. By the 1990s privatization had become a key element of many government policies around the world. The primary argument for the privatization of nationalized businesses was that it improved the performance of those industries.

Privatization can also be typified as being the transformation of what had been a state-owned monopoly into a competitive market by liberalizing and deregulating the industry itself. It has been argued that whilst privatization has seen some improvement in performance, the main purposes of privatization were to break the power of the trade unions within those nationalized industries and to provide considerable sums of money which could then be reinvested in other forms of public spending, as opposed to increasing taxation levels.

Clifton, Judith, Comin, Francisco and Fuentes, Daniel Diaz, *Privatisation in the European Union: Public Enterprises and Integration.* New York: Kluwer Academic Publishers, 2003.

Pro forma

The term 'pro forma' is most closely associated with **balance sheets** or **income statements** (which account for sales, expenses and net profits over a given period of time). Pro formas are essentially financial statements which have assumptions built into the data which is included, in preparation for transference to income statements or balance sheets.

Productivity

Productivity is a measure of an organization's outputs divided by its inputs. In other words, an assessment of the value of products and services produced and offered by the business, compared with the costs of employees, capital and materials, and other associated costs.

Profit

At its simplest, profit can be described as difference, or excess, between the selling price of raw materials, products or services and the costs associated with providing them to a third party. This is to say that profit can be expressed as either gross (before tax, expenses, etc.) or net (after taxes and expenses, etc.). Profits can, therefore, be calculated using the following simple formula:

evenue – costs (before or after tax and expenses) = profit

The term 'profit' equally applies to a surplus of **net assets** at the end of a trading period, compared with the net assets which were available to the business at the start of the trading period. The profit figure, clearly, has to be adjusted to take into account the fact that capital may have been added or taken out of the business during that period.

Given profit's importance, it remains one of the most difficult figures to calculate objectively. A business's true profits can be measured in a variety of different ways and it is not just a simple task of identifying the figure which is ultimately taxed and then, perhaps, distributed in the form of dividends to shareholders. Profit can be reinvested in the business, of course, and often is, in order to produce greater profits in the future. Profit, as recorded by the business in whatever form, can be found most clearly in its **profit and loss statement (account)** or **profit and loss account**.

Profit and loss account

The overall purpose of a profit and loss account, often referred to as an **income statement**, is to set out the financial result of a business's trading operations over a particular period of time, usually a year. It is important to understand that a profit and loss account refers to a period of time, whereas a **balance sheet** refers to a point in time. Together with the balance sheet, the profit and loss account is often referred to as a business's final accounts. The profit and loss account details any increases or decreases in **capital** which result from trading and is, essentially, a summary of those increases and decreases.

In the profit and loss account, each source of revenue generated and each type of expense incurred is detailed. A typical, if simplified, version of the calculations used to produce a profit and loss account can be seen in the example in Table 5.

O'Gill, James, *How to Understand Financial Statements: Get to Grips with Profit and Loss Accounts, Balance Sheets and Business Plans*. London: Kogan Page, 1991.

P

Profit and loss statement

A profit and loss statement, in US terms, is broadly the equivalent of a **profit and loss account** or **income statement**. It seeks to provide a view of the balance of money flowing through a business over a period of time. In essence, it seeks to identify the following:

$$Revenue - expenses = \frac{income}{profit}$$

Table 5 Example of a profit and loss account

Calculation	Item	Running total in £000	Notes
	Revenue	1070	This is the sum total of all income to the business.
Less	Cost of sales	550	This is the total of all direct costs related to the sale of products and services.
Equals	Gross Profit	520	This is the total arrived at by subtracting the cost of sales from the revenue.
Less	Overheads	120	These are the additional overheads of the business not directly related to trading operations.
Equals	Trading or operating profit	400	This is the net profit having taken into account the cost of sales and overheads.
Plus	One-off or exceptional items	(40)	This represents a £40,000 loss.
Equals	Pre-tax profit	360	After subtracting exceptional costs, this represents the net profit before taxation.
Less	Tax	(90)	This assumes a tax rate of 25%.
Equals	Profit after tax	250	This figure represents the potentially distributable proceeds of trade.
Less	Dividend payment	110	This is the figure which will be distributed to shareholders in the form of dividends.
Equals	Retained profit	140	This is the figure which has been decided by the board of directors to be reinvested or retained, rather than distributed in the form of dividends.

P

A profit and loss statement details the revenues and incomes, less the expenses, and then reveals the profit in terms of the balance which is remaining from this calculation.

Clearly, a profit and loss statement is one of the easiest ways to judge whether the business has made a profit or a loss. As with profit and loss accounts, the format is suggested by the **generally accepted accounting principles (GAAT)**, but in reality the ways in which profit and loss statements are constructed allow a certain degree of creativity. The key aspects of the profit and loss statement are:

- Sales and income are listed first.
- Costs of goods sold follow, which relate to any expenses which are directly related to producing a product or providing a service. It is not generally the practice to include overheads, or items which are not directly related to production or service delivery.
- The gross margin or the gross profit is now listed, which is, in effect, the result of subtracting the cost of goods sold from the sales or income. Optionally, the gross margin or gross profit can also be expressed as a ratio or a percentage of the sales. In many cases industry norms for the percentage or the ratio have been established, allowing investors to compare easily the performance of the business in relation to figures using the industry benchmark or standard.
- General administrative and selling overheads are now deducted, as these are expenses. They reveal the degree of support and the associated costs which the business requires to assist its core activities. Again many industries have established benchmark figures and the ratio or percentage between these overhead expenses and sales can be compared.
- Normally the next sections of the profit and loss statement deduct interest expenses and then taxation.
- The final line of the profit and loss statement is the net income, which is often referred to as the 'final bottom line'.

P

Profit and loss statements have slightly different inclusions from profit and loss accounts and indeed the order in which some of the calculations are carried out and the ways in which they are expressed also differ. Normally a US business would produce a profit and loss statement on a quarterly or an annual basis. The profit and loss statement provides precisely the same information as a profit and loss account, as it incorporates earnings and expenses in order to reveal net profit. Profit and loss statements are also known as income statements or earnings reports.

O'Gill, James, *How to Understand Financial Statements: Get to Grips with Profit and Loss Accounts, Balance Sheets and Business Plans*. London: Kogan Page, 1991.

Profit before interest and tax (PBIT)

The operating profit of a business is the gross profit less all other expenses (except for interest and tax), and it is often referred to as 'profit before interest and tax'. Technically, however, the PBIT is calculated by adding in any income from associates (subsidiaries etc.) and deducting charges for the head office, research & development, and other costs. This figure is then divided by the capital employed in order to calculate the return on capital employed.

Profit centre

A profit centre is an area of a business to which revenue can be traced. Part of the process in establishing the profitability of a particular part of a business is to compare the revenue derived from that section or department against the costs of running that operation.

Profit margin

A business's profit margin can be calculated in different ways, but essentially it is described as being the profit proportion of a business's sales revenue.

Effectively, the profit margin can be expressed in two different ways. The first uses the following formula:

$$\frac{Profit}{Selling\ price} \times 100$$

If the profit is $100 for an item and the selling price was $500, then:

$$\frac{100}{50} \times 100 = 20\%$$

In this case, the profit margin on the item is 20%. Alternatively, the business could use **mark-up** as the primary calculation methodology – the mark-up being the gross profit added by the business to each unit of the product being sold. Using the mark-up method, the following formula is applied:

$$\frac{Gross\ profit}{Cost} \times 100$$

In the same case with the same item, the following calculation can therefore be made, if we assume that the cost (of sales) or direct costs involved are some $400 per unit:

P

$$\frac{100}{400} \times 100 = 25\%$$

Whilst this figure appears more desirable, it is in fact telling us exactly the same thing, although it has factored in the actual direct cost of sales for that unit, rather than simply addressing the gross profit difference between the sales revenues and profit figures.

Profit sharing

This is a term which is applied to a number of schemes offered by an employer which aim to give the employees a stake in the business; many were prompted in the UK by the Finance Acts (1978, 1980 and 1984).

Around 20 per cent of UK business has some form of employee share ownership and the move is seen as being a form of employee participation and industrial democracy. In reality, however, the level of share ownership is low and the employees have little or no real control over the business (mainly as the shares tend to have non-voting rights).

The three most common forms of profit sharing are:

- Employee Share Ownership Plans (ESOP), which were brought to the UK from the US and provide a means by which employees can gain equity in the business. A trust is formed and the dividends on the preference shares pay off the loans used to purchase the shares on behalf of the employees. The shares are held in trust, but employees have the right to sell them.
- Profit Sharing schemes (PSS) usually take the form of Approved Profit Sharing (APS) schemes, which involve the distribution of shares to employees free of charge. Shares are purchased through a trust which is financed from the profits of the business. Alternatively, employees can become involved in SAYE (Save As You Earn), which is when employees sign a savings contract with the option to purchase shares at the end of a contract period at a predetermined price. Both of these methods are more popular as they have tax benefits attached to them.
- Profit-related Pay (PRP) schemes are present in around 20% of private sector business and are, essentially, an element in the total employee pay package. Profit-related pay is variable according to the profits made by the business, making a direct link between the activities of the employees, and their productivity, and the extra pay that they ultimately receive in the form of PRP.

Profit sharing is seen as an effective means by which a business can encourage individual performance and motivation. Employees have a

P

direct interest in the success of the business and therefore greater commitment and profit-consciousness.

The obvious downside as far as employees are concerned is that they are tying both their jobs and their savings to the success or failure of the business. As far as the business is concerned there is also a worry that increasing staff involvement (particularly in share ownership) may mean that the employees will make increasing demands on the business, asking to have a greater role in the decision making. Management may be unwilling to make concessions in the strategic decision making which can affect profitability and employee pay, as they may be considering longer-term issues.

Project accounting (PA)

Project accounting is neither project management nor financial accounting. Project accounting takes traditional accounting data and measures variations between estimated and actual costs. It does this on a real-time, project-by-project basis, allowing adjustments to be made to correct variances. Project accounting has grown out of the need by businesses to analyse their performance at a micro-level in order to become more efficient and competitive.

Public sector

Typically, the public sector is services provided by the government. The precise composition of the public sector varies from economy to economy. Typically, however, they would include education, public transport, health care, public infrastructure, the armed forces, and any associated local or regional government structures. The public sector is not differentiated from the **private sector** in the sense that both sets of operations require the organizations to operate within a budget.

Rather than receiving revenue through trade, public sector organizations receive a budget allocation derived from taxation. Within this budget they are required to provide certain levels of service. Increasingly, public sector organizations are expected to provide a level of service consistent with identified benchmark organizations within the same sector, or at broadly comparable levels. In terms of private enterprise finance, the activities of the public sector and their varying levels of expenditure, **outsourcing** and subcontracted work have immediate and long-term implications. Increasingly the public sector subcontracts a number of its support, service and core functions to the private sector, establishing contracts with, or alliances with, private sector organizations who can provide expertise or a guaranteed supply of certain products or services.

Ultimately, the expenditure and importance of the public sector within the economy is dependent upon the budgeted allocations of cash received from central, regional and local government.

In the past, the public sector provided public services which were not considered to be financially viable for private sector organizations. Equally, these public sector services were considered to be of such prime importance that market forces could not be allowed to influence or impede the level of service provided. Successive governments in many countries have sought to reduce or limit the size of the public sector. In the past, the public sector incorporated many state-owned industries and public corporations which have, over the past 20 or 30 years, been privatized and are now private sector organizations.

Purchase acquisition

Purchase acquisition is an accounting methodology which does not use the **pooling of interests** as a means of merging or consolidating the acquired business onto the buyer's own **balance sheet**. Using the purchase acquisition methodology, the acquiring business treats the merged business as an investment and adds the acquired business's assets to its own balance sheet. It also records the amount which it paid above the market price for the business as **goodwill**, which it will charge against future earnings.

P

Qualified opinion

The term 'qualified opinion' refers to either an auditor's or an accountant's professional opinion regarding a business's financial statement. It is described as a qualified opinion because the information may not necessarily be complete, or some financial data may be subject to changes in the near future which may still be under discussion or whose effect on the financial statement is not yet known.

> *See also* **unqualified opinion**.

Quantize

Quantizing is the process of converting the currency of an asset or a liability from the currency in which it is normally expressed, into another currency or denomination.

Quarterly report

The **Securities and Exchange Commission (SEC)** in the US requires that all American public companies submit an unaudited document, or Form 10-Q, on a quarterly basis. This set of financial results for the preceding quarter notes any significant changes in that quarter. The quarterly report contains a financial statement, a list of events which have occurred, such as **stock splits** or **acquisitions**, and an explanation of these events by the management of the business.

Quick assets

Quick assets are variously known as liquid assets, liquid capital or realizable assets. 'Quick assets' therefore refers to any assets which can easily be converted into cash. Typical quick assets include:

- trade debts;
- marketable investments;
- deposits in bank accounts (current accounts).

A significant measure of the business's solvency or liquidity is revealed by the relationship between the quick assets and the **current liabilities** of the business.

See also **liquidity ratio**.

Quick ratio

See **acid-test ratio**.

Q

Real asset

A real asset is an intrinsically valuable asset that has a physical presence. Typically, real assets include equipment or land; they are otherwise known as **tangible assets**.

Copeland, Tom, Koller, Tim and Murrin, Jack, *Valuation: Measuring and Managing the Value of Companies*. New York: John Wiley, 2002.

Damodaran, Aswath, *Asset Valuation: Tools and Techniques for Determining the Value of any Asset*. New York: John Wiley, 2000.

Real capital

'Real capital' is another way in which the **fixed assets** of a business, including its equipment and machinery, are described. The real capital assets are integral to the business's ability to produce products or deliver services. Real capital is acquired by the use of **financial capital** in as much as financial capital represents the funds required to buy these real assets.

Realized profit and loss

In accounting terms, a profit (or loss) is made when an asset has been disposed of, not necessarily when payment has been received for that asset. Simply recording the disposal of an asset does not necessarily mean that the business will receive payment either in the short or medium term or, in fact, ever. Ultimately, the debt may never be paid.

'Realized profits and losses' therefore refers to transactions which have been completed. In other words, a *true* profit or a loss has been made as a result of the sale of an asset, product or service only when revenue derived from the transaction has been recorded as having been received.

Receivables/receivables turnover

'Receivables' is a general term used to describe any money which is

R

owed to the business, regardless of the fact that those receivables may or may not be currently due for payment. In other words, receivables include the sales revenue derived from the business's operations. Receivables may also include any other payments, such as returns on investments, which are technically owed to the business at a particular point in time.

An associated term is 'receivables turnover', otherwise known as '**accounts receivable** turnover'. The formula used to calculate the average duration of an account receivable is:

$$\frac{Total\ credit\ sales}{Accounts\ receivable}$$

Cooke, Robert A., *Positive Cash Flow: Powerful Tools and Techniques to Collect Your Receivables, Manage Your Payables and Fuel Your Growth.* Franklin Lakes, NJ: Career Press, 2003.

Receiver

A receiver is an individual or a business appointed by the creditors of a business which has entered a state of bankruptcy. The receiver's primary function is to sell the business as a **going concern** and to raise as much capital as possible to pay off the creditors. Should the receiver fail to raise enough capital, then the business is put into **liquidation**.

Recession

Recession is part of the economic or **business cycle** in as much as it represents a period when there is a slowing down of demand. In effect a recession occurs when there is a fall in the growth of a nation's **gross national product**. It is typified by a reduction in the level of investment, poor business confidence and, consequently, a growth in unemployment. In financial terms, a recession represents a formidable challenge to businesses as they must continue to operate, perhaps reducing output and cutting back on **overheads**, while remaining ready to take advantage of an upturn in the business cycle.

Serious and long-term recessions are often referred to as depressions, reflecting the fact that demand and business activity are significantly reduced during these periods. Ultimately the recession will break; but not before imprudent organizations have been driven out of business.

Allen, Roy, *Financial Crises and Recession in the Global Economy.* Farnborough: Edward Elgar, 2000.

R

Recognize

'Recognize' is the term used to describe the actual recording of income or expenditure related to particular items within an accounting period. When an item of revenue or expenditure is recorded, it is officially recognized within the accounting system and now becomes a factor and an item in the preparation of any financial statements from that point.

Businesses will choose to recognize various transactions according to their own preferred means of recording their accounting information. Some may recognize these items before they have actually received payment or made a payment. Others will decide only to recognize these payments for accounting purposes once the payment has been received or the goods or services have actually been paid for.

Record date

The record date is variously known as either the **date of record** or the ex-dividend date. In effect the record date is a date which is declared by the issuing business, stating the date upon which an investor must own shares in order to become entitled to a future declared dividend or distribution of capital gains.

Recovery

'Recovery' is a term used in relation to the economic or **business cycle**. Typically, a recovery describes the period directly after a **recession**. It is a period of time when the **gross domestic product** rises. Recoveries involve a gradual period of increasing demand and therefore businesses need to ensure that financially they are prepared, in order to exploit this increase in demand by being in a position to increase their output.

The recovery part of the cycle will eventually grow into a boom period, or at least reach a plateau where the demand and overall trading activity are significantly higher than had been experienced during the recession period. Whilst businesses brace themselves financially through a series of measures to cut costs during a recession, a recovery period requires both faith and determination that investments made during this period will result in a growing demand level for the business's products and services.

Reducing balance depreciation

The reducing balance method is a fixed percentage rate which is applied to depreciating assets. A fixed percentage is deducted from the cost of the asset on the first year; in subsequent years, the same percentage deduction is made of that reduced balance. In other words, after the first year deduction, the subsequent deductions are made from the cost less the depreciation which has already been charged.

If we were to assume that a vehicle cost a business £20,000 and depreciation using this method was charged at 20%, then at the end of the first year the value of the vehicle would stand at £16,000. In the second year, the depreciation, still charged at 20% reduces the value of the vehicle from £16,000 to £12,800. In the third year, the depreciation charged at 20% would reduce the value of the vehicle by another £2,560 and so on.

This form of depreciation is often considered to be more realistic as the business depreciates a new asset by a considerable amount in the earlier years, but as the asset ages, the depreciation is lower. This offsets the increasing costs of repairs and maintenance of the asset. The reducing balance method is therefore seen as a means by which the business can spread the costs of the asset over a period of time. The reducing balance method is also known as the 'diminishing balance method'.

See also **depreciation**.

Refinancing

Refinancing involves the replacement of one loan with another. Typically, a business will obtain a new loan commensurate with the size of the outstanding balance of an existing loan and use this new loan capital, probably with the same property as collateral, to eliminate the original loan. This is usually undertaken in order to take advantage of a more preferable interest rate, although there are implications financially regarding the fees for such a refinancing deal.

Businesses also use refinancing to reduce the term of a longer loan, or perhaps to switch from a fixed rate loan to an adjustable rate loan, taking advantage of recent falls in the interest rate.

Refinancing is not always an option for businesses, particularly if there are what is known as pre-payment or early settlement fees attached to the existing loan. These penalty charges often offset the advantages of shifting to another loan under a refinancing package.

Friedman, Jack P. and Harris, Jack C., *Keys to Mortgage Financing and Refinancing.* Hauppauge, NY: Barrons Educational Series, 2001.

Re-flation

Re-flation is an economic policy adopted by governments to stimulate a growth in output in order to give the economy a much-needed fillip.

Re-flationary policies have both immediate and long-term implications for businesses as the government may consider the following:

- An increase in the money supply (which may lead to inflation).
- A commitment to increase public expenditure and investment (which could lead to difficulty in recruiting and retaining employees).
- A reduction in the tax burden (which could stimulate demand and lead to a rise in prices).
- A reduction in the interest rate (which could mean that retained profits or cash reserves are better spent on inward investment, rather than remaining in the bank).

Wilson, John Pearson, *Inflation, Deflation, Reflation: Management and Accounting in Economic Uncertainty*. New York: Random House Business Books, 1980.

Reinvestment

Reinvestment is essentially the process of **ploughback** in as much as the business chooses to use money which would otherwise have been paid out to **shareholders** in the form of **dividends**. In this way, interest received, money which would have been paid out as dividends, or other profits which have been made by the business, are reinvested to purchase more **assets**. Reinvestment effectively delays and perhaps reduces any **liabilities** in relation to **capital gains**.

Reinvestment date

'Reinvestment date' is a term most closely associated with the ex-dividend date. The reinvestment date is the first day of the ex-dividend period. Effectively the reinvestment date allows all transactions which are still pending to be completed before the **record date**. By the record date, of course, if the stock is not officially owned by an investor, the investor will be ineligible for dividends. This is equally true of the reinvestment date. If any pending transactions have not been fully completed by the reinvestment date, the value of that stock is automatically reduced by the amount of the dividend. There are practical reasons for this move because the dividend payment would have reduced the value of the business, but the investor would still be paying a price for the stock based on the assumption that the dividend would have been paid to them. In order to compensate the investor for the loss of the dividend, the value of the stock is reduced in proportion to that dividend. The impact of the dividend payment would otherwise not have been beneficial either to the seller or to the buyer, as neither would have been eligible for the dividend.

Replacement cost/replacement cost accounting/replacement cost insurance

The replacement cost is clearly the amount a business would have to pay in order to replace an asset. It is complicated by the fact that the value of the assets of a business may have depreciated as a result of their age or condition. None the less, in the event of the loss of an asset, perhaps through it being destroyed, lost or stolen, a business may face the difficulty of replacing it with a like asset in like condition at a depreciation value equivalent to that which the original asset had reached.

This can make replacement cost accounting somewhat complex, in as much as the depreciation attributed to assets must take account of the fact that theoretically the business needs to place a realistic value on the asset under the assumption that circumstances may arise where the asset has to be replaced. Replacement cost accounting therefore involves allowances for depreciation based on the depreciating asset's original cost as well as its replacement cost.

An additional complication is any relevant replacement cost insurance. Insurance obviously covers a business for the loss, by whatever means, of its assets. Normally replacement cost insurance covers a business for the replacement of assets at current market prices, rather than the current depreciated value of the asset which has been insured. In other words, assuming a suitable replacement asset is available, the replacement cost insurance will replace the lost asset on a new-for-old basis.

Replacement value

The term 'replacement value' refers to asset valuation in terms of its **replacement cost**.

R

Reserves

Reserves are funds held by a business which either have not been earmarked for a particular investment, or are destined to be distributed as dividends to shareholders. Reserves often represent capital derived from **retained profits**. Reserves are distinguished from what is known as 'provisions' in the sense that the latter have been set aside to cover the **depreciation** (or perhaps the replacement) of an asset, or perhaps to cover a known liability that will arise in the near future.

Normally reserves, or the general net assets of the business, are divided into the following funds:

- The revenue reserves (from retained profits) which will ultimately be distributed as dividends to shareholders.
- Capital reserves, which are not distributed as dividends but may be converted in the future into share capital (perhaps with a bonus issue of shares).

Residual value

The term 'residual value' refers to the actual value of a **fixed asset** which has **fully depreciated** and is now at the end of its useful life. In effect, residual value is equal to either the scrap value or the **salvage value** of an asset.

Retail Price Index (RPI)

The Retail Price Index (RPI) is the UK equivalent of the **Consumer Price Index (CPI)** in the US.

The RPI represents an index of prices of products and services aimed at the consumer market (in other words regularly purchased by average householders). The shifts between years are calculated by selecting a base year which is given a value of 100. Each change, in subsequent years, in the price of a **basket** of products and services is expressed as a percentage change from that base figure.

If, for example, the base year was set in relation to 1995, then the RPI could be expressed as shown in Table 6.

Table 6 The Retail Price Index

Year	RPI	% Change from base index
1995	100	–
1996	108	8%
1997	110	10%
1998	112	12%
1999	114	14%
2000	118	18%
2001	120	20%
2002	125	25%
2003	128	28%
2004	130	30%

R

In this fictitious case, the RPI shows that the basket of products and services is 30% more expensive in 2004 than it had been in 1995.

Retail Sales Index

The Retail Sales Index is a US monthly figure which measures products sold by retailers. Each month a sample of retail outlets of varying types and sizes is chosen in order to calculate the volume of trade undertaken in the previous month. The Retail Sales Index is widely believed to be a prime indicator of consumer confidence. It is released in the middle of each month and relates to data collated from the previous month. The report only deals with products and not services and therefore does not cover the entire range of consumer purchases in a given month. None the less, many businesses and government agencies consider that the Retail Sales Index is an indicator of great value, showing in which direction the economy is currently moving.

Retained earnings

Retained earnings are often referred to as 'retentions'. They represent cash which has been derived from profits, but has not been distributed to **shareholders** in the form of **dividends**. These earnings are also known as **reserves** and provide a business with much-needed capital.

Retained profits

Retained profits are also known as 'ploughed back profits'. As the term implies, they are a proportion of a business's profits which has not been distributed in the form of **dividends** to the **shareholders**.

The retained profits are usually earmarked for reinvestment in assets. This is common practice for businesses on the basis that it is considerably cheaper to use retained profits rather than borrow money in the form of loans, which would require interest payments as well as repayment of the principle.

See also **retained earnings.**

R

Retention rate

'Retention rate' refers to the amount of earnings which are retained by a business, either to be placed as a **reserve** or for **reinvestment**. The retention rate of a business can be calculated using the following equation:

$$\frac{Retained\ earnings}{Total\ earnings\ (after\ tax)} \times 100$$

Return on assets (ROA)

Return on assets is one of a number of calculations which can be undertaken in order to assess the profitability of a business. Return on assets (or ROA) uses the following equation:

$$\frac{Earnings}{Total\ assets} \times 100$$

Troy, Leo, *Almanac of Business and Industrial Financial Ratios*. New York: Aspen Publishers, 2003.

Walsh, Ciaran, *Key Management Ratios: Master the Management Metrics that Drive and Control your Business*. London: Financial Times, Prentice-Hall, 2003.

Return on capital employed (ROCE) ratio

The ROCE ratio aims to express the profit which is made available to suppliers of long-term capital as a percentage of the long-term capital employed. Obviously, the profit made available to these long-term suppliers of capital is net profit (before interest and taxation).

ROCE is considered to be a vital measure of performance. It measures input (capital employed) and output (profits). ROCE is calculated in the following manner:

$$ROCE = \frac{net\ profit\ (before\ interest\ and\ taxation)}{share\ capital\ and\ reserves\ and\ long\text{-}term\ loans} \times 100$$

R

If a business had a net profit (before interest and taxation) of some $350,000 and a total figure of some $2,900,000 (the sum of share capital, reserves and long-term loans), then the calculation would be:

$$\frac{350,000}{2,900,000} \times 100 = 12.06\%$$

Typically, this figure would then be compared with the industry standard in order to assess the relative effectiveness of the business in returning a decent reward for its investors. In this case the return on the investment (capital employed) represents 12.06% of that capital employed.

Troy, Leo, *Almanac of Business and Industrial Financial Ratios*. New York: Aspen Publishers, 2003.

Walsh, Ciaran, *Key Management Ratios: Master the Management Metrics that Drive and Control your Business*. London: Financial Times, Prentice-Hall, 2003.

Return on equity (ROE) ratio

This ratio seeks to display the profit made available to equity or ordinary shareholders as a percentage of their stake in the business. The ratio is:

$$Return\ on\ equity\ = \frac{net\ profit\ (after\ tax\ and\ preference\ dividends)}{ordinary\ share\ capital\ plus\ reserves} \times 100$$

The primary purpose of the ratio is to show exactly what investors are receiving in return for their investment in the business. Normally, the figures for the ordinary share capital plus reserve are taken from the business's end-of-year figures. In certain cases, the business may prefer to use opening and closing balances.

Assuming the following, a business can make the return on equity calculations as follows:

- The net profit was $200,000.
- The ordinary share capital plus reserves amounted to $1,800,000.

Therefore:

$$\frac{200,000}{1,800,000} \times 100 = 11.11\%$$

This figure reveals that the business is providing an 11.11% return on the $1,800,000 invested in the business by equity shareholders, based on a net profit figure of $200,000.

Troy, Leo, *Almanac of Business and Industrial Financial Ratios*. New York: Aspen Publishers, 2003.

Walsh, Ciaran, *Key Management Ratios: Master the Management Metrics that Drive and Control your Business*. London: Financial Times, Prentice-Hall, 2003.

R

Return on invested capital (ROIC)

Return on invested capital (ROIC) is used to assess the effectiveness of a business's use of money, whether that money was borrowed or already owned by the business, and no matter how this money has been invested in its operations. Typically, ROIC is calculated using the following equation:

$$\frac{Net\ income\ after\ tax}{Total\ assets\ -\ excess\ cash\ -\ non\text{-}interest\ liabilities}$$

Troy, Leo, *Almanac of Business and Industrial Financial Ratios.* New York: Aspen Publishers, 2003.

Walsh, Ciaran, *Key Management Ratios: Master the Management Metrics that Drive and Control your Business.* London: Financial Times, Prentice-Hall, 2003.

Return on investment (ROI)

This is the US equivalent of **return on capital employed (ROCE)**. Whilst management may use this formula, assessing profit before tax and interest as a percentage of total assets, shareholders are more interested in the figures for profit after interest, and comparing this with the assets less the liabilities.

Friedlob, George T. and Plewa, Franklin J., *Essentials of Corporate Performance Measurement.* New York: John Wiley, 2002.

Troy, Leo, *Almanac of Business and Industrial Financial Ratios.* New York: Aspen Publishers, 2003.

Walsh, Ciaran, *Key Management Ratios: Master the Management Metrics that Drive and Control your Business.* London: Financial Times, Prentice-Hall, 2003.

Return on investment (ROI) ratio

Return on investment is another ratio which seeks to identify the net profit (after tax) as a percentage of the total assets of the business. The ratio is:

$$Return\ on\ investment\ =\ \frac{net\ profit\ (after\ tax)}{total\ assets} \times 100$$

This ratio is extremely important as it measures the profits available after all charges have been deducted, compared with the assets owned by the business. Typically, the total asset figures are the year-end figures, but they can be an average of the opening and closing figures.

A business with a net profit of $250,000 (after tax) and total assets to the value of $3,200,000 would calculate as follows:

$$\frac{250,000}{3,200,000} \times 100 = 7.81\%$$

This figure would then be compared with the industry standard. A complication may be the age and **depreciation** of the **fixed assets** of the business. If depreciation is a factor then the business will reveal a higher ROI. Conversely, if the business has relatively new fixed assets valued on or near the purchase price, then the ROI will be significantly lower.

Troy, Leo, *Almanac of Business and Industrial Financial Ratios*. New York: Aspen Publishers, 2003.

Walsh, Ciaran, *Key Management Ratios: Master the Management Metrics that Drive and Control your Business*. London: Financial Times, Prentice-Hall, 2003.

Return on sales (ROS)

Return on sales, or ROS, is another alternative means by which a business's profitability can be assessed. On this occasion the focus of the profitability is upon sales in comparison to pre-tax income. The standard equation is:

$$\frac{Pre\text{-}tax\ income}{Total\ sales}$$

Troy, Leo, *Almanac of Business and Industrial Financial Ratios*. New York: Aspen Publishers, 2003.

Walsh, Ciaran, *Key Management Ratios: Master the Management Metrics that Drive and Control your Business*. London: Financial Times, Prentice-Hall, 2003.

Return on total assets (ROTA)

Return on total assets (ROTA), as the term implies, is a measurement of whether or not a business is effectively using the assets which it owns. Typically, the equation takes the following form:

$$\frac{Income\ before\ interest\ and\ tax}{Fixed\ assets\ +\ current\ assets}$$

Troy, Leo, *Almanac of Business and Industrial Financial Ratios*. New York: Aspen Publishers, 2003.

Walsh, Ciaran, *Key Management Ratios: Master the Management Metrics that Drive and Control your Business*. London: Financial Times, Prentice-Hall, 2003.

R

Revaluation reserve

The revaluation reserve is also known as investment revaluation reserve, property revaluation reserve, and unrealized capital gains on valuation.

The revaluation reserve is the difference between the current value of an asset (such as a building) and what it cost to buy. Although the reserve can only be realized by selling the building, it is useful to a business as it increases its capacity (in the form of collateral) to borrow more money in the future.

The revaluation reserve can also represent a temporary decrease in the valuation of assets compared with their historical costs.

Revenue

Technically, revenue is received income which has been received in recompense for products and services provided by the business. There is, however, a complication regarding revenue and when that revenue should be considered to have been received. This question regarding when to **recognize** the arrival of revenue is somewhat blurred. Some businesses choose to recognize revenue when a transaction is agreed. Others date the revenue arrival when the products or services are invoiced or delivered. Others, on the other hand, wait until they have the certainty that the money has arrived in their bank account.

A business's revenue figures are normally net of discounts or any other payments (such as returns) which may be payable to the customer. Revenue is extremely important as a measurement, as a business's net income can be calculated from the revenue by simply subtracting the expenses. Technically, of course, revenue should be recognized when the products or services have been transferred to the ownership of the customer, and when it is clear that the actual revenue will be received, or when its being received can be counted on.

Revenue reserve

See **reserve**.

Reverse leverage

Reverse leverage, or indeed reverse **gearing** (its alternative UK description) can refer either to a situation where a business is experiencing a negative cash flow, or to a situation where a business is borrowing money at a higher interest rate than the return it can confidently expect in investing the money which has been borrowed. Both sets of circumstances produce negative situations, hence the term 'reverse' leverage or gearing.

Rights issues

A rights issue involves the offering of new shares to the market in an attempt by the business to secure additional funds. The term has certain implications which relate to the existing **shareholders** of the business. In a rights issue, existing shareholders must be offered new shares in proportion to their existing holdings of shares in the business.

Typically, existing shareholders will be asked to purchase a single new share for a specific number of shares which they already own (e.g. one new share for each five held). As the existing shareholders are entitled to this rights issue, they are offered the new shares at a discounted price. Should they not wish to take up the offer, they can sell their rights to another investor in the market.

Risk adjusted return

The term 'risk adjusted return' is often used in relation to investments, and the amount of money which that investment returns in relation to the degree of risk involved. Using risk adjusted return methodology it is therefore possible to compare investments which have provided a low return for a low risk with those which have provided a high return for a high risk.

Royalty

A royalty is a payment usually consisting of a percentage of **revenues** received for a third party's use of another's property. Royalties are frequently paid in return for the right to use patents, franchises, intellectual property or other copyrighted materials. Royalties may be payable to individuals or businesses who hold the rights to the property, by a third party who is in a more influential position to exploit the value of that property. From the point of view of finance and accounting, a record of the revenues received as a result of offering the property for sale to customers has to be meticulously kept and an agreed percentage of that revenue has to be forwarded regularly, on an agreed basis, to the original owner of that property.

R

Run rate

The term 'run rate' refers to the extrapolation of financial information. The run rate process involves using financial data, collected over a period of less than a year, and converting those figures into a full year's set of financial data. Clearly a number of assumptions are made in extrapolating this data and converting it into full-year result figures. The data is often used in order to forecast the probable financial figures for a full year once reliable data has been collected for perhaps a three- to six-month period. Obviously, the less time the existing data covers, the more likely it is that the extrapolation will be inaccurate or lacking, and the more assumptions have to be made.

R

Sale and leaseback

Sale and leaseback is a transaction in which the owner of an **asset** sells it to a third party and then immediately purchases back the right to use that asset under a **lease**. The **capital** released by this process is used to enable the organization to either expand or survive during a difficult trading period. The key to successful sale and leaseback is to ensure that the profits which are generated by the sale are in excess of the lease payments.

Sales

Sales represent the **revenue** which has been collected by a business in return for products and services which it has provided to customers. Sales can be differentiated from revenue in as much as sales relate purely to income derived from the trading of products and services, rather than other forms of income, which may include interest from other investments. It is normally the case that sales are recorded only at the point when the transaction has been confirmed and the business is assured that payment will be received in respect of that transaction in the foreseeable future. Many businesses do not count a sale as having been completed until they have actually received payment for the products or services.

Sales ledger

A sales ledger is simply a record of the daily **sales** which have been completed by a business. The **ledger** contains the customers' personal accounts; sales which have been made on **credit** are logged as such and those customers officially become the business's debtors. All information contained in the sales ledger is eventually transferred to the **general ledger**.

Salvage value

The term 'salvage value' relates to the value of an item once it is has become obsolete and cannot be sold. Retailers and manufacturers who find themselves with obsolete products often find an organization specializing in salvage to buy the items on their inventory that have become obsolete. The salvage organization then sells on the parts, products or components at their normal **book value**.

Same-store sales

The term 'same-store sales' refers to the **investment appraisal** of the financial statements made by retail operations. In complex retail chains, which are constantly opening new stores or outlets, it is notoriously difficult to identify the actual underlying sales figures and performance of the group as a whole. Each time a new outlet is established, assuming that the business has chosen the correct location, then that outlet's sales should be comparatively brisk and will therefore represent a considerable contribution to the overall sales figures of the group, perhaps disproportionately so. 'Same-store sales' seeks to identify outlets which have been open for more than a year. By investigating the sales figures of these established outlets, investors are able to assess the underlying trends and performance of the group as a whole, rather than incorporating the perhaps distorted figures which are created by new openings. In this way, investors can assess the overall sales growth which can be attributed to existing outlets as well as the sales growth that can be attributed to new outlet openings.

SAYE

SAYE is an acronym for 'Save As You Earn'. In most cases SAYE schemes are set up by employers, giving employees the right to purchase a number of shares in the organization at a fixed price. SAYEs are also known as share saves, where a fixed monthly sum is deducted from an employee's pay by the employer for between three and seven years, at the end of which the employee receives a bonus. The bonus payment is derived from a calculation of the total amount of savings over the three- to seven-year period. In the UK, upwards of 1.75 million employees are involved in SAYE schemes in over 1,000 organizations.

Second preferred stock

Second preferred stock is a variant form of **preferred stock** which is subordinate to **first preferred stock**, but has precedence over other forms of preferred stock in relation to the payment of dividends and the receiving of cash in the case of the liquidation of assets.

Secular

Although the term 'secular' has many other connotations, in financial terms it refers to a long-term trend which is neither **cyclical** nor temporary.

Securities and Exchange Commission (SEC)

The Securities and Exchange Commission (SEC) aims to protect US investors against malpractice in the securities market. It is the lead Federal regulatory agency and enforces the Securities Act (1933), the Securities Exchange Act (1934), the Trust Indenture Act (1939), the Investment Company Act (1940) and the Investment Advisers Act (1941).

The SEC is essentially a quasi-judicial agency, which is independent and has five commissioners, each of whom is appointed for a five-year period. It has four divisions, which are:

- The Division of Corporate Finance (which ensures that publicly traded businesses disclose any required financial information to actual or potential investors).
- The Division of Market Regulation (which deals with legislation appertaining to brokerage).
- The Division of Investment Management (which deals with investment advisors and mutual funds).
- The Division of Enforcement (which deals with the enforcement of securities legislation, as well as investigating reported violations of these pieces of legislation).

www.sec.gov

Security

The term 'security' has two radically different meanings in relation to accounts and finance. The first definition refers to loans and the concept of a lender requiring some form of guarantee, or security, should the borrower fail to keep up with payments of interest or be unable to repay the principal capital. Security, or collateral, can also be provided by the business's own property (such as buildings or land).

The alternative definition relates to any form of share, stock, government bond, debenture, or trust. Normally the term 'security' does not extend to insurance policies, but it may also refer to the right to money which has been deposited or loaned.

Hirschey, T., *Investments: Theory and Practice*. Mason, OH: South Western College Publishing, 2004.

Tuckman, Bruce, *Fixed Income Securities: Tools for Today's Markets*. New York: John Wiley, 2002.

Selling, general and administrative expenses (SGA)

'Selling, general and administrative expenses' is a US term which is used on **income statements**. Typically, SGA will include the following:

- the combined **payroll** expenses of the business (including salaries, travel expenses, commissions, etc.);
- advertising expenses.

Businesses will be keen to limit the level of SGA expenses and try to link these expenses to a maximum percentage of their **revenue**. Clearly, whilst savings can be made by more targeted advertising, the normal procedure for cutting back SGA is to lay off staff.

Share capital

See **capital**.

Shareholder

A shareholder is the owner of shares in a **limited company**. In the US, shareholders are known as stockholders.

See also **shareholder of record, shareholder value, shareholder value analysis** and **shareholder's equity**.

Rappaport, Alfred, *Creating Shareholder Value: The New Standard for Business Performance*. New York: Simon and Schuster, 1998.

Shareholder of record

A shareholder of record is the registered holder, but not necessarily the beneficial owner of a **security**. A shareholder of record is variously known as a stockholder of record, holder of record or owner of record. Legally, a business or a **paying agent** can only pay **dividends** or other **distributions** to the shareholder of record.

Shareholder value

Shareholder value is a measurement of the benefits which shareholders receive from their investment in a business. It is the sum total of all of the **payouts** which a business makes to its shareholders. Therefore shareholder value is the sum of dividend payments, capital gains or other proceeds received from the business as the result of the shareholder's investment.

> Doyle, Peter, *Value-based Marketing: Marketing Strategies for Corporate Growth and Shareholder Value*. New York: John Wiley, 2000.

Shareholder value analysis (SVA)

Shareholder value analysis is a means by which the actual economic value, or market value, of a business can be assessed, by discounting **cash flows** resulting from the cost of capital. The primary aim of SVA is to:

- establish a benchmark valuation for the measurement of business and management performance;
- identify factors which add value to a business's operations;
- assess a shareholder's decision making with regard to disposing of stocks or shares in a given business;
- provide a framework which can calculate rates of return to enable the shareholder or investor to make strategic plans.

There is a difference between **shareholder value** and strategic shareholder value. Strategic shareholder value analysis aims to forecast any acquisition premiums and corresponding acquisition values of a business. The principal methodologies employed in SVA include analysis of the following:

- the business's cost of debts, equity and cost of capital;
- the financial model of the business and projected capital requirements;
- the **free cash flow** generated;
- the implied **return on investments**;
- financial performance ratios, including **return on equity**, **return on assets** and other turnover ratios;
- the trends in value creation and the main drivers behind that value creation;
- industrial trends and comparable businesses to establish valuation benchmarks;
- typical acquisition premiums and other valuations.

S

Cleland, Alan S. and Bruno, Albert V., *The Market Value Process: Bridging Customer and Shareholder Value.* New York: Jossey-Bass Wiley, 1996.

Morin, Roger and Jarrell, Sherry, *Driving Shareholder Value: Value-building Techniques for Creating Shareholder Value.* New York: McGraw-Hill Education, 2000.

Shareholders' equity

Shareholders' equity, or net asset value, refers to the total assets of a business less its liabilities, which include any **debentures**, loan stock or preference shares **(preferred stock)**.

Shareholders' equity is often referred to as the actual **net worth** of the business. A related issue is the net asset value per share, which has the following calculation:

$$\frac{\textit{Net asset value}}{\textit{Total number of ordinary (common stock) shares}}$$

Share premium account

A share premium account can often be found on a balance sheet and represents the amount of money paid (or set aside and promised to be paid) by a shareholder. The share premium account, therefore, represents the money paid in by shareholders on allotment of shares over and above their nominal value. Typically, the share premium account may be used to issue bonus shares or to write-off equity-related expenses such as underwriting costs. The share premium account is not distributable.

On the balance sheet, therefore, the share premium value represents the nominal value of the shares purchased in the business by (usually) the original shareholders. If the original shareholders paid a premium compared to the nominal value for their shares, the difference is placed in the share premium account.

S

Shareholder value analysis (SVA)

Shareholder value analysis (SVA) estimates the economic value of the equity of a business by discounting forecast cash-flows by the cost of capital. The primary goals of SVA are:

- to establish a baseline valuation for measuring managerial performance;
- to identify valuation drivers;
- to assist exit strategy considerations;
- to provide rate of return targets for strategic planning.

Shareholder value is simply defined as being the fair market value of the investor's equity in a business. SVA is therefore used to estimate the shareholder value for a business whose shares are not publicly quoted and may therefore have a nominal cash value. The SVA approach therefore makes a valuation based on the business's activities.

Shareholder funds provide a reasonable starting point for valuation. An amount of goodwill can also be added to this. In cases when there are similar listed companies to the one that is being valued, SVA can take into account these findings. There are three essential steps to estimating shareholder value:

- establishing the operating cash flows from the business on the basis of the existing value drivers;
- determining the cost of capital for similar listed companies;
- calculating the terminal or residual value.

Shipping terms

Shipping terms are essentially price quotations which include the cost of merchandise plus the cost of any other services which a beneficiary of a **letter of credit** is required to pay for shipping the merchandise. Typically, the following forms of shipping terms include a number of different pre-paid services:

- CFR (Cost and freight) – which includes the cost of the merchandise, transportation to the dock, loading onto the vessel, forwarder's fees for preparing the documents, and ocean freight.
- CIF (Cost, insurance and freight) – which includes the cost of the merchandise, transportation to the dock, loading onto the vessel, forwarder's fees for the shipping documents, ocean freight and an insurance premium.
- CIP (Cost and insurance) – which includes the cost of the merchandise, marine insurance and transportation charges, with the exception of the ocean freight to the named place of destination.
- DDP (ex-dock duty paid) – which includes the cost of the merchandise, transportation to the dock, loading onto the vessel, forwarder's fees for preparing the documents, ocean freight, insurance premium, unloading of the merchandise at the dock, import duties and delivery to a named destination.
- EXW (ex-factory) – which only includes the cost of the merchandise.
- FAS (free alongside) – which includes the cost of the merchandise, transportation to the dock, but not the forwarder's fees for the shipping documentation.

S

- FOB (free, or freight, onboard) – which includes the cost of the merchandise, transportation to the dock, loading onto the vessel and freight forwarder's fees for preparing the shipping documents.

Branch, Alan E., *Shipping and Airfreight Documentation for Importers and Exporters, and Associated Terms*. London: Witherby, 2000.

Shortage cost

Shortage costs are those which are incurred by a manufacturing organization when it is unable to supply customers because of a '**stock out**'. Shortages clearly arise when demand exceeds the supply at a particular time. Shortage costs can be calculated purely in terms of lost sales which could not be converted into **back orders**, although the true cost of shortages may be far more complex as they may include the permanent loss of customers who have successfully sought an alternate product from a different supplier, or those who have decided not to stock that item because of its variable availability.

Short-term assets

Short-term assets are, rather predictably, assets which a business does not expect to still retain possession of by the end of the coming financial period. Typically, short-term assets will have been purchased for specific purposes or, perhaps, to offset other acquisitions as a form of insurance against possible falls in value.

Peterson, Raymond H., *Accounting for Fixed Assets*. New York: John Wiley, 2002.

Shrinkage

'Shrinkage' is a commonly used term for the situation where an organization's physical inventory is less than that which appears in the paperwork or computer database. Usually this non-tallying of figures, or shrinkage, can be attributed to theft, loss, storage in the wrong place, delivery to the wrong location, or unreported breakages.

Single-entry book-keeping

Single-entry book-keeping is an accounting methodology which is employed primarily by small businesses who only need to create relatively straightforward financial statements. Transactions are recorded as a single entry, as opposed to the debit and credit system which is used in **double-entry book-keeping**. Businesses using single-entry book-keeping assess their taxable income purely as the difference between their cash receipts and their cash expenses over a given period.

Soft currency

A soft currency is a national currency which is notoriously difficult to exchange. Usually soft currencies belong to countries that have enormous deficits in their **balance of payments** and have only minimal exchange reserves.

Soft loan

'Soft loan' is normally associated with loans made by international banks, or agencies, to help encourage economic activity in developing countries. They may also be granted to support other non-commercial activities. A soft loan is typified by the interest rate being pegged at lower than the normal market interest rate, thus making the loan more attractive and affordable to the developing country.

Special dividend

A special dividend is a dividend which is received by **shareholders** – usually on a non-recurring basis – that is considered exceptional either in its timing or in the size of the dividend itself. Special dividends are received by shareholders only under exceptional circumstances, such as the disposal of a considerable asset, or the redistribution of earnings which had hitherto been retained for a particular purpose, but are now no longer required.

S

Special drawing rights

Special drawing rights were created by the **International Monetary Fund** in 1970 and are, in effect, international reserve assets which are allocated to each of the member nations. Provided a country adheres to the conditions set by the IMF, special drawing rights can be used to help deal with deficits in its **balance of payments**. In effect they can help settle debts that the country has with another nation, or with the IMF itself. The value of special drawing rights is calculated as a weighted average of several internationally traded currencies.

Squeeze

In financial and accounting terms 'squeeze' has three distinct meanings:

- Income or pay squeeze – in which there is a government-led move to control any possible increases in wages or salaries.
- **Credit squeeze** – in which limitations are imposed to control the lending of money.
- **Dividend** or profit squeeze – which is a restriction in increases in dividend payments to shareholders.

Essentially, squeezes are designed to help control **inflation** and are led by either the government and/or the **central banks.**

Standard cost

Standard cost is the means by which manufacturers seek to measure the exact cost of processing and delivering a single unit of a product or service. The exact way in which the standard cost is calculated differs from organization to organization, but the underlying principle is that standard cost is the ideal cost. In reality, of course, the actual cost will differ over time as different circumstances impinge upon the associated costs involved. Typically there may be fluctuations in the price of raw materials, parts and components, or there may be an increase or decrease in the number of defects. Note that the standard cost may not, necessarily, be the ideal cost.

Stated value

The stated value is a valuation which is placed on a business purely by internal accounting methodologies and usually as directed by its board of directors. The stated value of the business in the majority of cases bears no relationship to the true market price of the business. This is a particularly difficult issue when a new board of directors, in a relatively new business, offers stocks or shares for the first time. They attach a value to the stocks and shares, perhaps with no real linkage to the true market price of the shares themselves.

Statement of condition

The term 'statement of condition' is interchangeable with the more common term **balance sheet**. The statement is, in effect, a quantitative summary, at a particular point in time, of the business's total **assets** and **liabilities** and hence its **net worth**. The statement of condition details all of the assets which are owned by the business and then balances the value of these assets by revealing the financing methods which were used to acquire them. These financing methods would, of course, include **shareholders' equity** and other liabilities in the form of loans or **overdrafts**.

Sterilization

Sterilization involves government intervention into the foreign exchange market with the intention of attempting to offset the impact of either inflation or deflation.

It would normally be the case that a government would take the following steps outlined in Figure 4 if the nation's currency is depreciating in value on the foreign exchange markets.

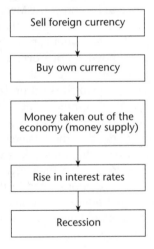

Figure 4   Government measures to influence the foreign exchange market

Sterilization seeks to prevent this chain of events by expanding the money supply at the right moment to prevent a rise in interest rates.

The reverse sterilization policy, adopted in cases when the currency is appreciating, involves restructuring the money supply at the right moment and allowing interest rates to rise slightly to prevent extra borrowing.

Stock

In more general business terms, 'stock' refers to any raw materials, components, work in progress or finished goods which may be owned by a business. Indeed, the ownership of this stock has financial implications as it is considered to be an asset of the business, and therefore, on a balance sheet for example, the financing methods which were used to acquire these stock items must be detailed.

Stock also has a further connotation with respect to ownership or equity in a business. 'Stock', which is an interchangeable word for the term 'share', indicates that an individual or another business has a claim to a proportion of a business's **assets** and **profits**. The exact proportion of that ownership is determined by the number of shares which that individual or business owns, but this figure has to be considered in relation to the total number of shares which have been distributed. Thus if a business has 10,000 shares, then an individual who owns 1,000 of these shares effectively owns 10% of the business.

Holding common stock, or **ordinary shares**, accords the owners the right to vote at Annual General Meetings (AGMs) and other meetings to which **shareholders** are invited. Effectively their voting power is in proportion to their proportionate ownership of the shares in the business. Other forms of stock, known as **preferred stock** or **preference shares**, do not afford the owners voting rights yet they do guarantee the owner a fixed interest payment, which is set preceding the purchase of the shares. Unlike the owners of common stock, or ordinary shareholders, these stockholders should receive a guaranteed income from their investment, assuming of course that the business is not suffering from financial difficulties. Owners of common stock or ordinary shareholders are entitled to a variable income from their investment based entirely upon the financial fortunes as demonstrated in the after-tax profits of the business, as a result of its trading operations.

The term 'stock' is also interchangeable with the terms 'equity', 'equity securities' or 'corporate stock'.

Elder, Alexander, *Come into My Trading Room: Complete Guide to Trading*. New York: John Wiley, 2002.

Stock dividend

A stock dividend is often offered to shareholders as an alternative to a cash dividend payment. A stock dividend involves the business offering additional shares to the **shareholder**, to effectively retain cash within the business and deepen the shareholder's investment in the business itself. The shareholder would inevitably pay tax on any cash dividends, but in the cases of stock dividends there are no tax implications until the shares are ultimately sold.

Spare, Anthony and Ciotti, Paul, *Relative Dividend Yield: Common Stock Investing for Income and Appreciation*. New York: John Wiley, 1999.

Weiss, Geraldine, *The Dividend Connection: How Dividends Create Value in the Stock Market*. Chicago, IL: Dearborn Trade Publishing, 1995.

Stock split

A stock split requires the approval of both the board of directors and the shareholders of the business. The process involves increasing the number of shares available by literally splitting the value of each share. The normal situation is a stock split of two new shares for every old one, with each new share now worth half the value of an old share. This ensures that existing shareholders retain their proportionate equity in the business.

The primary purpose behind stock splits is to reduce the value of each share in order to attract more investors in the now cheaper shares.

Nelson, Miles and Nelson, Darlene, *Stock Split Secrets: Profiting from a Predictable Price-Moving Event*. New York: Lighthouse Publishing Group, 2000.

Stock turnover ratio

The stock turnover ratio seeks to establish the relationship between the average stock holding of a business and the cost of sales. The standard formula is:

$$Stock\ turnover\ ratio = \frac{Cost\ of\ sales}{Average\ stock\ held}$$

The 'average stock' figure is calculated by arriving at the average of the opening and closing stock figures. In cases where the closing stock is not representative of the average stock holding (such as in the case of businesses selling seasonal products), a true average stock figure is calculated by considering the actual stock figures at the end of each month.

In order to calculate the average period of stockholding, the following formula is used:

$$Average\ period\ of\ stockholding = \frac{Average\ stock\ held}{Cost\ of\ sales} \times 12$$

Multiplying the figure by 12 gives the period in months of the stockholding. If the figure needs to be expressed as days, then the 12 is replaced by 365.

Using the two formulae, a business can calculate the following, given these assumptions:

S

- Cost of sales = £2,500,000.
- Average stock held = 300,000.

The stock turnover ratio is therefore:

$$\frac{2,500,000}{300,000} = 8.3$$

This indicates that the stock has been turned over 8.3 times to achieve sales of £2,500,000.

The average stockholding is therefore:

$$\frac{300,000}{2,500,000} \times 12 = 1.44 \text{ months}$$

Expressed as days:

$$\frac{300,000}{2,500,000} \times 365 = 43.8 \text{ days}$$

High stockholding periods may indicate slow moving stock (or perhaps obsolete stock). Other reasons could include:

- increased stockholding due to unpredictable supply;
- a predicted rise in the cost of stock;
- anticipation of higher sales figures;
- stock accumulation for a major sales campaign.

Low stockholding periods may simply be a result of poor stock management systems, or conversely, extremely efficient stock control. Other considerations may be:

- low stock leading to low sales and lost **goodwill** from customers;
- excellent relationships with reliable suppliers.

Stockholder

The term 'stockholder' is interchangeable with the term **shareholder**. It is essentially a US term which is used to describe an individual or a business that owns shares of stock in a business or a mutual fund.

Stockholder of record

See **shareholder of record**.

Stockholders' equity

See **shareholders' equity**.

Straight-line depreciation

The straight-line depreciation method is a means by which an **asset** can be depreciated, based on the assumption that the asset will depreciate by an equal value each year of its useful life. It is used in order to spread the cost of a **fixed asset** over its useful lifetime. The assumption behind straight-line depreciation is that the cost of the asset is equal to the original purchase price of the asset less its scrap value, divided by the number of years of the asset's useful life. Normally the following formula is used to calculate straight-line depreciation:

$$\text{Straight-line depreciation} = \frac{\text{Historical cost} - \text{residual value}}{\text{Years of useful life}}$$

In this instance **historical cost** is taken to mean the original purchase price and the residual value is equal to the asset's scrap value. Therefore, if a business has purchased a machine which is valued at £2m and its scrap value is assessed to be £50,000, and the assumption is made that the machine will be operative for 10 years, the following calculation can be made:

$$2,000,000 - 50,000 = \frac{1,950,000}{10} = £195,000 \text{ per year depreciation}$$

The straight-line depreciation method assumes that the asset will be used equally over its useful life. The methodology does not reflect the fact that the asset is likely to depreciate more in the first year than in subsequent years, which leads to a tendency for fixed assets to be somewhat over-valued on the **balance sheet**. The method also assumes that the business has got two crucial figures correct, i.e. the asset's length of useful life and the true residual value of the asset.

Stranded asset

A stranded asset is a **fixed asset** that has effectively become obsolete before it has been fully **depreciated**. The stranded asset's market value is considerably less than its value on the business's **balance sheet**.

Sum-of-the-years'-digits method

Sum-of-the-years'-digits method can be seen as an alternative **depreciation** methodology to **straight-line depreciation**. It assumes a higher level of depreciation and therefore greater tax benefits in the earlier years of an asset's life. This more realistically reflects the true depreciation of **fixed assets** in as much as fixed assets tend to depreciate at a higher rate in the first years of their ownership, and the depreciation, comparatively speaking, tails off towards the end of the asset's useful life.

Surplus

'Surplus' is a term which is used to describe an excess in favour of the business. Surplus can be applied to situations where a business's **assets** exceed its **liabilities**. It can also be used to describe profit which still exists after any operating expenses, interest, taxes or other charges have been deducted.

Suspense account

A suspense account is a temporary account created by a business which allows it the opportunity to record balances in the following circumstances:

- when mistakes have been made;
- when balances have not been finalized, as a transaction has not yet been fully completed.

Swap

The term 'swap' refers to exchanges of payment streams, the most common of which is known as an interest rate swap, in which one of the parties receives an adjustable rate of interest and the other agrees to be paid a fixed rate of interest.

Swap rate

The term 'swap rate' has two specific definitions. The first is in relation to an interest rate swap, in which the market rate of interest is paid by the party which was responsible for the fixed payment. When swaps are begun, the fixed rate is usually close to the market swap rate. As the swap matures, the fixed rate paid remains constant, while the swap rate may change.

The alternative definition is the difference between the spot rate and the forward exchange rate for a particular currency. It is expressed in points, as either a positive or a negative figure.

S

Systematic risk

Systematic risk recognizes that the value of overseas investments may decline over a period of time as a result of economic change. International businesses use the potential threats which may arise from systematic risk as a key factor determining how they choose to allocate their assets and diversify in different markets. By becoming involved in different overseas markets they can, to some extent, insulate themselves from events which would have a detrimental impact on a specific market. By spreading their risk they avoid the dangers of systematic risk affecting their whole operations. In making investments in different overseas countries international businesses can afford the detrimental impacts of under-performance in certain markets at different times, provided that this under-performance is not widespread across all of the markets in which they operate.

'Systematic risk' is also known as 'market risk'.

Systemic risk

Systemic risk can be differentiated from **systematic risk** in the sense that it affects an entire market or system. It is notoriously difficult to avoid the negative impacts of systemic risk by diversifying into new markets.

S

Tangible asset

Tangible assets are items which have a physical substance, and may well be used in the production or supply of products and services. In accounting terms, tangible assets also include **leases** or company **shares**. They are, in effect, the fixed assets of the organization and can be differentiated from **intangible assets**, such as **goodwill**, trademarks or patents, which do not have a physical substance but are still valuable concepts and assets.

Damodaran, Aswath, *Investment Valuation: Tools and Techniques for Determining the Value of Any Asset*. New York: John Wiley, 2002.
Gardner, Mona, Mills, Dixie and Cooperman, Elizabeth, *Managing Financial Institutions: An Asset/Liability Approach*. London: Thomson Learning, 1999.

Tangible net worth

Tangible net worth is a measure of the true physical assets of a business. The calculation is a simple one which requires the value of the business's **intangible assets** to be deducted from the business's total **net worth**.

Tax arbitrage

Tax arbitrage involves the creation of transactions or financial instruments which allow two businesses to exploit the loopholes or differences in their tax exposures at home. The purpose of tax arbitrage is to ensure that both parties pay the minimum amount of relevant tax – less than the amount which would otherwise have been due had the tax arbitrage not taken place.

Ballard, Jr, Frederic L., *ABCs of Arbitrage: Tax Rules for Investment of Bond Proceeds by Municipalities*. Chicago, IL: American Bar Association, 2002.

Tax haven

A tax haven is often known as an offshore financial centre. It is a term which is usually applied to low-tax economies which aim to attract foreign investment. The United Nations, for example, defines an 'offshore' institution as 'any bank anywhere in the world that accepts deposits and manages funds on behalf of persons legally domiciled elsewhere'. The US has a far more practical definition, as framed by its Financial Stability Forum, describing offshore financial centres as 'jurisdictions that attract a high level of non-resident activity'.

There are undoubtedly a large number of tax havens around the world. The United Nations again recognizes between 60 and 90 nations and territories. The US Department of State recognizes 52, including the US itself. The Organization for Economic Cooperation and Development identifies 41 low-tax jurisdictions. Countries such as the Cayman Islands, Bermuda and the Bahamas have no income tax, whilst others, such as Guernsey, Lichtenstein and Hong Kong have low flat-rate taxation systems.

Many commercial banks, however, and government **central banks**, consider tax havens to be nothing more than undesirable tax competition that has entirely different rules on disclosure, the protection of minority shareholder rights, and many other missing features in regulatory competition rules.

Finkelstein, Ken H., *The Tax Haven Guidebook*. Chicago, IL: Independent Publishers Group, 1999.

Tax treaty

A tax treaty defines and specifies precisely how particular income is to be taxed in the event that two countries have jurisdiction over the income in question. A new tax treaty between the UK and the US was ratified in March 2003. It was originally signed in July 2001 and amended by a protocol in July 2002. The treaty in this case affects income tax and capital gains tax, corporation tax, federal income taxes and the withholding of tax in both countries. These elements were all phased in between April 2003 and January 2004.

Phillips, John S., *International Tax Treaty Networks*. Surbiton, Surrey: Deanwood Publishing, 1997.

T

Tight monetary policy

A tight monetary policy is an approach often adopted by a nation's **central bank** as a means by which **inflation** can be controlled. Tight monetary policy involves the reduction of the **reserves** of commercial banks; in other words, a restriction of the money supply. Tight monetary policy is also known as 'tight money'.

See also **monetary policy** *and* **squeeze**.

Times interest earned

Times interest earned is a calculation which is made to assess whether a business is creditworthy. The standard calculation is:

$$\frac{Earnings\ before\ interest\ and\ taxes}{Interest}$$

Top line

'Top line' is an alternative term for **total revenue**. 'Top line' refers to the fact that the total revenue figure appears at the very top of an **income statement**.

See also **bottom line**.

Total absorption costing

Total absorption costing is an alternative means by which a business can attribute and proportion both direct and indirect costs (or **overheads**) and thereby allocate them as part of the cost associated with producing goods (or providing services).

Total absorption costing ensures that the business considers and factors into the equation all of its costs, that all overheads are covered by the prices charged for products and services, and that a contribution is always made to the overheads.

Total asset turnover ratio

This ratio is a variation on the **fixed asset turnover ratio** and also measures the business's effectiveness in using its assets to generate sales. In this case, the formula is:

$$Total\ asset\ turnover\ ratio\ =\ \frac{sales}{total\ assets}$$

A business which has sales of some £3,200,000 has a total asset figure of £2,850,000. Again the figure for total assets may be calculated as an average of the opening or closing values (used for expanding businesses primarily), or simply the closing value of the assets at the year end. The relevant calculation would therefore be:

$$\frac{3,200,000}{2,850,000}\ =\ 1.12\ times$$

The total asset turnover ratio therefore reveals that the business is generating £1.12 in sales for every £1 invested in assets.

A low ratio suggests that the business is having **productivity** problems. A high ratio may suggest that the business is **overtrading** on its assets; in other words, the business does not have sufficient assets to support the sales which are being generated. This is often a problem facing new businesses which are expanding. As sales increase, they do not have sufficient cash to invest in additional **fixed assets** and may also have **working capital** difficulties. Ultimately, the business may suffer from liquidity problems, which means that they may not be able to supply customers as they do not have sufficient funds to replace the stock.

Temple, Peter, *Magic Numbers: The 33 Key Ratios that Every Investor Should Know*. New York: John Wiley, 2001.

Total assets

The total assets of a business are taken to be the sum of its current and long-term assets, the current assets being those which the business can reasonably expect to turn over within the next financial year and the longer-term assets those which they expect to own for a considerable number of years. 'Long-term asset' in this sense can often refer to assets which are likely to be owned for at least 10 years.

Damodaran, Aswath, *Investment Valuation: Tools and Techniques for Determining the Value of Any Asset*. New York: John Wiley, 2002.
Gardner, Mona, Mills, Dixie and Cooperman, Elizabeth, *Managing Financial Institutions: An Asset/Liability Approach*. London: Thomson Learning, 1999.

Total cost

Total cost has two different definitions, one associated with accounting and the other with general finance. In accounting terms, 'total cost' is the equivalent of the sum of a business's **fixed costs**, semi-variable and **variable costs**. The total cost figure is used to describe the complete expenditure in relation to the business's operations, taking into account its **overheads**, its costs related to production, and other costs related to the output level of its operations.

In financial terms, 'total costs' can refer to investments, and the amount that has been spent in acquiring a particular investment. The cost of investment is not simply the cost of a **security** as it needs to

T

incorporate any associated transaction costs, such as commissions or fees, and indeed any taxation liabilities arising out of the investment.

Campanella, Jack (ed.), *Principles of Quality Costs: Principles, Implementation and Use.* London: McGraw-Hill Education. 2000.

Trade credit

Trade credit is provided by either exporting businesses, multinationals, government or governments, to other businesses or organizations. It usually takes the form of a delay in the payment for products or services received.

When trade credit is offered it is common practice to obtain trade credit insurance, which minimizes the risk of possible default and insolvency. Trade credit insurance can cover a business against the risk of a **bad debt** and is an essential tool in the export business. Trade credit insurance effectively replaces **working capital** when bad debts or late payments have an impact on the **cash flow** of a business.

A number of different insurance companies underwrite trade credit insurance. International businesses could choose to seek to cover what is known as whole turnover, which covers the whole of the policy holder's business and allows the granting of credit up to a stated limited. Alternatively, businesses may choose to take out a specific account policy, which can be either fixed or adjustable to cover a number of named buyers. The premiums are usually based on the amounts of debts outstanding. In determining the correct trade credit insurance policy for the business, and for insurers to set the premium rate, the following criteria are usually examined:

- the annual turnover of the exporting business;
- the previous experience of bad debts;
- the efficiency of the business's credit control systems;
- the length of credit granted by the business;
- the historical and current status of the buyers;
- the trade sector in which the exporting business operates;
- the size of individual accounts and the proportion they actually represent in relation to the whole of the exporting business's total turnover.

Trade credit insurance does not necessarily cover the exporting business for all of its loss, and normally covers between 75% and 95% of any given loss.

Briggs, Peter, *Principles of International Trade and Payments.* Oxford: Blackwell, 1994.

Total return

'Total return' is usually taken to mean the full return on any particular investment. The total return would include any income which has been derived from either a dividend or interest, and will incorporate any **appreciation** or **depreciation** on the value of the investment over a given period of time. Total return figures can be calculated on a yearly basis or at the end of a specific project, or in some cases at the end of an asset's useful life.

Total return can also be referred to as **yield**.

Madden, Bartley J., *Cash Flow Return on Investment Valuation: A Total System Approach to Valuing the Firm*. Oxford: Butterworth Heinemann, 1999.

Trading dividends

See **dividend capture**.

Transaction

The term 'transaction' has both a general definition and a definition which is directly related to accounting. The term 'transaction' can refer to any agreement between two parties to exchange the ownership of an asset in return for a payment. The payment need not necessarily be in cash, and therefore a transaction in its most general sense can include any form of trade, including **barter**.

In accounting terms, 'transaction' refers to an event which has occurred and which has been subsequently recorded in any book of accounts. This may include **ledgers**, or indeed any form of **financial statement**.

Transaction exposure

Transaction exposure is a form of currency risk that can occur when an international business deals with either another business or a subsidiary in an overseas market. Transaction exposure refers to gains and losses which may be incurred when transactions are paid for in a foreign currency. The funds received from the transaction may have to be converted to the home currency, but are obviously subject to fluctuations in the foreign exchange market. Transaction exposure can occur when a company buys or sells on credit in a foreign currency, or when a business borrows or lends in a foreign currency.

T

Treasury management

Treasury management is the provision of management reporting and performance measurement which aims to support decision making, assess performance and monitor compliance. Treasury management takes a key role in managing the liquidity of a business, examining its funding and financial risk taking. Treasury management has come into sharp focus as many businesses are under considerable pressure to optimize their **shareholder** value. Treasury management assists a business in examining financial risks which it may face. Treasury management is, in effect, a form of structured risk management which incorporates the examination of liquidity, funding, bank relationships and the control of all systems related to finance.

Collier, Paul A., Cooke, Terry E. and Glynn, John J., *Financial and Treasury Management.* Oxford: Butterworth Heinemann, 1988.

Trial balance

Theoretically, if a business has scrupulously kept its **double-entry book-keeping** system in order, then a trial balance should be a simple process. The debit balances and the credit balances are transferred to the trial balance and the totals of these columns should match.

In cases where they do not match, it is an accountancy function to search for the discrepancies. Adjustments to the trial balance may be necessary for the following items:

- prepayments and accruals;
- closing stock;
- depreciation.

The trial balance, once balanced, is then used in the completion of the business's final accounts, which consist of the **balance sheet** and the **profit and loss account**.

T

Trickle-down theory

Trickle-down theory is advocated by those who believe that the lack of government intervention in **free markets**, thereby allowing **free enterprise** to flourish, is a desirable state of affairs. Trickle-down theory suggests that profits which are made by private businesses will ultimately be distributed throughout the economy, notably through wages, which stimulates additional demand, which in turn creates more employment in other parts of the economy.

Turnover

Turnover is the aggregated total of sales of an organization over a given period of time. It is the total revenue for all products and services, less any trade discounts or tax based on the revenue.

Many companies use turnover to determine other measures, such as how quickly some assets are turned over. For example, stock turnover is obtained by dividing the total sales figures by the number of units sold.

A turnover ratio is an accounting ratio which effectively shows the number of times an item of capital has been replaced within a given financial period.

T

U u

Un-appropriated profit

Un-appropriated profit is variously known as 'earned surplus' or 'accumulated' earnings. Technically, un-appropriated profit is an integral part of **shareholders' equity**. In effect, un-appropriated profit is earmarked for reinvestment as **retained profit**. The un-appropriated profit is usually reinvested into the core business activities, or may be used to pay off long-term debts.

Un-audited opinion

The term 'un-audited opinion' refers to opinion as stated by a Certified Accountant in respect of a business's **financial statements**. The opinion is given as to the authenticity or the credibility of the financial statements, in spite of the fact that this accountant has not audited the accounts of the business. It is, therefore, equivalent to a second opinion, or professional opinion.

Undersubscription

Undersubscription refers to situations where a new stock or share issue has attracted fewer buyers than had been anticipated. The business, technically speaking, is left in the position of having more shares available than are required by investors. In order to protect itself against such a situation, the business would have engaged the services of a brokerage firm, which would have undertaken to underwrite the share issue and effectively purchase any balance of unwanted shares. Clearly the business will have paid the brokerage company a premium for this service, but the fact still remains that the market is unconvinced that the shares offer a reasonable investment opportunity.

Unleveraged

The term 'unleveraged' refers to businesses that are able to operate without having to secure finance in the form, usually, of loans. Clearly an unleveraged business is a balanced operation that offers a reduced level of risk to potential investors. Having said this, an unleveraged business may not have sufficient access to capital in order to rapidly increase its output, or take advantage of an external investment opportunity.

Unpaid dividend

An unpaid dividend is a declared dividend which will be paid to **shareholders** who have invested in the business, but which, for some reason, perhaps related to timing issues, has not yet been **distributed** in the form of dividends to those shareholders.

Unqualified opinion

An unqualified opinion is an opinion which is most closely associated with remarks made by an **auditor** regarding a **financial statement**. The auditor offers an opinion of the financial statement of the business without any conditions or reservations. The opinion effectively states that the financial reports are a true and accurate reflection of the present financial state or condition of the business and that the business has followed all conventional accounting rules and regulations in the formulation of its financial reports.

See also **qualified opinion**.

Unrealized

The term 'unrealized' can be applied to gains, losses and profit. In effect, the term 'unrealized' relates to transactions which were expected to take place but have not yet occurred. In respect of losses, a business or an investor may be aware of the fact that when a transaction ultimately takes place, the value of an asset or stock which they still own will actually be less than its current value. This is known as a paper loss.

'Unrealized profit' refers to the possibility of a transaction in relation to an investment or a sale which, when it occurs, will deliver the business or the investor a profit on an item which they currently own. Since the transaction has not yet taken place, the unrealized gain is known as either a book profit or a paper gain.

U

Valuation reserve

A valuation reserve is an allowance of cash which is set aside from a business's earnings in order to provide a pool of cash to cover changes in the value of the business's **assets**. Typically, this valuation reserve will assist the business in dealing with problems such as **bad debts** or **accumulated depreciation**.

See also **reserve**.

Value added

Value added, or added value, is an increase in the market value of a product, part or component which excludes the cost of materials and services used. In other words, this is a cost-plus-profit concept, defining value added as either the difference between the cost of producing a product and the price obtained for it (the selling price), or an additional benefit offered to a purchaser in order to convince them to buy. Added value is the key concept in both the internal and the external accounting systems of an organization and is a useful means of identifying the relative efficiency of a business. It should be noted that the value-added concept looks at the internal input costs in such a way that they are not confused with the external output costs, which may be beyond the control of the organization.

The value of the goods or services supplied may depend on a number of different variables. Obviously, if the organization is processing raw materials into finished products and is responsible for all stages of the production process, then it has a relatively high degree of control over the level of added value involved. Organizations which buy in components or part-finished products do not have this depth and length of control. They purchase products which have had value added to them already. The supplier will have gone through a similar set of calculations prior to selling the components or part-finished products on to the organization, which in turn will continue their processing. In the final analysis, the level of value added to the goods or services supplied is directly related to the price the customer is willing to pay. An organization may decide to add value which would raise the price beyond what the average customer is willing to accept. In such a case, the supplier would have either to accept that it cannot receive the price it expected, or to drastically reduce the costs which have contributed to the end-user price.

The most common definition of 'value added' is profit. Before the profit is realized, however, it is necessary to be able to cover the directly applied or overhead costs of the organization. If the organization is able to cover the various costs, then it has gone a considerable distance towards being able to break even. It is only when added value exceeds the **breakeven point** that the organization moves into real profit. It is, perhaps, this part of the value-added concept that is most important. Profit means a number of things to an organization: for example, additional investment potential, expansion, reorganization or **acquisition**. The nature of value added has a tendency to push up the end user price from the moment the raw materials are extracted. In stages, some more dramatic than others, added value will be heaped upon the product. Each layer of the supply chain will demand its rightful profit in handling the product or service. Consequently, if an organization is not involved in the total extraction, processing and sale of a product or service, then it may not be able to curb unnecessary levels of added value elsewhere in the trading cycle.

Sherrington, Mark, *Added Value: The Alchemy of Brand-led Growth*. Basingstoke: Palgrave Macmillan, 2003.

Value Added Tax (VAT)

Value Added Tax is a consumption tax which is assessed on the **value added** to products and services. It is, in effect, a consumption tax charged as a percentage of the final price of a product or service. It is also charged at each stage of the production and distribution chain. In other words, it is collected fractionally. This means that there is a system of deductions, with taxable individuals or businesses allowed to deduct from their liability the amount of tax they have paid to other individuals or businesses for purchases for their own activities.

VAT was brought in under the first VAT Directive (11 April 1967), requiring that European Union member states replace any of their indirect taxes by a common system of value added tax. The national laws of each of the member states in respect of VAT were specified by the Directive 77/388/EEC. Non-EU businesses which export to the European Union are taxed at import stage, whilst export goods are zero-rated and not subject to VAT.

Directive 2001/4/EC requires all member states to set a minimum standard VAT rate of 15% to be effective until at least December 2005.

www.europa.eu.int/eur-lex/en/lif/reg/en_register_093010.html

Ogley, Adrian, *Principles of Value Added Tax: A European Perspective*. The Hague: Interfisc, 1998.

Variable costs

Variable costs are expenditure which varies directly with changes in output. In other words they are inextricably linked to the level of activity. Variable costs would include raw materials, components, labour and energy, which would vary according to the degree of production.

Variance

'Variance' is used in standard costing and budgetary control and describes the difference between budgeted costs or income, and the actual costs or income which were achieved or incurred. Should the variance be better than what had been predicted or budgeted, then it is considered to be a favourable variance. Conversely, if the variance is worse than had been predicted, it is known as an adverse variance.

Velocity

Velocity has three associated sub-definitions, all of which are related to the movement of currency in the economy:

- *Velocity of circulation* – broadly the amount of times a unit of currency is used in a specific period of time. This is calculated by dividing the total amount of money spent, by the amount of money which is in circulation in the economy.
- *Income velocity (of circulation)* – which refers to the number of times a unit of currency is part of an individual's income in a specified period of time. This is calculated by working out the ratio of the **gross national product** compared with the amount of money which is in circulation in the economy.
- *Transactions velocity (of circulation)* – which refers to the number of times that a unit of currency is used in transactions over a specified period of time. This is calculated by working out the ratio between the money spent (on products and services) compared with the amount of money which is in circulation in the economy.

V

Venture capital

A venture capitalist is an individual who invests money in a start-up company. Many venture capitalist organizations are run as part of investment banks. The venture capitalist provides the funding for fledgling businesses which lack the financial muscle to put their ideas into the marketplace. The venture capitalists often retain a controlling share in the business and should the business prove to be successful, then their initial investment is hugely rewarded by future returns.

Gompers, Paul and Lerner, Josh, *The Venture Capital Cycle*. Cambridge, MA: MIT Press, 2002.

Warranty

Although the term 'warranty' is most closely associated with an agreement made between a buyer and a seller, it does have a strictly accounting and finance implication. The standard use of the term 'warranty' deals with the conditions under which sellers agree to make repairs, or deal with problems, at their own cost and not at the cost of the buyer.

In accountancy terms, however, 'warranty' has a completely different meaning and relates to an expert's statement of opinion, or indeed fact, concerning a business's financial state and condition. The warranty may be made by an independent accounting professional or a financial analyst.

Wash sale

'Wash sale' is a US slang term known in the UK as 'bed and breakfast'. It involves either a solitary investor, or a group of investors, selling and purchasing blocks of securities over a relatively short period of time, which gives the impression that there is considerable trading in that security. The colluding investors seek to make quick profits from the resulting increase in the value of the security.

Wasting asset

A wasting asset is either a lease which will have a zero value at the end of the lease term, or, more generally, any other form of asset. It is classed as a wasting asset if it is considered to be a depreciating asset that, at the end of its useful life, will have a very low or nil market value (except for its scrap value).

Winding up

'Winding up' is an alternative term used to describe the **liquidation** of a business. Under the terms of the British 1986 Insolvency Act, a court could place a winding up order on a business, compelling it to go into liquidation.

Working capital

Working capital is the capital which is employed by a business in its day-to-day trading operations. It is calculated by subtracting the business's **current liabilities**, such as trade creditors, from its **current assets**, which would include stock, **debtors** and cash. Ideally, the working capital should be sufficient for the business to be able to pay its immediate debts, otherwise it will struggle to continue its operations and this may well indicate that the business needs to reappraise the relationship between its assets and its liabilities.

Rao, P. M. and Pramanik, A. K., *Working Capital Management*. New Delhi: Deep and Deep Publications, 2002.

World Bank

The World Bank began its operations in 1946 in close cooperation with the **International Monetary Fund (IMF)**. It was formerly known as the International Bank for Reconstruction and Development. It was an institution created with the IMF at Bretton Woods in 1944. The World Bank has three main areas: the International Bank for Reconstruction and Development (IBRD), the International Development Agency (IDA) and the International Finance Corporation (IFC).

The World Bank is essentially one of the specialized agencies of the United Nations, which now has a total of 184 member countries. The World Bank has 109 country offices and some 10,000 development professionals, in virtually every country in the world. Currently the bank is involved in over 1,800 projects in almost all countries and sectors of the world. On average it lends $30 billion each year.

With approximately three-quarters of all of the World Bank's loans designated for specific development projects, each of these development projects must pass along a six-step project cycle. The cycle consists of:

- an identification phase, which determines whether the project is suitable for funding;
- the preparation phase, during which the borrower conducts a feasibility and design study, as well as an implementation strategy;
- the appraisal phase, during which the bank conducts its own assessment of the project;
- a negotiation and approval phase, where the bank and the borrower negotiate the loan agreement;
- the implementation of the project phase in accordance with the terms of the loan agreement;

- the evaluation phase, where the bank evaluates the borrower's reports and considers its own project study.

www.worldbank.org

World Federation of Development Financing Institutions (WFDFI)

The WFDFI was created in 1979 and aims to improve the technical operations and coordination amongst worldwide development banking. Its members include development financing institutions.

www.wfdfi.org.pe

Write down

'Write down' is an accounting process which consists of a downward adjustment in the valuation of an **asset**. The write down process may occur in order to reflect more clearly the true depreciated value of a particular asset, or indeed it may reflect the fact that the asset was over-valued in the first place. Clearly, write down is the opposite of **write up**.

Write up

'Write up' is an accounting process which consists of an upward adjustment in the valuation of an asset. The write up process may occur in order to reflect more clearly the true value of a particular asset, or indeed it may reflect the fact that the asset was under-valued in the first place. Clearly, write up is the opposite of **write down**.

Write-off

The process of writing off applies either to an asset or to a debt. In effect, they both reduce the value to zero. The two different applications of write-off are:

- *Asset write-off* – reducing the value of an asset to zero on the **balance sheet** in the case of obsolete plant or machinery, the end of a lease, or a poor investment.
- *Debt write-off* – reducing a debt to zero as it cannot be collected (**bad debt**).

Written-off losses also appear on the **profit and loss account** in the case of written-off bad debts.

Written-down value

The written-down value is the value of an **asset** which takes into account the result of its reduction in value as it has been used. Typically, for tax purposes, a written-down value allowance of 25% is available in the year of purchase. This is deducted from the initial cost to establish the new written-down value. In the following year the written-down value is reduced by another 25% off the value remaining after the first reduction. In essence, the written-down value shows the accumulated depreciation of an asset.

Year-over-year

'Year-over-year' is an accounting and finance term which refers to a comparison with the same time period in a previous year. Businesses will use year-over-year in order to predict trends and fluctuations in business activity and trade, as a means by which they can hope to predict the current year's trends. Year-over-year can be a useful means of establishing budgets, or ensuring stock and employees are available, or indeed as a basis for making adjustments to a business's operations to reflect predicted trends.

Year-to-date (YTD)

The term 'year-to-date' can be applied to a wide variety of accountancy calculations. The year-to-date refers to the beginning of the current financial year and all financial transactions which have taken place until the present day. Year-to-date can be used in order to provide a running total of the operations of the business in financial terms for any part of the year, without having to wait for the full financial figures at the end of the financial year.

Yield

'Yield' is a term used to describe income from investments. There are a number of different forms of yield, which include the following:

- *Nominal yield* – from a fixed interest security
- *Current yield* – which is the present value of the earnings from an investment.

The current yield is also known as 'running yield', 'interest yield' or 'earnings yield'.

Barnhill, Theodore, Schenkman, Mark and Maxwell, William, *High Yield Bonds: Market Structure, Valuation and Portfolio Strategies*. London: McGraw-Hill Education, 1999.

Ingold, Anthony, McMahon-Beattie, Una and Yeoman, Ian, *Yield Management: Strategies for the Service Industries*. London: Thomson Learning, 2000.

Yield advantage

A business's yield advantage can be calculated with regard to its convertible securities by using the following equation:

Convertible securities – common stock dividend yield

In this case the business's 'convertible securities' refers to **bonds**, **preferred stock** or **debentures**, which are exchangeable at the request of the holder for common stock.

Barnhill, Theodore, Schenkman, Mark and Maxwell, William, *High Yield Bonds: Market Structure, Valuation and Portfolio Strategies*. London: McGraw-Hill Education, 1999.
Ingold, Anthony, McMahon-Beattie, Una and Yeoman, Ian, *Yield Management: Strategies for the Service Industries*. London: Thomson Learning, 2000.

Yield management

Yield management is real-time demand forecasting, which is also known as revenue management or real-time pricing. It is used by organizations to calculate the best pricing policy for optimizing profits. Yield management is based on real-time modelling and forecasting of demand behaviour per market segment.

This methodology was first adopted by the airline industry in the early 1980s as a means of comparing supply and demand against differentiated pricing, and control of the inventory for each price category. The concept rests on the premise that the producer gains in increased turnover and revenue, while the customer enjoys lower prices for the same quality of service.

Yield management is a tactical weapon which aims to ensure the profitability of manufacturers in a competitive environment. From the early 1990s the concept began to penetrate other sectors of activity, initially in the United States and then in Europe.

Barnhill, Theodore, Schenkman, Mark and Maxwell, William, *High Yield Bonds: Market Structure, Valuation and Portfolio Strategies*. London: McGraw-Hill Education, 1999.
Ingold, Anthony, McMahon-Beattie, Una and Yeoman, Ian, *Yield Management: Strategies for the Service Industries*. London: Thomson Learning, 2000.

Zero-based budgeting (ZBB)

Zero-based budgeting, or zero budgeting, is used to prepare and justify all budget expenditure from a zero base. It is designed to prevent budgets from gradually increasing year-on-year. The technique sets the budget at zero and the manager responsible for that budget has to justify each and every item of expenditure. Zero-based budgeting allows businesses to identify areas of their work which do not require high budgets, thereby allowing them to place investment in areas of the business which need finance. It is also a means by which the overall base costs of the business can be reduced.

Zero budgeting does require considerable management time in identifying and adjusting the budgeting levels, but allows scope for more devious managers to justify higher budgets than others.

Pyhrr, Peter A., *Zero-base Budgeting: A Practical Management Tool for Evaluating Expenses*. New York: John Wiley, 1978.

Z

Index